WOMEN
and the
JOURNEY

THE FEMALE TRAVEL EXPERIENCE

WOMEN and the JOURNEY

THE FEMALE TRAVEL EXPERIENCE

EDITED BY BONNIE FREDERICK & SUSAN H. MCLEOD

ILLUSTRATED BY JO HOCKENHULL

WITH A FOREWORD BY CATHARINE R. STIMPSON

Washington State University Press
Pullman, Washington

Washington State University Press, Pullman, Washington 99164-5910

Library of Congress Cataloging-in-Publication Data
Women and the journey : the female travel experience / edited by Bonnie
    Frederick and Susan H. McLeod.
            p.   c.m.
    Includes bibliographical references.
    ISBN 0-87422-100-5 (pbk.)
    1. Women travelers.   I. Frederick, Bonnie.   II. McLeod, Susan H.
G 200.W65   1993
910'.82 – dc20   93-29498
                                                                      CIP

Contents

List of Illustrations

All illustrations by *Jo Hockenhull*

Foreword

THE FOURTH OF JULY in New York City in 1993 was hot, hazy, and humid. Driving alone on the New Jersey Turnpike, which runs parallel to the City, I tooled past an airport, a football stadium, office buildings, a hotel — all those cement conquerors of an ancient meadowlands. The heat was muddling my driver's reflexes, but the antics of the other drivers, on their sweaty holidays, kept these reflexes on edge. People threw firecrackers from a car as if they were beer cans. They threw beer cans, too. As cars cut in front of me with but feet to spare, I began to wonder if my Toyota and I were invisible, if something horrible and magical had not happened during America's patriotic celebration of its official birthday.

The need to stop at a tollbooth and pay $1.70 reassured me of my visibility. In my purse I also carry a photograph of the sweet baby daughter of my god-daughter. In it, the baby is standing erect, on her own two legs, about to touch my exercise bike, as she smiles in triumph.

This double image that I have just conjured up — an American woman in a car, paying a toll, carrying a favorite picture of a toddler in her purse — might seem very ordinary, a stupid commonplace. However, the appearance of ordinariness is deceiving. It obscures how extraordinary this image really is.

For it represents a woman driving a car on a trip. She is alone, Jane without Dick, Thelma without Louise. To be sure, the automobile is a part of the long history of the evolving technology of transportation, but the automobile is still very new, a phenomenon even younger than America. Karl Benz and Gottlieb Daimler did not develop the internal combustion engine until the mid-1880s. Unfortunately, the brief history of the automobile tells yet another infuriating story about gender. To be sure, women can now drive in most places; I was at the wheel of my Toyota on that July 4, 1993. Yet, the "lady driver" is still a much-mocked stereotype, and in some places, the law forbids women to drive at all.

Moreover and more cheerfully, in this image a child stands and walks unaided. Her feet had once been no longer than a hen's egg. She could do little more with them than kick out and stir the air. Now, she launches out on journeys of her own, her destination an exercise bike or a door. When she falls, she picks herself up and goes on. Because she is well-nurtured and well-nourished and on track, she is usually happy. She takes her spills in stride. For months before I took the photo, I had watched the child learn the intricate language of mobility. I had seen, once again, the miracle of the unfolding and growing of the human mind and body.

This double image is also compatible with *Women and the Journey,* a fascinating and original book. Written and designed by a group of women colleagues at Washington State University and the University of Idaho, it takes up two great themes. The first is the human appetite and need for journeys, for departures and arrivals, for picking up and moving on. Many of our journeys are full of splendors and achievements, but very few of them are pure of motive and smooth in execution. Significantly, Washington State University is located in Pullman, in the southeast corner of the State of Washington, a location only a little above the fork of the Oregon Trail that 19th-century pioneers cut west, a few decades before the automobile, through Idaho, Washington, and Oregon. As the pioneers did so, they drew on the older routes of fur traders and paths of Indians. The relations between the pioneers and the environment were both grand and terrible. The relationships between the pioneers and the indigenous peoples were often the stuff of tragedy.

The second theme is the differences between the experiences of women and men who embark on journeys. Working with texts by both women and men, the authors plausibly suggest that women do experience and have experienced travel differently from men. For example, women often pay more attention to the process of the journey than men do. Moreover, we see and write about women's travels differently from those of men.

Yet, the authors refuse to overgeneralize about "the female experience." They are aware of the differences among women. Because of this respect for diversity, *Women and the Journey* has a welcome historical and geographical range. It takes up women in Medieval Islam; Chinese women immigrating to 19th-century America, many of them as enslaved prostitutes; the "real" travelling women in the Victorian period; the narratives of captive women in Hispanic America; and the reshaping of the quest narrative when women take up a quest.

A virtue of *Women and the Journey* is that one wants to know still more – still more about black women on the Middle Passage from Africa to America; still more about women in the great migrations, many of them compelled, of the 20th century; still more about women and the spaces beyond this globe, a drama that will provide material for the big travel narratives of the 21st century. One wishes to know more for several reasons. First, the pieces in *Women and the Journey* are intrinsically interesting. They provoke our curiosity. How, they ask, could a woman of Greek Christian origin, who then married a Moslem of some standing, pass back and forth over the border between her family of birth and her family of marriage, Christian on one side, Moslem on the other? How, these articles also ask, could Victorian and Edwardian women travel in *those* clothes, climb mountains and march through jungles in *those* crinolines and corsets? More profoundly, *Women and the Journey* makes us wonder about our own mobility. Why do we travel? Why do we drive down turnpikes in the heat? Why does a child seem programmed to walk and run?

Next, despite its diversity, the bits and pieces in *Women and the Journey* have a unifying attitude. They are intellectually scrupulous. They are aware of what anthropology and history can and cannot be; they are equally aware of the power of our dominant narratives to shape our sense of things, to impose old patterns on new experiences. The essays refuse to indulge in sensationalism, tourism, and a voyeuristic *frisson* because of the presence of an exotic "Other." They do, however, praise curiosity, the ability to see old things with a fresh eye and new things with a clear eye. *Women and the Journey* asks us to dwell with diversity, but to do so judiciously and fairly. Such an attitude is, I believe, a necessity for citizenship in the global village. In this village, we can journey across physical distances swiftly, either in person or through the global media, but our drives across cultural, social, and gender differences are still arduous and threatening. Too often, we sally forth in a battle tank rather than in a peaceable Ford or Toyota. In brief, read *Women and the Journey,* learn from it, take pleasure in it. I hope that the toddler whose picture I carry will do so someday.

Catharine R. Stimpson
New York City
August 1993

Prologue

Susan H. McLeod and *Bonnie Frederick*

T HIS IS AN unusual book, not so much in its character as in its conceptualization and execution. Unlike most editions of essays, it began not with one person's idea but with the emergence of a collective idea. This idea was nurtured and developed not by one editor but by all the essayists. During the time we worked on the project our guiding metaphor was that most female of activities, quiltmaking— each of us had a part to contribute, each of us had some say in how the final product went together. Like quiltmaking, the process was both satisfying and frustrating: not everyone's contribution fit the pattern we finally decided upon; at times people committed to the project had to drop out; one person we had invited to be part of the group became such a disruptive force that the process was stalled for a time. Since almost all decisions were made through consensus rather than by a single editor, the process of putting the essays together was time consuming. Still, we all feel that the final product is a piece to be proud of.

The core group of faculty that began the project first met in the spring of 1987 under the auspices of a seed grant from Washington State University's Graduate School. That first small group, formed for interdisciplinary research and discussion, made two key decisions. The first was the theme of our group study: travel. This theme seemed large enough to include everyone's research interests, and it also seemed an area where we could make an original contribution. While women's journeys have become more noticed by women critics and historians in the last few years, the existing body of travel criticism is still overwhelmingly male-centered. Birgitta Ingemanson, who was studying the travel narratives of women who observed the Russian Revolution of 1917, was central in helping us define our thematic core. The next decision was to produce tangible results from our study and discussion.

Several of us had been in feminist study groups before and we knew the experience of losing focus without a goal in mind. The junior faculty among us were particularly committed to publishing something, probably individual articles with the group's editorial help.

With these decisions in mind, the group invited women from all over WSU and the University of Idaho (our sister university seven miles away) to join. Over the next two years we became, in Birgitta Ingemanson's words, a "research collective." Although the group's membership has varied over time, it has always been firmly interdisciplinary. Principally made up of specialists in literature, languages, history, and art, the group represents many cultures and areas of study. The composition of the study group itself is not representative of Washington State University, the University of Idaho, or women in general. We make no claims of being particularly diverse. Those whose names you find included here are the ones whose ongoing research lent itself to this project, whose pieces fit the final pattern, and who were committed enough to complete the project.

Our working method was to meet once a month (later twice a month) in the late afternoon to discuss one person's essay draft. The paper was read aloud, then discussed by the group, each person commenting from her own area of expertise. Straggling in after a day of teaching, we at first looked and felt like travelers weary of the road. But as we began to comment on the paper presented we gained energy and became refreshed through the pleasurable exchange of ideas. Susan McLeod, then Director of Composition in the English Department at WSU, called the meetings, kept the discussion on track, and served as final reader of the essays. Calling on her knowledge of writing communities and women's ways of interacting, Susan provided the theoretical framework for the group process as well as its practical application. When Susan was on sabbatical leave, Bonnie Frederick took over her duties and helped focus essay revisions for the final version of our project.

Though we ranged in academic rank from graduate students to full professors, we all soon realized that we knew only part of the field we had decided to study. With each an expert in her own area but none expert in all, the group became remarkably egalitarian. As each member presented her paper to the group for discussion, it became clear that we all could learn from each other. No one's paper was perfect the first time, but it wasn't always easy to give or accept criticism.

It was a humbling yet inspiring experience, and we are all better writers for having submitted our work to the group process.

As travelers do, we broke the routine of the journey with memorable meals. Early on, we breakfasted with Catharine Stimpson, then Graduate Dean at Rutgers and generous advocate of women's research. After listening to us describing our ideas, she said firmly, "You realize that what you are talking about here is a book." And so we were. The next year, combining inspirational meals with the American female ritual of the slumber party, we spent a weekend at the university's Camp Larson on Lake Coeur d'Alene in northern Idaho. It was a marathon night-and-day session of discussing papers. The sustained discourse added greatly to the book's overall coherence; it also made us even more aware of how rare and precious is uninterrupted time.

As the group discussed ideas we came to share a common language with which to discuss travel and we swapped knowledge and ideas at every opportunity. These common discussions are evident in many ways. The role of clothing, for instance, appears repeatedly; the issue of rape and fear of rape is also present in many papers. Features of the quest also recur in these pages, even in accounts of otherwise pragmatic journeys. Yet, though we came to share a discourse and a core of ideas, our articles reflect differences in disciplinary rhetoric, theoretical approach, and personal style. This book is an anthology of many voices, not a single one. We have enjoyed our differences and never have intended to edit our chapters into a homogeneous discourse. Therefore, each reader will find some chapters more personally interesting than others; we hope that our readers will venture into unfamiliar areas as we did. At a time when university academics are increasingly isolated from each other and unable (or unwilling) to understand each other's disciplines, this project has been an exhilarating chance to expand our narrow specialties and personal styles.

Our own university has been very supportive of this group, and we particularly want to thank Robert Smith, Dean and Vice Provost for Research in the Graduate School, under whose auspices we received the original seed grant and who funded the weekend retreat at Camp Larson. We owe a great deal to Catharine Stimpson, whose encouragement in the beginning stages meant so much to us. We are indebted to Mary Field Belenky who, during a most timely visit, helped us rethink the nature of the group process. We also thank the various deans and departments who have recognized this book as a valuable scholarly project, and the Humanities Research Center, which provided logistical support for the manuscript. Chris Bergum, the secretary of Women Studies, contributed her organizational skills by coordinating memos, current drafts, and keeping track of the changing *dramatis personae* of our group. Jeanne Richeson was our sharp-eyed and knowledgeable editorial assistant. Finally, we are grateful to the dedicated women who were unable to write or complete essays themselves but who generously joined in our discussions: Radha Balasubramanian, Barbara Kemp, Barbara Meldrum, Joan West, and especially Shelley Spear.

Introduction

Bonnie Frederick and *Virginia Hyde*

...as a woman, I have no country. As a woman,
I want no country. As a woman my country is the whole world.
Virginia Woolf, *Three Guineas*

T HIS BOOK DEALS with a wide variety of women travelers, or women
on the move, from both fiction and non-fiction. Their experiences
are so diverse that it is difficult to generalize about the meanings of
their journeys. But gendered meanings they all do share, for the journeys prove significant transits, in which each woman's gender invests
her journey with a meaning that both comments on and differs from
that of men's journeys. A study of women's journeying is especially
timely today when women's lives, past and present, are being reinterpreted and retold with women's voices doing the telling. Only a few
of these essays concern materials that can be considered "travel literature," but the category supplies a useful frame for our work.

While travel literature seems an essentially masculine genre if one
judges only from studies and anthologies of it,[1] women have also written of their journeys—the 1990 *Women Travel*, edited by Natania Jansz
and Miranda Davies, contains more than 100 contemporary women's
accounts of their journeys in 43 countries. Jane Robinson's *Wayward
Women: A Guide to Women Travellers* catalogues the biographies of some
400 women travelers; even this impressive number is incomplete, since
the guide focuses primarily on women from English-speaking countries. Nor can the omission of women travel writers from anthologies
be attributed to poor quality of writing: Rebecca West's *Black Lamb
and Grey Falcon: A Journey through Yugoslavia,* for example, is a master-
piece of the genre.[2] When women tell their own stories and construct
their own histories, many examples of women travelers become visible.

The historical record begins early: Etheria (or Egeria) made a pilgrimage to the Holy Land around the year 385 — and she wrote about it in a wholly new way, creating "the subject of travel literature as we know it now."[3] Following in her footsteps, modern authors give a new mobility to female characters, not simply in their geographical movements, but also in their roles; current science fiction, for instance, often uses the journey structure to hypothesize women's roles in the future as contrasted with those of the present (Ursula K. LeGuin's novels are examples). Literary critics have also been formulating new theories — of quest romance, of mythology, and of the *Bildungsroman* — in relation to the woman traveler.

To contribute to the growing body of material that helps us understand women's lives, this collection of essays, written by a women's interdisciplinary study group at Washington State University, focuses on women's activity in fiction and history. Voices from different levels of textuality form a "conversation" with each other throughout this volume. The interpenetrations between fiction and non-fiction in both travelogues and novels are well known,[4] and our study complicates them further by its consideration of gender differences. Our essays concentrate on women's accounts but also include some men's accounts of women's journeys and some women's accounts of men's. These interrelationships become intricate indeed when a female writer uses data or definitions from men or when a male writer invests a female character with some of his own adventures or ideologies. In acknowledging these complexities, however, we affirm the richness and resonance of the "dialogues" put into play — those between fiction and history and those between male and female.

Women may travel for pleasure, curiosity, business, adventure, altruism, health, self-discovery, scientific research, or some combination of all these reasons. Their travel may follow an established pattern, as in the case of religious pilgrimages, or the women may simply wander as the mood strikes them. Their journeys may end when they return to their homes or when they establish new ones; nomadic women carry their homes along with them. Women also experience journeys of fear and horror: they may suffer forced exile; be taken into captivity; or flee slavery, war, or natural disaster. Because of this enormous diversity of journey patterns, certain limits on our study needed to be established. Therefore, for the purposes of this book, we decided to focus on physical movement, not just mental journeys or journeys as metaphors for life. Certainly the physical journey leads to the metaphysical and the metaphorical, but we believe that an understanding of the metaphysical must begin in the physical. Our concept of mobility does not necessarily imply long distances, but it does focus on the ability to move about and the degree to which the woman's will shapes her journey. Though we chose gender as our fundamental study concept, we do not conceive of gender as timeless or independent of race and class. It may be true, for example, that a wealthy woman's journey is more similar to a wealthy man's journey than to a poor woman's journey. Certainly, British ladies having tea in the jungle have little in common with Chinese immigrant women arriving at an unknown destiny in America. Similarly, while pilgrimage is common to Christianity, Islam, and Hinduism, the pilgrim of one religion surely would find the others' pilgrimages very different from her own. To suggest the great variety of women's travel, therefore, we include examples of journeys from different historical periods, countries, classes, and ethnic groups. Our essays do not pretend to be definitive or encyclopedic; instead, we hope to surprise other researchers into seeing their own areas of study in new and productive ways.

Crossing the Threshold

Women's journeys are as much about departure as they are about arrival. Home is both the literal and metaphorical point of departure; whatever home might be (and it is frequently awful), it is the fixed point to which other places will be explicitly or implicitly compared. If, for example, a woman rejoices in the freedom of travel, the underlying comment is that such freedom does not exist at home. It probably is no coincidence that the sudden increase in women's travels in the Victorian period coincided not only with the era's great prosperity, but also with some restrictive concepts of home life and women's domestic duty. "Claustrophobic" describes much of middle- and upper-class Victorian homelife: its interior decoration, cumbersome clothing, closed windows, and some social mores (the African traveler Mary Kingsley's childhood home had only one window that was not bricked up).[5] The cluttered, airless sitting room in England or America is the point of comparison when 19th-century women travelers write of the expanse of the American plains, the functional minimalness of African clothing, or the sweetness of the air in the Himalayas.

For many women, the family house, and particularly the Anglo-Germanic notion of home, is at once a romantic dream of peace and contentment and a nightmare of suffocation. Indeed, for some women of all social classes, home can be a place of sexual danger, as the narratives of incest victims, slave women, and abused wives reveal.[6] It is no accident that women writers such as Harriet Beecher Stowe and Edith Wharton wrote both books on ideal interior decoration and novels of perverse households.[7] This alternating attraction to and horror of domestic life is not just a literary device; it haunts many women travelers. Saint Teresa of Avila, for example, witnessed with horror the death of her mother in childbirth; she left the family home with its memories of sexual death and entered another house, equally closed but celibate: the convent. Under the respectable protection of her house, Teresa was able to wander over all of Spain, traveling for God's glory, as her brothers had earlier traveled to America in search of personal glory.[8] Similarly, the world traveler Isabella Bird was an invalid at home – and a tireless explorer elsewhere. Yet she continued to return home and make the effort to be a more conventional woman. She married at age 50, which "kept Isabella at home for a few years (she had thought of visiting New Guinea, but that was hardly the sort of place to which one took one's husband)." When her husband died five years later, Bird immediately began traveling again: "her own ill health blew away with a good sea-breeze."[9]

Other women depart in despair and fear. The Chinese women described in Annette White-Parks's essay, for example, begin their journey as captives, slaves, or duped mail-order brides. African-American slave women, too, were impelled to flight by the violence of their captivity. As Bonnie Frederick's essay discusses, women's captivity can involve the special horrors of rape and separation from their own families (especially children). For example, in *Incidents in the Life of a Slave Girl: Written by Herself* (1861) Harriet Jacobs (using the name Linda Brent),[10] does not flee slavery for herself though she continually has to connive to resist sexual violation by her master. She even wishes at times for the death of her son: "Alas, what mockery it is for a slave mother to try to pray back her dying child to life! Death is better than slavery."[11] But the birth of a daughter makes her resolve to escape:

> When they told me my new-born babe was a girl, my heart was heavier than it had ever been before. Slavery is terrible for men; but it is far more terrible for women. Superadded to the burden common to all, *they* have wrongs, and sufferings, and mortifications peculiarly their own.[12]

Jacobs's journey to freedom is the inverse of that of her white, wealthy contemporaries; while they flee *away* from their homes, Jacobs and other fugitive slaves flee *toward* their imagined homes. The slaves' mythic flight to freedom and their search for their true homes have been played out in many variations in the lives of African-American women after emancipation: Josephine Baker journeyed to Paris to find artistic freedom; Ida B. Wells roamed the country in search of the truth about lynching; Maya Angelou traveled to Africa, where she hoped to find home; and in an ironic version of the flight pattern, Rosa Parks brought a bus — and an oppressive way of life — to a dead stop by refusing to move at all.[13]

For women alienated from the "home" given to them by their society, the journey may become an end in itself; it may not have a projected arrival point at all, as in the case of the wanderers studied in Sheila O'Brien's essay on *Housekeeping*. Movement becomes a way to combat a feeling of homelessness that has nothing to do with the physical site of home. The young Maya Angelou rebels at living in St. Louis, saying, "I carried the same shield I had used in Stamps [Arkansas]: 'I didn't come to stay.' "[14] Hseih Pingying in *Girl Rebel* (1940) says much the same thing about the new house built for her wedding, which she, after being a soldier for several years, does not want:

> I did not feel much concerned about it because I did not intend to stay in this little town.... Escape would be more difficult hereafter, but I must watch for an opportunity at any time.... Thus when everyone thought I had surrendered to the old conventions, I was planning my fourth escape.[15]

Similarly, Stephen Gorden in Radclyffe Hall's *The Well of Loneliness* (1928) is not a willing wanderer. Her gender is a tissue of ironies: because she is a woman, she cannot inherit her father's house. However, by acting like the man she feels she truly is, she becomes an outcast. Her travels are restless wanderings that, on the one hand, allow her to live as a man, yet do not satisfy her upper-class English vision of home and domesticity.[16]

Whatever the reasons for embarking on a journey, women travelers both accept and embrace risk. When the poet Rosario Ferr says, "I did not like the protected existence I had led until then in the sanctuary of my home, free from all danger but also from any responsibilities,"[17] she pinpoints the common trap of the domestic shelter: no danger means no freedom. The awareness that one is challenging the expectation of safety and security is at the heart of women's travels in both fact and fiction; when the journeyer exults in danger and celebrates her survival, she is glorying in the *freedom* to be in danger. As Ellen Moers shows in her study of "traveling heroinism," the rise of the Gothic novel in the 18th and 19th centuries was, in part, caused by the appeal to women readers of its female characters' forbidden travel: "It was *only* indoors. . .that the heroine. . .could travel brave and free, and stay respectable."[18] The "danger" of the journey often means sexual danger, whether moral or physical. Leaving home has overtones of sexual freedom, a burden many women travelers resented but one that others, such as Radclyffe Hall, welcomed.[19] More horrifying, however, is the danger of rape, which, as Charlotte Perkins Gilman eloquently points out, is a threat used by society to restrict women's movements:

> [Women] must be guarded in the only place of safety, the home. Guarded from what? From men. From the womanless men who may be prowling about while all women stay at home. The home is safe because women are there. Out of doors is unsafe because women are not there. If women were there, everywhere, in the world which belongs to them as much as to men, then everywhere would be safe. We try to make the women safe in the home, and keep them there; to make the world safe for women and children has not occurred to us. So the boy grows, in the world as far as he can reach it, and the girl does not grow equally, being confined to the home.[20]

Even such a seasoned traveler as Katherine Mansfield, who visited and wrote about numerous locations, from her native New Zealand to the fashionable spots of Europe, noted in 1915 that a woman traveling by herself attracted "an impertinent, arrogant and slightly amused attitude" and that she herself had the uncomfortable sense "that everybody and everything. . .was secretly 'in the know,' waiting for that ominous infallible thing to happen to her, which always did happen, which was bound to happen, to every woman on earth who travelled alone!"[21] Therefore, the simple act of embarking on a journey may already be a risk for a woman.

In spite of society's warnings of harm on the road, however, many women travelers defy the convention of ladylike timidity by acknowledging danger with casual, flippant, or even boasting words, such as Delia Akeley's: "I'm always frightened in the jungle – always prepared for a violent death. I never go without taking along the means to end it quickly if I am mortally hurt. But I love it."[22] The journey is often presented not only as a risk but as a risk well worth taking, a means of self-transformation and self-discovery. Coming to grips with her feelings about home, danger, and accepted notions of womanhood inevitably changes the woman traveler, setting her apart from other women who remain behind. As Robyn Davidson says in *Tracks*,

> I'm amazed at how quickly and absolutely this sense of the importance of social custom fell away from me. And the awareness of its absurdity has never really left me. I have slowly regained a sense of the niceties, but I will always see the obsession with social graces and female modesty for the perverted crippling insanity it really is.[23]

Even when nearing death from tuberculosis, Katherine Mansfield still turns to the idea of the journey to validate her self-identity:

> I want to enter into [the world], to be part of it, to live in it, to learn from it, to lose all that is superficial and acquired in me and to become a conscious direct human being. I want, by understanding myself, to understand others. I want to be all that I am capable of being so that I may be...a *child of the sun*.[24]

To fulfill her whole potential through interactions beyond herself, in nature and society, takes on a therapeutic and almost religious function.

Writing and Reading About the Journey

Simone de Beauvoir once deplored that man "in song and story" is generally the active hero while woman remains "locked in a tower, a palace, a garden, a cave, she is chained to a rock, a captive, sound asleep: she waits."[25] More recently, Sandra Gilbert and Susan Gubar have confirmed that "most Western literary genres are...essentially male,"[26] leaving little room for a woman's voice and experience.

For a woman to write about the journey is frequently, then, to create a female model differing from the male one. Recent scholarship on the *Bildungsroman*, a form of the novel whose action may include extensive travel experience, shows that women have seldom been favored as its protagonists.[27] The picaresque tradition, it is true, has included some active women – but Daniel Defoe's Moll Flanders is rendered more acceptable by her self-righteous repudiation of her actions, and the male writer of such "female" picaresques as *La lozana andaluza* (1528) subverts his anti-heroine's autonomy when he "creates her, puts words into her mouth, and allows a male-dominated society to defeat her."[28] The picaresque does defend the pícara's identity and actions, however, when the writer is also female, as in the case of Elena Poniatowska's *Hasta no verte Jesús mío* (1969), Rita Mae Brown's *Rubyfruit Jungle* (1973), and Erica Jong's *Fanny* (1980).[29]

Of even greater interest is the way women writers have altered and reinterpreted the quest theme in a wide variety of literary works. Although the essays in this collection all deal with literal movement, the journeys often have features of the quest – the search for self-development – so that the metaphorical journey is superimposed on the literal one. Carol Christ has revealed a pattern of "spiritual quest" in modern women's literature, one eventually integrating the woman's inner search with an outer "social quest." In the works Christ explores, the woman's pursuit of "wholeness" includes stages reminiscent of those of mysticism – including a "dark night of the soul," an "awakening," new insight, and a "new naming" of female reality; this experience is "a movement overcoming the dualisms. . .which have plagued Western consciousness," and it may therefore offer important alternative views to society.[30] Dana Heller, too, in *The Feminization of Quest Romance* (1991), points to modern works of literature by women that focus on successful searches for female identity and fellowship. Carol Pearson and Katherine Pope even trace the "female hero" through her own version of slaying a "dragon" and gaining the "reward of community."[31]

But the male-centered quest has long dominated the literature and scholarship on the genre. Joseph Campbell, in his widely influential *Hero With a Thousand Faces* (1949), assumes that an initiation archetype – of a traveler seeking a life-validating boon – is available to both women and men, but this traveler's most typical activity is "the winning of a bride" and his success is figured in terms of "going to the father"[32] – that is, gaining his own maturity as a man and negotiating his peace with his fathers and their society. Underlying Campbell's theory (like Northrop Frye's later criteria for quest romance) are the findings of Sigmund Freud and Carl G. Jung about the mind's projection of symbolic objects, such as landscapes, and about its "journeys" or forays into unconscious experience — concepts which themselves are being revalued today by feminists and others.[33]

Particularly pertinent is Jung's assertion of the necessary human attempt to combine both male and female within each individual, making the goal of a quest the gaining of an inner androgyny. Despite some "androgynous" features of Campbell's and Frye's paradigms, however, both tend to imply a male protagonist whose fulfillment is uppermost, more central than that of female characters. Frye's book on romance, *The Secular Scripture*, even associates the female ("the womb of the earth-mother") with the purgatorial wasteland in which the hero struggles to win and internalize female powers from mother nature.[34] A feminist reading notes that this struggle does not symbolize real unity with the feminine but a triumph over it, thus making the female the "spoils" of combat.[35] Besides hinting at this cosmic battle between the sexes, Frye elsewhere describes the staple female character of quest romance as a passive figure waiting for a man to return from his adventures.[36]

Thus quest theory itself raises issues of gender that ultimately involve the difference between women and the male concept of the "female"—what Jung terms the anima — and the difference between the female and male rewards of questing. Presumably both questers seek the same inner harmony and validation from others. If, however, the male quester's wholeness is signified by his returning home and gaining a "bride," women searchers have often found the patriarchal home an inadequate end of the quest. Working with a body of literature entirely by women, Pratt adapts the theory of archetypes to the female quester, who, somewhat like Campbell's heroes, separates radically from "societal norms," but often by "marital rebellion" or other "social protest."[37] Whereas the heroes of Campbell's paradigm return to society with their winnings and new illumination, those of Pratt's version are often unable to reenter a society in which they are no longer the norm, no longer the passive figures in a patriarchy.[38] Our essays reveal this kind of exile from "home" in *Housekeeping* as well as, curiously, in some works by D. H. Lawrence.

This book's discussions of Lawrence, John Bunyan, the Victorian men who retold Godiva's story, and Latin American captivity stories raise the question of how, or how well, a male author can project the journeys of women characters. This question and the various answers our essays offer are related to another gender issue: how do women readers and writers relate to male protagonists? A revealing example of this complex process occurs in Rebecca West's use of the legendary Theseus and Ariadne in one of her most striking comments on travel:

> my journey moved me...because it was like picking up a strand of wool that would lead me out of a labyrinth in which...I had found myself immured. It might be that when I followed the thread to its end I would find myself faced by locked gates, and that this labyrinth was my sole portion on earth. But at least I now knew its twists and turns, and what corridor led into what vaulted chamber, and nothing in my life before I went...[had made plain these mysteries].[39]

As an active traveler, West has identified herself with the heroic Theseus who escapes from the Cretan labyrinth by following a thread provided by the more passive Ariadne. But a woman's journey, whatever its "epic" and life-altering aspects, may not be entirely definable in terms of the traditional male quest. West, for example, has adapted the myth to her own circumstances, for she is not only Theseus but also Ariadne, weaving the threads of her travel narrative to provide a means of liberating knowledge for her readers and herself. Even the way the old myths are read may prove to be gender-related. In recent feminist studies of other classical myths, for example, the stories of Persephone and Psyche are retold to reveal the female protagonists and messages beneath layers of patriarchal interpretation.[40] Although a man had earlier recognized in Psyche a "feminine Heracles" and a "feminine Prometheus,"[41] her daring journeys (presumably unbecoming to a lady) were not allowed truly heroic — and admirable — standing until recently.

Faced with a scarcity of woman-centered paradigms for their travel narratives, many authors adapt and piece together the aspects of male narrative patterns that can be used to represent female experience. The precedent for this adaptation to male models has already occurred in women's childhood, when they began to read for pleasure. Feminist reader-response theory has shown that women learn to read male narratives as if they too were men for the duration of the work.[42] This is certainly true of travel tales, particularly the ones aimed at boys. It is not at all uncommon to find women referring to childhood reading of "boys' books"; little girls still read *Little Women*, but they also read *Treasure Island*.[43] Rebecca West, for instance, had clearly experienced the sense of "being" Theseus as well as Ariadne when she referred to the myth of the labyrinth in her travel book. Similarly, Harriet Tubman, who led her family to freedom, took on the role of "Moses," not "Miriam," because she did more than watch over and protect her people. Suspending their own gender for a while in order to identify with the other-sex hero seems more often the privilege of girls than of boys: "The very fact that little onus was attached to girls reading boys' books, while boys reading girls' books was surreptitious and was experienced as somehow shameful, revealed to every child the existence of a hierarchy of value favoring the male."[44] Perhaps this difference explains the omission of women travelers in, for instance, Bruce Chatwin's *Songlines*, while Robyn Davidson's *Tracks*, which also documents a contemporary journey across Australia, refers to both female and male journeys. Arguably, Davidson's readings are wider and richer for including more than just men; but the fact that she — like most women — reads men's works *and acts on their inspiration* reveals a reading process that absorbs male experience and retells the story in the reader's own terms. Experiencing a male hero's adventures may not be explicitly possible in the text itself (it is hard to imagine Huck Finn as a girl), yet the power of the text as a whole can be understood in a distinctly feminine way. Kathryn Shevelow reminds us that

> Not all rhetorical appeal in a text is the direct result of conscious authorial intention. We must distinguish between a rhetoric consciously exercised by the author. . .and that generated only by the interaction between the text and the reader. . . . The overt [level of persuasion] is the didactic message that comprises the content of the text; the covert is the rhetorical power surrounding the text, which is entirely dependent on the way in which the intended readers read the text (which is in turn dependent on their social and psychological backgrounds).[45]

By filtering male-centered texts through a woman's consciousness, the woman traveler can recognize that adventurous journeys are conventionally made by men, while simultaneously interpreting the text's rhetorical power to open the possibility of her own travel.

There is one travel text available to women that has no gender identification of its own: a map. Maps are romantic, magic objects that enchant the future traveler with possibilities. Unlike fictional or historical discourse, the words on maps are subjectless, verbless suggestions, evocative by their very sparseness. Amelia Earhart describes how she, along with her sister and cousins, used maps in childhood games of make-believe, "imaginary journeys full of fabulous perils," in an old carriage stored in a barn:

> The maps of far places that fell into our clutches supplemented the hair-raising experiences of the decrepit carriage. Map-traveling took its place beside window-shopping as an accepted diversion. The map of Africa was a favorite. The very word meant mystery. Blithely we rolled on our tongues such names as Senegal, Timbuctu, Ngami, El Fasher, and Khartoum.[46]

As she reads the map, Earhart is aware that travel has been male-identified, but she refuses to accept the gender restriction:

> Here was shining adventure, beckoning with new experiences, added knowledge of flying, of people – of myself. . . . Then, too, there was my belief that now and then women should do for themselves what men have already done – and occasionally what men have not done – thereby establishing themselves as persons, and perhaps encouraging other women toward greater independence of thought and action.[47]

Earhart clearly reads as a woman, transforming the map of Africa into her own map of personal fulfillment, and becoming doer as well as reader. She will provide the subjects and the verbs to complete the sentence suggested by the map.

Travelers, readers, writers – the women studied in this collection of essays undergo journeys mapped according to their own womanly conditions. Sometimes conforming to conventional standards of propriety, sometimes rebelling in defiance, the women all seek to transform themselves, and sometimes others, through the simple (and often not-so-simple) act of traveling. For some, travel leads to salvation, as in Bunyan's *Pilgrim's Progress*, Part II, while for others it brings utter loss, as in the tales of captive women. There are surprises here even for the knowledgeable reader of women's travels; for example, the journeys of Muslim women are not well known and certainly not expected, given the stereotypes of the harem sensationalized in the West. In all these instances, the act of traveling strips away the illusions of women's condition, revealing their struggle for personal discovery and social change in the face of cultural ideologies constructed to restrict their mobility and independence.

Notes

1. Bruce Chatwin, for example, does not quote women travelers in his *Songlines* (New York: Penguin, 1987) though he quotes an enormous number of male writers. He at least has an inkling that women want to travel; he describes his aunts sighing over the romantic sound of place names such as Xanadu and Samarkand (6). However, it is quite clear that the Chatwin men travel, and the Chatwin women stay home. Worse still is the promising chapter "Space and Gender: Women's Mediations" in Eric J. Leed's *The Mind of the Traveler: From Gilgamesh to Modern Tourism* (New York: Basic Books, 1991); it turns out to be about prostitutes whom male travelers encounter.
2. *Women Travel: Adventures, Advice, and Experience, A Real Guide Special,* ed. Natania Jancz and Miranda Davies with Alisa Joyce and Jane Parkin (New York: Prentice Hall, 1990); *Wayward Women: A Guide to Women Travellers,* ed. Jane Robinson (New York: Oxford University Press, 1990); Rebecca West, *Black Lamb and Grey Falcon: A Journey through Yugoslavia,* 2 volumes (New York: Viking, 1941).
3. Mary B. Campbell, *The Witness and the Other World: Exotic European Travel Writing, 400-1600* (Ithaca and London: Cornell University Press, 1988), 21. There are two available translations of Etheria's text: *The Pilgrimage of St. Silvia of Aquitania to the Holy Places c. 385 A.D.,* trans. John H. Bernard (London: The Palestine Pilgrims' Text Society, 1891), and *Egeria's Travels,* trans. John Wilkinson (London: SPCK, 1971).
4. See, for example, Percy G. Adams who, in *Travel Literature and the Evolution of the Novel* (Lexington: University Press of Kentucky, 1983), 93, 97, 160, points to the commingling of fiction with history and of the false with the actual in travel literature. He also notes the "similarities between the journey structure of fiction and the journey structure of travel literature." Terry Caesar's "The Book in the Travel: Paul Theroux's *The Old Patagonian Express,*" *Arizona Quarterly* 46 (Summer 1990): 101-110 examines what travelers read along the way, and how the reading informs the writing of the journey.
5. Dea Birkett, *Spinsters Abroad: Victorian Lady Explorers* (New York: Blackwell, 1989), 6.
6. Even the powerful American salvation myth of the westward journey offers no escape for women. See, for example, Melody Graulich, "Violence Against Women: Power Dynamics in Literature of the Western Family," *The Women's West,* ed. Susan Armitage and Elizabeth Jameson (Norman: University of Oklahoma Press, 1987), 111-25.
7. Ambivalence about women's domestic role is pervasive in popular literature; see, for example, the discussion by Sally Allen McNall, *Who is in the House?* (New York: Elsevier, 1981). William C. Spengemann has suggested that even in Susannah Rowson's *Charlotte Temple,* "the most rigidly programmatic sentimental novel ever written" with "its blind devotion to

the domestic ethos," "it is hard to ignore the antidomestic forces working within it." *The Adventurous Muse: The Poetics of American Fiction, 1789-1900* (New Haven: Yale University Press, 1977), 92.

8. St. Teresa of Jesus, *The Life of the Holy Mother Teresa of Jesus*, vol. 1, *Complete Works of St. Teresa of Jesus*, ed. E. Allison Peers (London: Sheed and Ward) 10-13. Notice how Teresa mixes together her mother's health and death with the various references to travel, whether going to fight the Moors or wandering in search of adventures as in the novels of chivalry and *Foundations*, vol. 3, *Complete Works*. *Foundations* is the record of Teresa's journeys across Spain, founding houses for her order. She, like Isabella Bird, alternates ill health with travel, though Teresa claims to travel only at God's command: "So far as I remember at the moment, no fear of trials ever kept me from making a foundation, though I particularly disliked journeys, especially long ones; but once I had started they troubled me very little, as I realized in Whose service they were being made." (88) For a discussion of Teresa's self-denying rhetoric and the implications of her travels, see Alison Weber, *Teresa of Avila and the Rhetoric of Femininity* (Princeton: Princeton University Press, 1990), 42-76. Also see Mariá Lourdes Soler, "El amor y el matrimonio profanos vistos por Santa Teresa," *Letras Femeninas* 26 (Spring-Fall 1990): 1-12.

9. Robinson, *Wayward Women*, 82.

10. For a discussion of the text's authorship and legacy, see Jean Fagan Yellin's "Text and Context of Harriet Jacobs' *Incidents in the Life of a Slave Girl: Written by Herself*," *The Slave's Narrative*, ed. Charles T. Davis and Henry Louis Gates, Jr. (Oxford: Oxford University Press, 1985), 262-82.

11. Harriet Jacobs, *Incidents in the Life of a Slave Girl: Written by Herself* (1861; Detroit: Negro History Press, 1969), 119. For a fascinating literary parallel of choosing a child's death over slavery, see Toni Morrison, *Beloved* (New York: Knopf, 1987).

12. Jacobs, *Incidents*, 96.

13. Ida B. Wells, *Crusade for Justice: The Autobiography of Ida B. Wells*, ed. Alfreda M. Duster (Chicago: University of Chicago Press, 1970); Maya Angelou, *All God's Children Need Traveling Shoes* (New York: Random House, 1986). The flight to Harlem in particular has been a powerful and recurring journey pattern in American history and literature; see, for example, James De Jongh, *Vicious Modernism: Black Harlem and the Literary Imagination* (Cambridge: Cambridge University Press, 1990).

14. Maya Angelou, *I Know Why the Caged Bird Sings* (New York: Random House, 1969), 68. Also see Elizabeth Schultz, "African and Afro-American Roots in Contemporary Afro-American Literature: The Difficult Search for Family Origins," *Studies in American Fiction* 8 (1980): 127-45.

15. Hsieh Pingying, "Girl Rebel," *Rice Bowl Women: Writings By and About the Women of China and Japan*, ed. Dorothy Blair Shimer (New York: Mentor, 1982), 134, 141.

16. This journey pattern is described as the "dying fall" by Catharine Stimpson; its more triumphant version is the "enabling escape." Catharine R.

Stimpson, "Zero Degree Deviancy: The Lesbian Novel in English," *Critical Inquiry* 8 (1981): 364. Also see Bonnie Zimmerman, "Exiting from Patriarchy: The Lesbian Novel of Development," *The Voyage In: Fictions of Female Development*, ed. Elizabeth Abel, Marianne Hirsch, and Elizabeth Langland (Hanover, N. H.: University Press of New England, 1983), 244-57.

17. Rosario Ferr, "The Writer's Kitchen," *Lives on the Line: The Testimony of Contemporary Latin American Authors*, ed. Doris Meyer (Berkeley: University of California Press, 1988), 215.

18. Ellen Moers, *Literary Women: The Great Writers* (New York: Doubleday, 1976), 122-40.

19. The sexual implications of a woman on a journey can be seen in the unfortunate titles concocted by editors: Jane Robinson, ed. *Wayward Women*; Margaret Fountaine's diary posthumously published as *Love Among the Butterflies: The Travels of a Victorian Lady*, ed. W. F. Cater (London: Collins, 1980); and the worst, *Ladies on the Loose: Women Travellers of the 18th and 19th Centuries*, ed. Leo Hamalian (New York: Dodd, Mead, 1981). The travelers themselves chose far less titillating titles, often incorporating that resonant word "lady": Mrs. F. D. Bridges, *Journal of a Lady's Travels Round the World* (London: Murray, 1883); Isabella Bird, *A Lady's Life in the Rocky Mountains* (London: Murray, 1879); etc.

20. Charlotte Perkins Gilman, *The Home: Its Work and Influence* (1903; Urbana: University of Illinois Press, 1972), 254.

21. Katherine Mansfield, *Journal of Katherine Mansfield*, ed. J. Middleton Murry (New York: Alfred A. Knopf, 1929), 33.

22. Elizabeth Fagg Olds, *Women of the Four Winds* (Boston: Houghton Mifflin, 1985), 153.

23. Robyn Davidson, *Tracks* (New York: Pantheon, 1980), 212. Davidson makes this statement after describing running out of toilet paper and tampons on her eight-month trek across Australia with four camels.

24. Mansfield, *Journal*, 254.

25. Simone de Beauvoir, *The Second Sex* (New York: Bantam Books; reprint 1970), 271-72.

26. Sandra Gilbert and Susan Gubar, *The Madwoman in the Attic: The Woman Writer and the Nineteenth Century Literary Imagination* (New Haven: Yale University Press, 1979), 76.

27. See, for example, Sandra Frieden's "Shadowing/Surfacing/Shedding: Contemporary German Writers in Search of a Female Bildungsroman," and Marianne Hirsch, "Spiritual Bildung: The Beautiful Soul as Paradigm," both in *The Voyage In*, 23-48, 304-16.

28. Edward H. Friedman, *The Antiheroine's Voice: Narrative Discourse and Transformations of the Picaresque* (Columbia: University of Missouri Press, 1987), 148.

29. Alison Weber points out that St. Teresa of Avila's *Book of Foundations* (1573) is, though a deeply religious text, also a female picaresque in which Teresa outwits the men who try to restrain her. For Teresa, whose

writings were under constant scrutiny by the Inquisition, the self-deprecating voice of the pícara was a strategem of survival: "as a woman she could not assume a heroic role in her epic of reform. The alternative was to be a pícara, an antiheroine in a mock epic" (134). But for the woman traveler who seeks to speak with a rhetoric of authority rather than the self-ironic voice of the pícara, the picaresque may be an unsuitable model.

30. Carol P. Christ, *Diving Deep and Surfacing: Women Writers on Spiritual Quest* (Boston: Beacon Press, 1980), 13-26.

31. Dana Heller, *The Feminization of Quest Romance* (Austin: University of Texas Press, 1991). See also sections entitled "The Journey" and "The Return" in Carol Pearson and Katherine Pope, *The Female Hero in American and British Literature* (New York and London: R. R. Bowker, 1981), 63-278.

32. Joseph Campbell, *The Hero With a Thousand Faces*, 2nd ed. Bollingen Series 17 (Princeton: Princeton University Press, 1968), 384-85. See also Northrop Frye, *The Anatomy of Criticism: Four Essays* (Princeton: Princeton University Press, 1981), 183, who agrees that winning the bride is the typical quest activity. See also Annis V. Pratt's discussion of Frye in her "Spinning Among Fields: Jung, Frye, Lévi-Strauss," in *Feminist Archetypal Theory: Interdisciplinary Re-Visions of Jungian Thought*, ed. Estella Lauter and Carol Schreier Rupprecht (Knoxville: University of Tennessee Press, 1985), 106-118.

33. See, for example, Demaris Wehr, *Jung and Feminism: Liberating Archetypes* (New Brunswick, N. J.: Rutgers University Press, 1987), reassessing the Jungian anima in light of feminist theory. See also Pratt, "Spinning Among Fields," 105-106.

34. Northrop Frye, *The Secular Scripture: A Study of the Structure of Romance* (Cambridge, Mass.: Harvard University Press, 1976), 119.

35. Pratt, "Spinning Among Fields," 111. The "battle" idea is present, too, in the figures of speech by which American frontiersmen described their forceful penetration and subjugation of the "virgin land," as discussed by Annette Kolodny, *The Land Before Her: Fantasy and Experience of the American Frontiers, 1630-1860* (Chapel Hill and London: University of North Carolina Press, 1984), 3-7. Also see the essays in *The Desert is No Lady: Women's Visions of Southwestern Landscapes, 1880-1980*, ed. Vera Norwood and Janice Monk (New Haven: Yale University Press, 1987).

36. Annis V. Pratt, with Barbara White, Andrea Loewenstein, and Mary Wyer, *Archetypal Patterns in Women's Fiction* (Bloomington: Indiana University Press, 1981), 139-40.

37. *Ibid.*, 142.

38. *Ibid.*, 141. See also Pratt, "Spinning Among Fields," 101-106.

39. West, *Black Lamb*, 1088-89.

40. On Persephone, see, for example, Pratt, "Spinning Among Fields," 112, and Carl Jung and C. Kerenyi, *Essays on a Science of Mythology: The Myth of the Divine Child and the Mysteries of Eleusis*, trans. R. F. C. Hull

(Princeton: Princeton University Press, 1950), 77. On Psyche, see Heller, "Remaking Psyche," 22-39; Lee Edwards, "The Labors of Psyche: Toward a Theory of Female Heroes," *Critical Inquiry* 6 (Autumn 1979): 33-49; and Mary Anne Ferguson, "The Female Novel of Development and the Myth of Psyche," in Abel, Hirsch, and Langland, *The Voyage In*, 228-43.

41. Eric Neumann, *The Origins and History of Consciousness*, trans. R. F. C. Hull, Bollingen Series 42 (Princeton: Princeton University Press, 1970), 93, 127. See also Neumann's *The Great Mother: An Analysis of the Archetype*, 2nd ed., trans. Ralph Manheim, Bollingen Series 47 (Princeton: Princeton University Press, 1963).

42. See, for example, Judith Fetterley, *The Resisting Reader: A Feminist Approach to American Fiction* (Bloomington: Indiana University Press, 1978).

43. Elizabeth Segal, " 'As the Twig is Bent...': Gender and Childhood Reading," *Gender and Reading: Essays on Readers, Texts, and Contexts*, ed. Elizabeth A. Flynn and Patrocinio P. Schweickart (Baltimore: Johns Hopkins University Press, 1986), 175. A recent example of a woman reading male-oriented stories is the *Parade* Police Officer of the Year for 1990, Katherine Heller (Pam Proctor, "I Didn't Have Time to Taste the Fear," *Parade*, September 30, 1990, 4-6). She cites childhood readings of works by Jack London, Louis L'Amour, and Alistair MacLean as inspiration for joining the police force. "I had lessons in piano and voice, but I wanted to break free.... I was a wild spirit. I wanted to be out there like Sea Wolf, pirating ships" (5). Heller's mother wouldn't let her play sports for fear she'd get hurt. Heller won the *Parade* award for shooting a man who was trying to kill her partner.

44. Segal, "As the Twig Is Bent," 177.

45. Kathryn Shevelow, "Fathers and Daughters: Women as Readers of the *Tatler*," in Flynn and Schweickart, *Gender and Reading*, 108.

46. Amelia Earhart, *Last Flight*, ed. George Palmer Putnam (New York: Orion, 1988; reprint of New York: Harcourt, Brace, 1937), 84.

47. *Ibid.*, 30.

Section I

Adventure, Class, and Clothing

IN VARIOUS ERAS and cultures, journeying may allow women to experience adventure in ways that both reveal and remake their gender imaging. The destination may not matter particularly nor the distance. What is important is mobility, for a change in a woman's surroundings may open possibilities for change in the traveler herself. Strange lands, odd customs, and unfamiliar faces are mere souvenirs from the road into an even less ponderable unknown: the limits and the possibilities of her femaleness. In the following three essays, women venture into the border regions of their gender as it has been defined at home. At home, their feminine roles may have been so automatic that they seem "natural." Away from home, however, the traveler's gender is isolated from its context and thus becomes unusually visible to the traveler herself and to others. In this defamiliarization of gender, clothing becomes a symbol of ideology that can be consciously manipulated or abandoned according to the traveler's needs. As Birgitta Ingemanson observes, female travel (and travel writing) can be a performance, the audience consisting not only of the imagined armchair travelers but also of the highly judgmental spectators along the way.

For the 19th-century women travelers in the first two essays, Birgitta Ingemanson's "Under Cover: The Paradox of Victorian Women's Travel Costume" and Susan Armitage's "Another Lady's Life in the Rocky Mountains," the adventure was to go on a journey while preserving, as Armitage says, their "gentility in the wilderness." They had to overcome their class's Victorian restrictions on ladylike behavior without losing decorum, to find ways of balancing the social expectations of propriety with their own newly awakened zestful sense of freedom — that thirst for mobility and active life that parlors did not accommodate.

In the accounts of these women's journeys one therefore finds an intriguing dichotomy: women's properly clad and mannered figures posed against grand backgrounds of wild nature that symbolize the soaring, exhilarating forces at work on their internal self-imaging.

Diane Gillespie's "The Ride of Godiva: Defiant Journeys in 20th-Century English Women's Plays" offers a counterpoint to the first two essays. These Godivas, traditional and modern, find freedom in undressing just as the women in Ingemanson's and Armitage's essays find freedom in dressing for the part. Their challenge is to move at a speed equivalent to the shock value of their nakedness. The Godivas remove more than their clothes; they also remove the ideological trappings that limit their activity. Their journeys are short, but they cross the frontiers of propriety, changing their communities as well as themselves along the way.

Under Cover:
The Paradox of Victorian Women's
Travel Costume

Birgitta Maria Ingemanson

Omnia mea mecum porto
(I carry all my things with me)
Cicero

DURING VICTORIAN AND EDWARDIAN times, in many ways so oppressive for women, European and American "ladies" traveled
in larger numbers, more widely, and with greater recognition than ever
before. Western society was beginning to tolerate small doses of female mobility, but more significantly, as Dorothy Middleton and Catherine Barnes Stevenson have pointed out, women themselves began to
use journeys as an instrument of personal and professional liberation.[1]
From a vantage point of 100 years later it may seem odd, then, that
in addition to breaking the chains of passivity forced upon them at home,
these women did not also rebel against the inhibitive clothing and etiquette prescribed in Victorian drawing rooms. On the contrary, even
in a period of dress reform and budding interest in women's sports,
the great women travelers coolly persisted in donning their corsets
and hats, dining in open nature on white linen cloths, and taking their
stoves and often-intricate household utensils – in effect their homes –
with them.[2]

Victorian dress and domesticity were certainly cumbersome and
restrictive, but their function on the road can also be considered supportive, even permissive. In strange surroundings, familiar clothing along
with well-known domestic props provided not only a reassuring sense

of stability but also a façade of propriety behind which the women were free to pursue the ulterior purpose of their travels: active participation in life. Rather than adopting a liberated "New Woman" (and thereby threatening) persona, these travelers cleverly expanded the one they already possessed: they were slightly mad but proper (and therefore harmless) ladies. Quite dramatically, this mask of normalcy offered mobility, influence, and a degree of power. Paradoxically, the very constraint of their costume, not unlike that of a shell, turned out to provide both the freedom and the shelter necessary to overcome the homelessness and alienation endemic to travel.

The actualities of female travel have caught the attention of relatively few scholars. While some, such as Middleton and Stevenson, have published ground-breaking studies with a focus on women's journeys in the Victorian era, most have dismissed female travel books as something faintly comical or as something questionable from a literary point of view. Thus, one anthologist compiling excerpts from original travel accounts by women cannot resist a hint of suggestiveness with his title *Ladies on the Loose*;[3] and another—the editor of the *Norton Book of Travel*—belittles women's travel writing even more concretely by including among his more than 50 entries a mere four female authors: Lady Montagu, Frances Trollope, Freya Stark, and Jan Morris. Quick to note that Morris is the former James Morris who accompanied the Mount Everest expedition in 1953 and who later had a sex-change operation, the Norton editor concludes inanely that "Although as a travel writer she can be tough when necessary, there seems something feminine (in the old-fashioned sense) in the 'niceness' of her vision."[4] The sexist tone of this remark is only marginally different from the resentful put-down of the hugely successful explorer May French Sheldon expressed in 1891 by one reporter who speculated that it is "the feminine spirit of unrest, and the uneasy jealousy that is for ever driving the fair sex into proving itself the equal of the other."[5]

There was ample reason for women in Victorian-Edwardian society to be "jealous" of men's position and rights, but the women travelers who so irked the scholarly and journalistic establishment presented a far from unified political front. Ranging from anti-imperialist activists like Mary Kingsley to opponents of women's suffrage such as Gertrude Bell, they sought ultimately not political power on the national scene but a wider scope of possibilities in their personal lives. For although Victorian and Edwardian women with the social background, education, and financial means to *choose* to travel did not face the dangers and humiliation of captive women or other travelers on forced journeys, all women who stepped out on the road had to confront the unnaturally passive ideals of their femininity. Unlike men, who were used to mobility and social participation, women were brought up not to stray alone from the home. The women travelers of these times were seldom outwardly flamboyant, but their very decision to travel challenged accepted norms and invited retribution. Along with the Bachelor Girl and the Old Maid, they became the butt of jokes; traveling heroines in novels often met unfortunate ends.[6] The progression of women travelers was thus fraught with difficulties that male travelers did not encounter; it can be described as an obstacle course with multiple hurdles: leaving home and living on the road, all the time facing society's disapproval. The intriguing ally the women seem to have chosen in this difficult pursuit was their clothing.

The most visible external impediment to women's mobility, Victorian and Edwardian female dress, with its vibrant colors, elegant fabrics, and fanciful shapes, was designed to titillate the senses, not to support a healthily active existence.[7] While English and American political activists at home argued for dress reform and a simplified code of behavior, women travelers on the road, by contrast, were far more concerned with maintaining a correctly feminine appearance, whatever the difficulties of doing so. Proving that "a woman could travel as easily and effectively as a man," as May French Sheldon wished to do,[8] would be meaningless if the woman also dressed like a man. Catherine Barnes Stevenson has summed up the negative political implication: "To wear trousers, even in the jungle of Africa or the mountains of Tibet, was to identify oneself as an advocate of female emancipation."[9] Considering the untamed landscapes these women traversed, it would seem reasonable to wear men's attire. Yet for fear of demeaning their social status Victorian women travelers were unwilling to neglect the strict dress code to which they were accustomed at home. In textbook parlance, they moved their "clothing zone" with them.[10] Thus, women steadfastly hiked, explored, and lived out-of-doors in their long skirts and tight waistlines (albeit supplemented on occasion with "Dr. Jaeger's Porous Woollen" underclothes). Photos from climbing expeditions during the late 19th century show women scaling mountains in crinolines and floppy hats, alpenstock in hand.[11] Professional travelers such as Isabella Bird, Kate Marsden, and May French Sheldon, first among women to become members of the prestigious Royal Geographical Society in London (in 1892) and consequently no strangers to controversy, were—at least initially—categorically opposed to wearing trousers. Although Bird's research interests frequently took her to wilderness areas in, for example, the Rocky Mountains and Tibet, and although she loved what she called "a good gallop," she was not about to pose in embarrassing costume, however agile it might make her. Amelia Edwards, who traveled widely in the spectacular Dolomites in northern Italy in the summer of 1872, agreed, advising her female readers on the absolute need to bring their own side-saddles, echoing the general notion that riding astride was unacceptably "inelegant."[12] Another formidable Victorian, Daisy Bates, who worked among the Australian aborigines and died in 1951, earnestly defended her clothes selection in the bush even decades after Queen Victoria's death. Admitting that it was hard to walk in her "high-heeled footwear," she nevertheless remained true to the dress ideals of her youth:

> It was a fastidious toilet, for throughout my life I have adhered to the simple but exact dictates of fashion as I left it, when Victoria was Queen—a neat white blouse, stiff collar and ribbon tie, a dark skirt and coat, stout, and serviceable trim shoes and neat black stockings, a sailor hat and a fly-veil, and, for my excursions to the camps, always a dust-coat and a sunshade. Not until I was in meticulous order would I emerge from my tent, dressed for the day.[13]

The clear gender difference in the understanding of what constituted proper dress made women's lives doubly circumspect. Living in Africa in the 1880s, Katharine Petherick did not forget the dress code and its special female restrictions, even in the jungle. Acutely aware of her upbringing, when visitors came she was far more perturbed by her own necessarily but only relatively ragged looks than by the much worse state of affairs of the male explorers around her.[14]

As these examples indicate, the strictures of female clothing in Victorian times were often in direct and absurd contrast to the vast scenery and boisterous activities of travel. A similar gap, between society's ideal of decorous but passive femininity and the reality of human inquisitiveness and hunger for life, was equally glaring. Despite the restrictive dress, women's imaginations soared: that they longed for adventure was certain. Repeatedly, these travel writers stressed a youthful dream very contrary to the accepted norm, namely "to go beyond the garden gate, to follow the road that passed it by, and to set out for the Unknown," as Alexandra David-Neel put it in the description of her childhood in 1870s Paris.[15] Hitting upon the same evocative symbol of the garden gate, Gertrude Bell, who by no stretch of the imagination could be said to challenge the established status of women, began her influential account of a 1905 journey to the Levant with a powerful paean to the excitement of breaking loose from closure and restraint:

> To those bred under an elaborate social order few such moments of exhilaration can come as that which stands at the threshold of wild travel. The gates of the enclosed garden are thrown open, the chain at the entrance of the sanctuary is lowered, with a wary glance to right and left you step forth, and, behold! the immeasurable world. The world of adventure and of enterprise, dark with hurrying storms, glittering in raw sunlight, an unanswered question and an unanswerable doubt hidden in the fold of every hill. . . . So you leave the sheltered close, and, like the man in the fairy story, you feel the bands break that were riveted about your heart as you enter the path that stretches across the rounded shoulder of the earth.[16]

Thus, having to turn to male role models for guidance and inspiration, the published women travelers were often spurred by a sense of indomitable excitement and wonder that helped them over the first obstacle on their course: they were out of the familiar home.

Once on the road, all travelers must define their relationship to it. For educated Victorian and Edwardian women, attuned as they were to the social requirements of dress and etiquette, it was easy to perceive the physical landscape as a kind of platform or moving stage and their costume a most suitable prop. Travel was drama; the travelers were the actors emerging in full view; there was an audience and a kind of script. That traveling and the road itself were understood in a generally theatrical light is indicated by the choice in numerous journeys, for instance the one by Amelia Edwards, of words such as "playground" and "amphitheatre" to describe the travel arena. Villagers and chance acquaintances became eager (while frequently critical) spectators, augmenting the dramatic atmosphere. Having just arrived in the *piazza* of a small northern Italian town, Edwards and her female companion noted a familiar scene: "the usual score or two of idle men and boys. . .immediately start up from nowhere in particular, and swarm, open-mouthed, about the carriage, staring at its occupants as if they were members of a travelling menagerie."[17] It was often the *type* of clothing, so necessary to the women travelers themselves, that roused the spectators' curiosity. As Daisy Bates walked down a lane in the intense summer heat of Australia, people would comment on her "funny clothes" and gloves.[18] The onlookers had no difficulty noting the dramatic qualities of the women's appearance, often subjectively taking sides as if discussing a performance. For example, news reports about Lady Hester Stanhope, who settled in Lebanon in the 1830s, observed with some condescension that "she has so long been acting a part...that she has begun to act it in earnest"; while a fascinated member of the audience at one of Mary Kingsley's public lectures interpreted Kingsley's black silk dress and extravagant cameo brooch as "a bit of stage-craft designed to heighten her achievements."[19]

The women's immediate agenda or "script" was to ensure their right of continued progress. As when they were setting out on the journey, this step, too, was closely related to their choice of traveling costume. For Gertrude Bell, being a good traveler meant juggling an imperialistic sense of righteousness on behalf of Great Britain with a certain polite respect for the laws and customs of others. Pointedly, she excluded clothing from the area of cultural tolerance and urged women to dress as lavishly and well as they would at home: "For a woman this rule is of the first importance, since a woman can never disguise herself effectually. That she should be known to come of a great and honoured stock, whose customs are inviolable, is her best claim to consideration."[20] Bell seems to acknowledge that the road is a stage and that the stage costume must reflect the grandeur of the company backing the troupe, whether in the theater or among nations. Benjamin Disraeli, the future British prime minister who visited Palestine and Turkey in 1830-31, observed in his novel *Contarini Fleming* (1832) that the only way to travel in the Middle East was "with an appearance of pomp."[21] Women travelers took this idea to extraordinary length, and were surprisingly successful in using their clothing to establish both wide mobility and a modicum of power. Mary Kingsley, for example, always eager not to disturb male sensibilities, preferred to operate from behind her carefully contrived trademark—that neat dress in black silk—to achieve her considerable scholarly and political goals. Advising single women who intended to travel in Africa not to try to explain their lack of a husband, she suggested that they say instead "you are searching for him and then...locate him [far] away in the direction in which you wish to travel"; this "elicits help and sympathy."[22] Although it was a ruse, the women would be able to go where they wanted. Other female travelers were less discreet in their power-play, aiming instead to influence with a bang. Bedecked in the outlandish attire of a British court gown, jewels, and an enormous blond wig, American-born May French Sheldon, who studied the Masai in East Africa, confirmed her credentials and commanded her native crew. It was calculatedly for show—the hair was false, the jewels artificial—but she succeeded in gaining the men's respect and was rewarded with Masai honorary titles such as "Sir," "Lady white man," or simply Bébé Bwana, lady boss or "Mrs. Mister."[23]

Although outwardly scoffing at the unseemly spectacle of being performers in a road show or circus troupe, inwardly Edwards (who described her entrance into the Italian *piazza*) and other travelers with her recognized this reality and arranged their lives accordingly. Yielding to centuries of travel wisdom, they took not as little luggage as possible but enough to be comfortable;[24] in turn, they created a *mise-en-scène* or stage setting with the props that best backed their roles. Bombastic as ever, Sheldon prepared a medical kit to rival a village pharmacy:

> there was carbolic acid, cascars, nitrate of silver for the cauterization of wounds, menthol and lanolin, besides a supply of "Livingstone's Rousers," which were tonics and aperients. There were pellets and tooth extractors and two large-sized pigskin cases, filled, two small leather emergency cases, one French-Sheldon medicine belt and lancets, splints, toilet soap, violet water, Eno's fruit salts and a traveller's surgical and medical guide.[25]

When leaving for Russia to care for Siberian lepers in 1891, Kate Marsden packed 40 pounds of plum pudding in addition to the usual sardines, biscuits, and tea. On a smaller scale than in England but nevertheless impressively, Amelia Edwards also proudly displayed her extensive preparations for all travel eventualities. She could manage light sickness as well as meet the requirements for that culinary necessity, a good sauce:

> we bought two convenient wicker-baskets, and wherewithal to stock them—tea, sugar, Reading biscuits in tins, chocolate in tablets, Liebig's Ramornie extract, two bottles of Cognac, four of Marsala, pepper, salt, arrowroot, a large metal flask of spirits of wine, and an Etna [stove]. Thus armed, we could at all events rely in case of need upon our own resources.[26]

Although spurred by different motivations, Victorian and Edwardian women travelers shared an astute sense of existential harmony with the philosopher in an alien land who, according to Cicero is said to have declared, "I carry all my things with me."[27] While his possessions were limited by the exigencies of forced exile and theirs were allowed to multiply thanks to servants and spacious vehicles, their need for unity and a meaning of life were the same. Just as the women's clothing helped confirm a small area or "circle" of familiarity, the food stuffs and other domestic staples constituted a center of calm and peaceful routine amidst the larger traveling reality of constant change.

In retrospect, we may find the costume and strident domesticity of Victorian women travelers cumbersome and inappropriate. But, precisely in the context of vigorous travel, these attributes had a deeper, eminently pragmatic function: as a barrier behind which the women were safe. In extreme cases, the costume and props served literally as a shield, protecting bodies and saving lives; one begins to sense the outline of a pass of safe conduct. Indeed, the very encumbrance of the clothing could be instrumental as a lifesaver. In 1883 Florence Dixie, a well-known British traveler temporarily at home, was stabbed on a street in Windsor, but "the steel of her stays" prevented the knife from reaching her body.[28] May French Sheldon, who adorned her walking stick with the command "Noli me tangere" [Touch me not], sat, slept, and traveled in a "palanquin," a covered carrying-chair of intricate and comfortable design. When it occurred that she was hurled off a bridge by accident, the chair constituted her "shell" of survival, functioning not so differently from Dixie's corset: "For a hazardous moment...I was whirled about, protected from injury by my Palanquin, but with my head down and completely submerged in thick yellow water."[29]

More frequently, the female travelers' clothing and domestic objects provided an official identity and façade behind which the women could develop not only their publicly condoned feminine role, but also their innermost human dimensions. Sadly, for many Victorian women travelers, the metaphor likening life to a journey, so common among male travel writers, was peculiarly and painfully poignant: in their experience, real life — active and mobile — was possible *only* on the road. They had to leave Victorian society in order to be allowed to take charge of their destiny, to make their own decisions, and to be healthy as women and professionals. To achieve this, they found it necessary and pragmatic to present an acceptable façade, to travel under cover as it were. Their disguise was not contrastive like that of female author George Sand who dressed in men's garb in order to be able to move undisturbed at night.[30] Rather, it was a virtually invisible mask like that of Miss Marple or Jessica Fletcher, fictional women detectives whose "first and foremost skill is to pretend that they are not what they are."[31] Similarly, Victorian and Edwardian women travelers arranged their cover. To some degree they were assisted in this enterprise by the Victorian penchant for projecting respectable but not necessarily genuine fronts; the intense social concern with outward appearance and "surface effects" offered women a degree of freedom in personal behavior.[32] While reformer Elizabeth Cady Stanton worried in 1857 that the restrictive nature of female dress cemented women's dependence on male support when they wished to move "up stairs [sic] and down, in the carriage and out, on the horse, up the hill, over the ditch and fence," Isabella Bird felt that it was precisely in motion and activity that decorative façades could best be exploited. She noted: "Travellers are privileged to do the most improper things with perfect propriety."[33] Dressed correctly, in other words, they were free to proceed as they pleased.

Just as the yearning for adventure and the "Unknown" first ignited their travel dreams and later spurred them on, the open expanses and dynamic motion of the journeying itself gave the travelers health and purpose. Scholars have documented the role of the Victorian medical profession in keeping females physically immobile: many women were ill simply from passivity, frail by an enforced sedentary existence without any outlet for action.[34] If society thus inhibited their natural desire for movement, illness — as if in a subterfuge — could allow it to blossom. In her book *High Albania* (1907), Edith Durham, who traveled on doctor's orders in an enlightened attempt to cure her depression, was at first tentative and somewhat perplexed in her relationship to the road: "There is a peculiar pleasure in riding out into the unknown." By the last page, however, she has grown in strength and enterprise, and has found a true vocation in relief work for the people of the war-torn Balkans. Seeing the lifeline into the future, for those nations as well as for herself, Durham finishes her account with the words, "I cannot write FINIS for the END is not yet."[35] Many other women who were at home plagued with serious ailments had similar "miraculous" cures on the road. Marianne North, severely rheumatic, went around the world drawing pictures of plants and animals. These paintings became the keystone of the North Gallery, which opened at Kew Gardens outside London in 1882. While May French Sheldon had asthma, and tuberculosis threatened Kate Marsden (who then suffered a mental breakdown), both accomplished extensive professional journeys to Africa and Russia respectively. Isabella Bird is a particularly interesting case. Burdened with a string of ailments including a weak heart, back trouble, and the dreaded "nervous fears," she nevertheless rode and hiked vigorously, exploring faraway destinations on four continents. Significantly, while on the road she was rarely ill; it was when she approached home that the medical problems flared up. Throughout her life, Bird never solved this indoors dilemma, and her yearning for action kept her incessantly moving from one newly furnished dwelling to another. But she remained unable to settle down within the four walls;[36] they, alas, did not move.

Numerous travel accounts attest to the benefits resulting from a felicitous traveling formula that blended a sense of "home" with the dynamics of "motion." I have noted the care and interest with which the women travelers built their stage with its costumes and props; equally life-affirming was the movement of travel itself. An essentially progressive enterprise that offers vistas of scenery as well as new knowledge, travel fosters an atmosphere of eager mental discovery. Julian Jaynes, in his book on the functions of the mind, refers to scientists who recognize "the three B's, the Bus, the Bath, and the Bed" as the kinds of places where "sudden flooding insights" can occur.[37] Although they intend by this primarily the seclusion and peace of privacy, the mention of "the Bus" also signals an awareness of the beneficial role of motion when human beings are trying to come to terms with life's questions. In 1807 during a 70-hours' journey by "heavy coach" across France, Jean Franois Champollion, the young Frenchman who 15 years later was to solve the mystery of the hieroglyphs, was jolted into clarity about the path his studies on the Rosetta Stone must take.[38] A similar illustration may be found in Leo Tolstoy's novel *Anna Karenina*. Dolly, the worn-out mother of a boisterous brood, goes by carriage to visit her sister-in-law Anna, and the traveling itself makes her thoughts spin into an uncharacteristic focus on her own life: "At home her care of the children never gave her leisure to think, but now, during this four hours' drive, all the thoughts she had repressed crowded suddenly into her mind, and she reviewed her whole life from all sides as she had never done before."[39]

If Victorian and Edwardian women travelers remained largely silent on their bed-and-bath experiences, they often emphasized their particular modes of transport. Virtual characters in the journeys, trains and carriages punctuate introspective passages with their rocking and jolting or with the speedy flickering of impressions outside. "Life rushes along like a wheel," wrote socialist agitator Aleksandra Kollontai in 1912, and then likened the English landscape beyond her train window to the flitting images of the cinema.[40] Amelia Edwards was more effusive. Reminding the reader of the poetry and "old romance" of places like Verona, Vicenza, and Padua, she declared, "I know no greater enjoyment than to pass them thus in rapid review, taking the journey straight through from Milan to Venice on a brilliant summer's day. What a series of impressions! What a chain of memories!...and the train flies on!"[41] Thus, the motion itself, coupled with the fresh views and insights, helped open up and develop the women's curiosity and abilities. Neatly corsetted and beveiled, they were no longer mere "grand tourists" or health cure patients, but became professionals in fields as varied as anthropology, archeology, botany, geology, history, and philosophy.[42]

The scholarly achievements of Victorian women travelers have been documented by writers such as Dorothy Middleton, Catherine Barnes Stevenson, and Marion Tinling, but in addition to recognizing the professional aspects of these women's journeys, it is illuminating to consider how they differed from those of men. Male travelers have written supremely interesting and literary travel accounts, as numerous anthologies make clear; men, too, had to establish their relationship to the road, often suffering hardships and obstacles on the way. Yet, in daily routine the women with their costumes and props seem to have fared generally better. Intensely goal-oriented, male travelers tended to charge ahead toward their destination, interested primarily in conquering the land and "getting there." Although they usually planned their journeys carefully and included provisions for emergencies, their inclination toward the result of the trip made them less likely to create a sustaining home environment on the way. For example, Robert Byron, whose travel book *The Road to Oxiana* (1937) has been likened to *Ulysses* and *The Wasteland* in terms of literary significance, and who was certainly not immune to comfort, nevertheless rarely mentioned the domestic side of his journey. By contrast, the account is full of phrases indicating the desire to arrive and to subjugate.[43] Victorian women, on the other hand, while certainly establishing precise goals and objectives for their journeys, tended rather to concentrate on the process of the thing: they traveled to travel, not merely to arrive. As a result they took a stronger and often more objective interest in the places and people they encountered; they had a generally less exalted view of themselves; and they better understood the need for and purpose of domesticity.[44]

The importance of Victorian and Edwardian women's travel costume and other props lay thus not solely in their role as a façade or sturdy armor; perhaps foremost, they were a life support system. Clothing is sometimes seen as an outer "skin,"[45] and the empathic nature of female travel as well as the Victorian feminine ideal seem to have afforded women a direct, practical understanding of this function. Again, the theater provides a useful parallel. The French acting phrase "to enter into the skin of one's part" ("entrer dans la peau de son personnage") approximates the Stanislavsky method of acting, which stresses the need not only to imagine but actually to experience *from within*, as it were, the character traits and circumstances of one's role: one must fuse with the part and live it at home as well as on stage.[46] In fact, the role becomes a mobile unit in which the actors perform. The situation for travelers is very similar: they, too, must find genuine harmony between their own person and "the road," their chosen stage. In addition to presenting the sights and an atmosphere of adventure, great travel books have always commented on metaphysical questions as well, and in such a context the precise wonders of, for example, "Italy" or "Japan" are ultimately of less significance than the traveling human being's relationship to life. Indeed, German literary critic Hans-Joachim Possin has suggested that the underlying, real purpose of all travel, no matter what the surface may seem to project, is to establish one's own identity and find the meaning of one's life. Whether consciously or not, he says, travelers are always encountering and attempting to deal with the homelessness (*Heimatlosigkeit*) and alienation that threaten every journey and all of human existence.[47] Robert Byron would agree, identifying the higher purpose of travel as a search for spiritual fusion in the form of "an organic harmony between all matter and all activity,"[48] a balance, then, between on the one hand the traveler's inner dreams and aspirations, and on the other the external reality of the surroundings that must start with his or her "skin."

Travelers who do not ensure a harmonious balance between their own progression and the forces and conditions around them invite rifts of catastrophic proportions. Whether from foolish pride or ignorance, Antarctic explorer Robert Scott paid less attention to the details of day-to-day living during his 1911-12 trek to the South Pole than to the speed with which the party was to advance. The inadequate preparations for food and transport eventually led to his and his men's death. Although reaching its goal and procuring valuable scientific information, the expedition neglected to establish a basic harmony between its own activities and the natural surroundings. Another example is equally vivid. In 1930 a young Frenchman, Michel Vieuchange, undertook a journey to a long-cherished goal in southern Morocco: Smara, the "forbidden" city. Dressing as a Berber woman, he hoped to advance where Christian men would be killed. The diary describing this journey is grueling to read, filled with almost constant despair broken by only occasional glimmers of hope. Having arrived at his goal, Vieuchange spent an hour in the city; on the return journey, he caught dysentery and died.[49]

The purely physical reasons for Vieuchange's untimely death cannot be disputed: his body, weak from the exigencies of harsh travel and illness, could not recharge and revive. But other travelers, including many Victorian women, had their share of exhaustion, anxiety, and nasty ailments, and lived. One might argue, in fact, that alienation killed Michel Vieuchange. He became a charge, allowing others to run his life and taking no part in the daily decisions about food and night stops. Remaining an outsider with little knowledge of the arena he had chosen, with time he became increasingly more alienated from the people and landscape around him. Although he desired the disguise of a woman and understood the possible benefits of this mask, he did not learn how to take advantage of it. The clothing was highly uncomfortable for him, not because it was female but because it was not his own. In the disguise of an Arab man, he felt equally hampered. His problems stemmed, I think, from the widening split between his external, chosen but not internalized persona, and his inner self. Put bluntly, he was in the wrong skin and did not have a chance of surviving.

For if the skin does not fit it must be changed. Perhaps the most remarkable example of being in the wrong skin, and of sensing the disjunction between the outer and inner beings, is the life journey of writer James Morris who, in the 1960s, became a woman. In travels that seemed to mirror his life, he was compelled to shed not only his masculine clothing but also his male body. In the book about this difficult quest, Jan Morris writes: "I spent half my life traveling in foreign places. I did it because I liked it, and to earn a living, and I have only lately come to see that incessant wandering as an outer expression of my inner journey."[50] In less drastic examples, adjustments of women's travel costume would come with changes in society and modes of transport. Just as train travel obliterated some of the rigors of journeys by coach and carriage in mid-19th century Europe, allowing more elegant dress and lighter shoes, so the widespread use of the bicycle by the end of the century influenced female dress in a more informal direction.[51] Yet, the changes of travel costume seem to have had less to do with a particular age or fashion than with the stage in a given traveler's need or development. The more confidence gained, the more physical—and philosophical—burdens shed. Thus, Isabella Bird designed a special riding suit that would allow easy movement without ignoring Victorian notions of decency: "full Turkish trousers and jauntily made dresses reaching to the ankles" in "tartan flannel," no less. Alexandra David-Neel in icy Tibet sometimes had to do without the warm and bulky coat that served as her shelter, and she learned to create a warm shell around her by meditation.[52] Robyn Davidson, who rode across the deserts of western Australia in 1980 with her dog and four camels, started out with detailed stores of everything that she at first thought essential. By the end of the journey, she "soared":

> I had pared my possessions to almost nothing—a survival kit, that's all. I had a filthy old sarong for hot weather and a jumper and woolly socks for cold weather and I had something to sleep on and something to eat and drink out of and that was all I needed. I felt free and untrammelled and light and I wanted to stay that way.[53]

If Davidson's literary and clothing style was decidedly different from that of her sisters of a century earlier, the women nonetheless shared the same hopes for success, the same difficulties and elation.

Although the Victorian and Edwardian women travelers were of a socio-economic class largely unburdened by poverty or lack of education, the price of their mobility was high. Few of them married; fewer yet had children. Instead, they seemed to turn their journeys into their life, publishing books and lecturing, some—such as Florence Dixie and Aleksandra Kollontai—writing novels about women travelers while they themselves waited for more work opportunities to mature.[54] What they all learned was, in Davidson's words, "that you are as powerful and strong as you allow yourself to be, and that the most difficult part of any endeavour is taking the first step."[55] By reaching into geographic areas where females had never traveled alone, the Victorian women travelers overcame several hurdles in one blow: they emerged from their homebound existence with its subordination to fathers, brothers, and husbands; left a society that granted women only exalted or down-trodden status; and went into the world, actively seeking mobility, con-fronting change, living life. One might say that they used the road as a practical laboratory to test their stamina, intelligence, and independ-ence. To a degree, this made them no different from male travelers who sometimes also sought escape from civilization and from socie-ties that stifled them;[56] it was not a new discovery to liken travel to life. But the women had to be more circumspect in this enterprise. Traveling "under cover," they took along their home not so they could constantly be in it but, ironically, to be able to go outside; they dressed in formal attire not to be conspicuous but, paradoxically, to appear nor-mal and proper. That elemental façade in place, they were ready to proceed.

Notes

1. Dorothy Middleton, *Victorian Lady Travellers* (London: Routledge & Kegan Paul, 1965), introduction; Catherine Barnes Stevenson, *Victorian Women Travel Writers in Africa* (Boston: Twayne, 1982), chapter one. The theme has been continued in more recent collections of materials on women travelers in the Victorian and Edwardian era, including Mary Russell's *The Blessings of a Good Thick Skirt: Women Travellers and Their World* (London: Collins, 1986). I am grateful to Gitta Bridges for alerting me to the existence of this book.
2. See for example Alexandra Allen, *Travelling Ladies* (London: Jupiter, 1980), 10, 22.
3. Leo Hamalian, ed., *Ladies on the Loose: Women Travellers of the 18th and 19th Centuries* (New York: Dodd, Mead & Co., 1981). A similar title is Jane Robinson's *Wayward Women: A Guide to Women Travellers* (Oxford and New York: Oxford University Press, 1990).
4. Paul Fussell, ed., *The Norton Book of Travel* (New York and London: W. W. Norton & Co., 1987), 715. The gender imbalance of this volume is to some extent counteracted by the following new compilation exclusively of women travelers: Marion Tinling, ed., *Women Into the Unknown: A Sourcebook on Women Explorers and Travelers* (New York; Westport, Connecticut; and London: Greenwood Press, 1989).
5. Cited in Allen, *Travelling Ladies*, 40. A fascinating postmodern literary analysis of the problems of reception and therefore of writing that British women travelers (plus the French Alexandra David-Neel) faced in the period 1850-1930 is provided in Sara Mills, *Discourses of Difference: An Analysis of Women's Travel Writing and Colonialism* (New York: Routledge, 1991).
6. For the jokes see Middleton, *Victorian Lady Travellers*, 75. Unlucky literary heroines are described by Shelley Spear in "The Female Traveler in George Eliot's Fiction," paper presented in the "Women in Literature" research group at Washington State University, 1989.
7. See for example Stella Mary Newton, *Health, Art & Reason: Dress Reformers of the 19th Century* (London: John Murray, 1974).
8. Quoted in Middleton, *Victorian Lady Travellers*, 94.
9. Stevenson, *Victorian Women Travel Writers*, 3.
10. Mary Ellen Roach and Joanne B. Eicher, *The Visible Self: Perspectives on Dress* (Englewood Cliffs, N. J.: Prentice-Hall, 1973), 64.
11. See Middleton, *Victorian Lady Travellers*, 136, for the note about the woolen underwear. For the photos see for example Nicholas Bentley, *The Victorian Scene: A Picture Book of the Period 1837-1901* (London: George Weidenfeld & Nicolson, 1968), 138; and Christopher Hibbert, *The Horizon Book of Daily Life in Victorian England* (New York: American Heritage Publishing Co., 1975), 96.
12. Amelia Edwards, *Untrodden Peaks and Unfrequented Valleys: A Midsummer Ramble in the Dolomites* (1873), with a new introduction by Philippa

Levine (Boston: Beacon Press, 1987), xxxii. See also Middleton, *Victorian Lady Travellers*, 139. The reference to Bird is on page 48.

13. Quoted in Allen, *Travelling Ladies*, 172, 186.
14. Middleton, *Victorian Lady Travellers*, 16.
15. Alexandra David-Neel, *My Journey to Lhasa: The Personal Story of the Only White Woman Who Succeeded in Entering the Forbidden City* (New York and London: Harper & Brothers, 1927), ix.
16. Gertrude Bell, *The Desert and the Sown* (1907), new introduction by Sarah Graham-Brown (Boston: Beacon Press, 1987), 1-2. The image of reaching out "Over the Garden Gate" is used prominently in Dea Birkett, *Spinsters Abroad: Victorian Lady Explorers* (Oxford and New York: B. Blackwell, 1989); see the chapter by that title.
17. Edwards, *Untrodden Peaks*, xxi, xxx, 21. For another instance of the Italian *piazza* being understood as a stage see Edith Wharton, *Italian Backgrounds* (1905; New York: The Ecco Press, 1989), the chapter "An Alpine Posting-Inn," 3-14. Furthermore, writers such as Decima Moore and Leonard Woolf describe travel as a dramatic performance; see Valerie Pakenham, *Out in the Noonday Sun: Edwardians in the Tropics* (New York: Random House, 1985), 182, 184. The basic idea that human relationships have theatrical dimensions has been researched by Erving Goffman; see for instance *The Presentation of Self in Everyday Life* (Edinburgh: University of Edinburgh, 1956). For an illustration of the theater's special advantages for women see Juliet Blair, "Private Parts in Public Places: The Case of Actresses," in Shirley Ardener, ed., *Woman and Space: Ground Rules and Social Maps* (New York: St. Martin's Press, 1981), 205-228.
18. Allen, *Travelling Ladies*, 185.
19. *Ibid.*, 89; and Katherine Frank, *A Voyager Out: The Life of Mary Kingsley* (Boston: Houghton Mifflin, 1986), 258.
20. Bell, *The Desert and the Sown*, xx.
21. Robert Blake, *Disraeli's Grand Tour: Benjamin Disraeli and the Holy Land 1830-31* (New York: Oxford University Press, 1982), 70.
22. Frank, *A Voyager Out*, 257.
23. Middleton, *Victorian Lady Travellers*, 96-98; Stevenson, *Victorian Women Travel Writers*, 4.
24. Winfried Löschburg, *A History of Travel*, English version Ruth Michaelis-Jena and Patrick Murray (Leipzig: Edition Leipzig, 1979), 84-85.
25. Allen, *Travelling Ladies*, 25.
26. Edwards, *Untrodden Peaks*, 11. The information about Kate Marsden is in Middleton, *Victorian Lady Travellers*, 136.
27. The epigraph at the beginning of this essay, "Omnia mea mecum porto," is from Cicero, *Paradoxa Stoicorum*, 1.8, and refers to the Greek philosopher Bias who was forced into a journey of exile c. 570 B. C. While the quotation is usually reproduced as I have, Cicero's word order is slightly different: "Omnia mecum porto mea." Rhonda Blair kindly helped me with this reference.

28. Stevenson, *Victorian Women Travel Writers*, 76. The incident is laced with ironic twists bearing on clothing. Dixie had been active in the movement for dress reform but was wearing formal Victorian clothes at the time of the assault, 74. Furthermore, her male attackers were disguised as women in order to be able to approach her less noticeably.
29. Middleton, *Victorian Lady Travellers*, 90; Allen, *Travelling Ladies*, 39.
30. Curtis Cate, *George Sand: A Biography* (Boston: Houghton Mifflin, 1975), for example 393. For a discussion of women wearing men's clothing, see, for example, Estelle C. Jelinek, "Disguise Autobiographies: Women Masquerading as Men," *Women's Studies International Forum*, 10:1 (1987): 53-62.
31. Melvin Maddocks, "Women of Mystery—the New Detectives," *Christian Science Monitor*, 22 January 1988: 19.
32. Bentley, *The Victorian Scene*, 44; Roach and Eicher, *The Visible Self*, 144. See also the monumental work on the Victorian age by Peter Gay, *The Bourgeois Experience: Victoria to Freud*, v. 2, *The Tender Passion* (New York and Oxford: Oxford University Press, 1986), 4, passim.
33. Stanton's observation has been cited by many researchers, for example Susan B. Kaiser, *The Social Psychology of Clothing and Personal Adornment* (New York: Macmillan; London: Collier Macmillan, 1985), 9. For Bird's stand see Pat Barr, *A Curious Life for a Lady: The Story of Isabella Bird* (London: Macmillan and John Murray, 1970), 54.
34. See for example Barbara Ehrenreich and Deirdre English, *For Her Own Good: 150 Years of the Experts' Advice to Women* (Garden City, N. Y.: Anchor Press/Doubleday, 1978).
35. Edith Durham, *High Albania* (1909), new introduction by John Hodgson (Boston: Beacon Press, 1987), ix-x, 39, 348. Durham was lucky in that several of the members of her family were physicians who could, thus, influence the medical decisions.
36. The references to Bird are in Middleton, *Victorian Lady Travellers*, 39, 53. For the other women's ailments, passim.
37. Julian Jaynes, *The Origin of Consciousness in the Breakdown of the Bicameral Mind* (Boston: Houghton Mifflin, 1976), 44. I am thankful to Robert V. Smith for sharing this and the next reference with me.
38. C. W. Ceram, *Gods, Graves, and Scholars: The Story of Archaeology*, trans. E. B. Garside and Sophie Wilkins, second ed. (New York: Alfred A. Knopf, 1967), 92-93.
39. Leo Tolstoy, *Anna Karenina: The Maude Translation, Backgrounds and Sources, Essays in Criticism*, ed. George Gibian (New York: W. W. Norton, 1970), 549.
40. A[leksandra] Kollontai, *Po burzhuaznoi Evrope: Iz zapisnoi knizhki agitatora 1909-1914* [Across bourgeois Europe: From an agitator's notebook 1909-1914] (Kazan': Gosudarstvennoe izdatel'stvo, 1921), 16, 45.
41. Edwards, *Untrodden Peaks*, 9.
42. Although the Grand Tour was an exclusively male enterprise in the 18th century, by the middle of the 19th women were increasingly using it for

their education, too. Thomas Mallon, *A Book of One's Own: People and Their Diaries* (New York: Ticknor & Fields, 1984), 57.

43. Robert Byron, *The Road to Oxiana* (1937), with a new introduction by Paul Fussell (New York: Oxford University Press, 1982), for example 116-17, 123. The literary comparison of Robert Byron to James Joyce and T. S. Eliot is in Paul Fussell, *Abroad: British Literary Traveling Between the Wars* (Oxford and New York: Oxford University Press, 1980), 95. For an absorbing study of the sexual aspects of men's attitude to the American frontier see Annette Kolodny, *The Lay of the Land: Metaphor as Experience and History in American Life and Letters* (Chapel Hill: The University of North Carolina Press, 1975).

44. Stevenson, *Victorian Women Travel Writers*, 5; Hamalian, *Ladies on the Loose*, 253; Witold Rybczynski, *Home: A Short History of an Idea* (New York: Viking Penguin Inc., 1986), viii.

45. For instance in Marilyn J. Horn, *The Second Skin: An Interdisciplinary Study of Clothing* (Boston: Houghton Mifflin, 1968).

46. Toby Cole, ed., *Acting: A Handbook of the Stanislavski* [sic] *Method*, introduction by Lee Strasburg (New York: Lear Publishers, 1947), 19-20, 221.

47. Hans-Joachim Possim, *Reisen und Literatur: Das Thema des Reisens in der englischen Literatur des 18. Jahrhunderts* (Tübingen: Max Niemeyer Verlag, 1972), 257.

48. Quoted in Fussell, *Abroad*, 91.

49. Michel Vieuchange, *Smara: The Forbidden City. Being the Journal of Michel Vieuchange While Traveling Among the Independent Tribes of South Morocco and Rio de Oro*, ed., introduction and epilogue by Jean Vieuchange, trans. Fletcher Allen (1932; New York: The Ecco Press, 1987). For the information on Robert Scott see Roland Huntford, *Scott and Amundsen* (1983), mentioned by Lloyd Rose in "Ice Follies: Arctic Explorers Go With the Floe," *The Village Voice Literary Supplement*, May 1989: 15.

50. Jan Morris, *Conundrum* (New York: Harcourt Brace Jovanovich, 1974), 101.

51. Löschburg, *A History of Travel*, 141; Eugen Weber, *France: Fin de Siècle* (Cambridge, Mass., and London: The Belknap Press of Harvard University Press, 1986), 104.

52. Barr, *A Curious Life*, 29; David-Neel, *My Journey to Lhasa*, 122.

53. Robyn Davidson, *Tracks* (New York: Pantheon Books, 1980), 252. A "jumper" in Australian parlance is what Americans know as a sweater.

54. Stevenson, *Victorian Women Travel Writers*, 80; Barbara Evans Clements, *Bolshevik Feminist: The Life of Aleksandra Kollontai* (Bloomington: Indiana University Press, 1979), 226.

55. Davidson, *Tracks*, 254.

56. Löschburg, *A History of Travel*, 123.

Another Lady's Life in the Rocky Mountains*

Susan Armitage

THE ENGLISHWOMAN Isabella Bird is well known for her charming, informative and adventurous travel account, *A Lady's Life in the Rocky Mountains.*[1] The title was surely intended to be both paradoxical and provocative, for Bird's contemporary readers cannot have expected that *ladies* would venture into the Rocky Mountain wilderness.

Bird's demonstration that ladies did indeed venture is encapsulated in her exciting account of her Colorado journey, especially of her celebrated solo ride from Colorado Springs to South Park and back to Denver in October and November of 1873. Moreover, Bird was not the only literary lady traveling in Colorado in 1873. Another woman, Hester McClung of Xenia, Ohio, traveled in Colorado with her family from May to October of that year. Her travel letters recording this unusual trip were printed in her hometown newspaper and later preserved as a family memento.[2] Indeed, the paradox was not the incongruity of gentility in the wilderness but the fact that the two ladies, Isabella Bird and Hester McClung, traveled much of the same route at almost the same time—and saw such different things.

Isabella Bird was certainly one of the most improbable adventurers that the world has known. Her Colorado visit was only an early portent of remarkable literary and personal success as a world traveler. Later trips took her to Japan and Malaya—which she wrote about as *The Golden Chersonese and The Way Thither*—and extended visits to China, Tibet, Persia, and Kurdistan followed, occupying in all, 30 years of travel.

---

*An earlier version of this article and the letters of Hester McClung appeared in *Essays and Monographs in Colorado History* 5 (1987): 79-138.

In 1873, Isabella Bird was 42 years old. She was the daughter of an English clergyman, to whom she had been devoted, and following his death she lived in Edinburgh with her sister, Henrietta, to whom she was also devoted. Nothing in the manner of Miss Bird of Edinburgh betrayed the adventuress who lived within: she was plain, soft-spoken, and timid. Furthermore, she was an invalid, incapacitated for months at a time with a chronic spinal disease. Unable to significantly affect either her physical or psychological distress, doctors urged the classic Victorian remedy of last resort, a sea voyage. In 1872, deeply depressed and unhappy, she embarked on the medically prescribed voyage, and in January of 1873 arrived in Hawaii—the Sandwich Islands as it then was—and found herself. Exotic lands—strange cultures and the chance to explore them in her own style—were what Bird needed. She blossomed with health and set off on her adventures, which sustained her, physically and mentally, for the rest of her life.[3]

Unlike Isabella Bird, Hester McClung would never have considered traveling alone. In 1873, at age 30, she had already assumed her lifelong role as maiden aunt to her sister's family, Lena and George Merritt of Indianapolis, Indiana. Cherished and highly regarded within the family, McClung was nevertheless dependent, her life dictated by family needs. She was, in short, a much more typical unmarried woman of her time and social class than Isabella Bird. But like Bird, health reasons brought McClung to the wilderness.

Early in 1873 the Merritts decided to take drastic action concerning the health of their young son George Junior, who had been diagnosed as preconsumptive. In May the party—composed of Lena and George, sons Ernest and George Jr., daughter Nettie, and "Aunt Hes"—traveled to Denver by railroad and thence to Canon City, where they bought a pack wagon, horses, beds, tent, and camping equipment. They embarked on a five-month "camp cure," as it was known, traveling slowly up to South and Middle Parks, and returning to Denver in October via Colorado Springs. Alas, they missed Isabella Bird, about to begin her famous ride, by two weeks.

The Merritts' trip was a success, their son's health was restored, and Hester McClung's travel letters achieved some brief local literary fame back home. Although the McClung letters are no match for Bird's in artistry and delight, they contain a wealth of information about the physical details of travel in early Colorado and human encounters along the way. They record the adventures the small party experienced, and adventures they were, however diligently this very proper family group tried to cloak them in a thick mantle of respectability. Within this protective family framework, Hester McClung had adventures of her own which, although much less spectacular than those of Bird, were clearly significant to her.

Isabella Bird had, at first, given no thought to making a solo ride. She had intended to travel by "the cars"—railroad—and stagecoach to Colorado Springs and South Park. She changed her mind in Denver, when ex-governor A. Cameron Hunt convinced her that travel by horseback was perfectly safe, drew her a map, provided her with a written introduction to the settlers from whom she would ask lodging, and reassuringly sent her on her way. So Isabella rode off on her horse Birdie, sidesaddle while still in Denver (although it hurt her spine) and later thankfully and restfully astride, wearing her "Hawaiian riding dress," a bloomer costume with full turkish trousers and an overdress, tailored in plaid flannel—a bit garish, one would think.[4] Isabella Bird's true adventurousness consisted of being intensely practical in an age when that was considered unladylike. She rode her horse thoughtfully, paying careful attention to Birdie's needs, which may have saved her life on at least one snowbound occasion. Then, too, the decision to ride astride, in a large Mexican saddle, proved eminently sensible for the trail conditions she encountered.

Contrast Bird's matter-of-fact practicality with McClung's flutter when *she* first rode astride:

> Next morning we learned that arrangements had been completed by our newly made friends for a trip to be made by both parties over the trail leading up Chalk Creek, to the falls or rapids five or six miles distant. Filled with interest we hurried to the cabin where we saw a confused collection of riding animals—horses, ponies, mustangs, mules and jacks, donkeys or buroes. . .all hands were busy cinching on the saddles. . .but we were filled with dismay when we noticed that among them all was but one lone side-saddle. . .and there were three ladies of us. . . . It seemed an impossibility at first, but we were encouraged by the refined Mr. M. who said. . .this would be the only safe way. . .we. . .soon found ourselves in the midst of the great Mexican saddles, which have very high pommels and cantles, and their great leather covered stirrups, that I have always called clumsy, now kindly enclosed our feet. Our impromptu riding habits consisted of our large water-proofs which completely enveloped us.

And so they traveled to the beautiful falls and back, a trip that for McClung culminated in an ironic confession:

> Our ride homeward was pleasant, not only because of the mountain scenery but also on account of the mere pleasure of the ride.... I think that letting a ballot slip through my fingers into the ballot box—that ungraceful, unwomanly act that is to convert us at some future day into masculine beings—I think that even that will not make me feel more free, more unfettered, in plain language, more man-like than I did while galloping on my great black charger.

As Isabella Bird's ride commenced, she promptly got caught in a snowstorm, which touched her romantic nature:

> I cannot describe my feelings on this ride, produced by the utter loneliness, the silence and dumbness of all things, the snow falling quietly without wind, the obliterated mountains, the darkness, the intense cold, and the unusual and appalling aspects of nature. All life was in a shroud, all work and travel suspended.[5]

Here, it seems to me, is the heart of Bird's artistry. Better than her fabulous encounters with desperados, better than the suspense evoked by her daring solo trips, the best of Isabella Bird is her deep and unawed feeling for the physical splendor of Colorado. She was challenged, not cowed, by the majesty and grandeur of the mountains. Isabella Bird was a great artist with words, but her literary style was not as spontaneous as it appeared. The published letters were the result of a multi-stage process. Every three or four days Isabella wrote a letter to Henrietta deliberately creating a window on the world for her stay-at-home sister. These letters were entertainment—certainly not fiction, but not plain, unadorned fact either. Like many travel writers, Isabella found a cheerful optimistic tone more suitable than dwelling on troubles. When Isabella returned from her travels she edited the letters her sister had saved, omitting much personal detail and adding chunks of historical and political information. Only then did they go to the publishers—spontaneous, entertaining, and informative, just as Isabella intended them to be.[6]

McClung's brief moment of literary fame was inadvertent. Her first letter, written from Denver to a friend, was so charged with the excitement of the trip and full of fascinating Western details that the friend arranged for publication of the series by the Xenia *Gazette*—which ran her "sprightly letters," as they called them, under the title "Far West

Correspondence." In contrast to Bird's, McClung's letters are immediate in their concentration on daily detail rather then remote scenery and in their composition; for once the letters went to Xenia, McClung had no opportunity to revise them.

Isabella Bird's ride began at Manitou, near Colorado Springs, and thence over Ute Pass along part of the customary wagon road. She then diverged to follow Tarryall Creek, went across South Park to the top of Breckenridge (now Boreas) Pass for the experience of actually seeing the mountain streams diverge—one to the west, one to the east—and then headed back to Denver via the stage road over Kenosha Pass. She traveled this circuit in 12 days, mostly alone, and stayed most nights with hospitable settlers (although on one night, she later discovered, her inhospitable host was part of a vigilante mob).

Contrast this solitary adventure with the leisurely pace and comparative luxury of Hester McClung's "camp cure." The family party arrived in Denver in late May, then traveled on narrow-gauge "baby cars" to Colorado Springs, Pueblo, and Canon City, where they hired a local guide and camp equipment—not backpacks and sleeping bags, but a sizable wagon with beds, seats, and a table, a large tent, lots of cooking equipment, a mule team, and a saddle horse—and set off for their "trial trip" of two weeks in the West Mountain Valley. It was a resounding success. The party returned their guide to his home in Canon City and set off for an extended tour on their own. Even such classic amateur errors as camping in a dry creek bed—only, inevitably, to have it rain and turn the dry creek into a large and very wet mountain stream—they gaily accepted. The scenery surpassed their expectations. Hester McClung had a good, observant eye, and she strained to convey the reality of the view:

> For several days we rode leisurely through enchanting lands. There were hills and dales and beautiful parks (rightly named) consisting of wide stretches of country interspersed with groups of pinions and variously shaped smooth mounds made beautiful by small cedars; and the scarlet-blossomed cactus gleaming among the less pretentious wild flowers which grow everywhere, the natural road as smooth as the drives in the parks of our large cities—the whole of this beauty surrounded, apparently without outlet by great mountain ranges.

Equal to the beauty of the scenery was a zestful sense of freedom. Hester McClung frankly—revealingly—states that "two miles of the way consisted of a little zigzag precipitous canyon, down which we were whirled with a velocity that at home, would have made us faint with fright; but here we are so reckless that had I been a man I should have tossed up my hat and shouted for joy." Several weeks later, Hester returned to the same topic:

> This total absence of nervousness is the best part of our traveling. We are not afraid of anything nor do we fear to attempt anything, and I only hope we may retain the feeling when we return to the states; but I fear we will not, for it is the purity and strength of this air and the elevating and strengthening effect of these mountains that make us strong and fearless.

Isabella Bird would certainly have agreed with this sentiment. Hester McClung attributed her sense of freedom to the "strength of this air," but Bird was more perceptive: she knew that the appeal of travel arose from the absence of the social burden of propriety and convention that weighed so heavily on "ladies" in the 1870s. Her basic principle, and the clue to her remarkable psychology, was her belief that travelers in strange lands were "privileged to do the most improper things with perfect propriety."[7]

For both women, travel in Colorado meant liberation, in the sense of freedom from conventional restraints. Isabella Bird took the greatest advantage of this freedom simply by traveling alone. That was precisely the sort of "most improper thing" that she could not have attempted in polite English society. The most daring thing that Hester McClung attempted physically was to ride astride; intellectually and emotionally, however, the Colorado trip posed new challenges even to this most settled woman.

The greatest challenge for both women travelers was to define the boundary between the new freedom they felt and the inescapable boundaries beyond which no lady dared to venture. In exploring the contours of womanly behavior, their shared response toward the pioneer women settlers they met reveals an interesting ambiguity. First they pity them for the conditions in which they live. Both travelers described a typical one-room log cabin in telling detail. Here is an exterior scene from McClung:

> [We came upon] the hewn log house with its one room, one door [sic] and two large windows. The latter possessions are here reckoned among the luxuries as most of the ranch cabins can boast of

but one window and that composed of three small panes of glass, placed side by side in an opening made of cutting out a piece of one of the logs. Hanging on the outside of the cabin, close under the sheltering eaves, were numerous tools, sets of harness, and innumerable and indescribable saddles and bridles.

And an interior from Bird:

> The cabin is long, low, mud roofed, and very dark. The middle place is full of raw meat, fowls, and gear. One end, almost dark, contains the cooking-stove, milk, crockery, a long deal table, two benches, and some wooden stools; the other end houses the English manager or partner, gear of all kinds, and sacks of beans and flour. . . . It was all very rough, dark, and comfortless.[8]

In addition to their rough, crude homes, pioneer women had to cope with isolation. Both accounts make clear that it was not the danger of being alone in wild country but the lack of contact with other women that made life so difficult. "Being seven miles distant from any lady friend," McClung states of one woman,

> she was almost famished for company, and gave us such a warm heartfelt welcome that we were friends from the first; and after lengthening our stay from day to day, we at last left her with much regret on our part, while she felt that, now since she had a taste of society, it would be insufferably lonely without us during the few weeks remaining before the snow drove them back to Denver.

Yet both travellers most admire not the women who make an adjustment to the environment but those who best fit the model of idealized, proper womanhood—McClung, in praise, describes one woman as "delicate and refined"—those who, ignoring the environment, replicate Eastern civilization:

> All this will perhaps convey the idea that the cabin presented an uncouth appearance, but the literary aspect given by the large round table in the center of the room furnished with writing materials and late papers and magazines, and the fine collection of handsome specimens of jasper, quartz and gold, silver, copper and iron ore together with curious specimens of petrifaction and fossils, and last but not least the refinement and culture of the inmates—all these served to cast a kind of halo over the little plain cabin and its rude furniture.

Similarly, Bird enthuses over one pioneer family in Deer Valley:

> It is a pleasant two-story log house, not only chinked but lined with planed timber. Each room has a great open chimney with logs

burning in it; there are pretty engravings on the walls, and baskets full of creepers hanging from the ceiling. This is the first settler's house I have been in in which the ornamental has had any place. There is a door to each room, the oak chairs are bright with rubbing, and the floor, though unplaned, is so clean that one might eat off it. The table is clean and abundant, and the mother and daughter, though they do all the work, look as trim as if they did none, and actually laugh heartily.[9]

Bird, so impressed by this encounter, lapsed into unaccustomed sentimentality, reporting with approval a freighter's remark that it "made him more of a man to spend a night in such a house."[10]

This is an interesting contradiction: both Bird and McClung delight in their own escape from propriety yet strongly admire the pioneer women who are tireless in their devotion to those same ideals. Neither Bird nor McClung mention what must have been the inevitable concomitant of this devotion to "civilized" standards in the mountain wilderness: endless hard work, exhaustion, and frustration.

Surely *this* is the central paradox of these ladies' lives on the frontier: travelers can maintain their ladylike status without the effort it entails, but settlers run the risk of being overwhelmed by the hard work of the civilizing mission. Bird and McClung could have their cake and eat it too: continuing to believe in the civilizing mission of women while delighting themselves in being temporarily free of the burden of work that maintaining proper standards required.

Equally telling are other encounters the two women experienced. The Merritt party, as Hester McClung's letters describe, met sheepherders, miners, and trout fishermen. They also must have met ranch wives, from whom they purchased bread, eggs, butter, and milk on a regular basis to supplement the fish and game they caught so easily. Yet the settlers whom McClung describes in detail are people of substance: a mineowner and his family; a German merchant; a former Chicago merchant who had come to Colorado for his health; a strange hunting party headed by a General L. of Denver, accompanied by three or four ladies and a black maid; and a large mineowner near Breckenridge. That the party conversed with many other people is clear from McClung's quite knowledgeable accounts of mining, but it also appears that the travelers generally felt comfortable only with people like themselves. Because of this process of selective description, the picture that emerges from the McClung letters is of a highly civilized, not to say refined, mountain wilderness.

There is one major exception to this genteel image. Twice the family group camped near a certain party of Ute Indians. McClung's first meeting with Indians had been in Denver: she recoiled in distaste. Stereotypically, she lamented that she would never enjoy reading *The Song of Hiawatha* again now that she knew how dirty Indians really were. The subsequent encounter ended more happily:

> When we saw them in Denver I thought nothing could induce me to touch them, but here upon closer acquaintance we considered some of them kind and agreeable friends, and our antipathy for them vanished to such an extent that three of them ate at the table with us the last morning.

McClung also reported, with some pleasure, that the head chief took a liking to her and tried to purchase her from her brother-in-law. She was quite flattered by how many ponies he was willing to swap for her and by how difficult it was to dissuade him from the attempt. During their second encounter with the Ute band, about two weeks later, the same Indian pursued his suit more actively, playfully picking up Hester and carrying her to his pony. Here is her response:

> To say that I was a little frightened is expressing my then feelings in the mildest possible manner. The others told me his eyes were twinkling with merriment, but as I could not see them that made no difference in my feelings. It has since been my opinion that the expressive gestures of the red man, of which we so often hear, though of use and interest in most instances, are, under some circumstances, frightfully suggestive.

Clearly, for McClung the boundaries of propriety, indeed of the imaginable, had been reached!

In comparison, most of Bird's meetings were with settlers with whom she spent the night, and, like the Merritt party, she was more comfortable with people of her own social class. Of them (such as a woman she considered to be "very agreeable" and "lady-like-looking")[11] long and favorable descriptions follow, while less pleasant company (for example, "two free-tongued, noisy Irish women")[12] get short shrift. We need to be aware that both Isabella Bird's and Hester McClung's assessments of individuals were based at least in part on elite social attitudes toward class and status. The Colorado mountain wilderness may have been new and fresh, but the attitudes these two tourists brought to it were apparently unaffected by frontier democracy. For example, Hester McClung describes the dugouts of the eastern Colorado plains but dismisses their inhabitants as being "of a lower order." This clear class bias limits the usefulness of both accounts. We cannot rely on them for an adequate portrait of the early settlers of Colorado because there are so many people with whom they had no contact. One reason that these accounts are limited is because they were written by women. Ladies—and McClung and Bird remained ladies—were constrained in their social acquaintance, even on the frontier. It was a self-limitation: they simply were not comfortable with rude and vulgar people and withdrew from them. Nineteenth century men had greater freedom to cross class lines, but their travel accounts are usually marred by their inability to see women clearly and unsentimentally.

Isabella Bird spent no time with Indians. She was not, in fact, particularly interested in them. Her opinion is brief and brutal: "The Americans will never solve the Indian problem," she states, "till the Indian is extinct."[13] Instead, she encountered a gentlemanly desperado, Comanche Bill, with whom she rode to the Continental Divide at Breckenridge Pass. She was definitely interested in desperados, especially the gentlemanly kind, as evidenced in her earlier attraction to "Mountain Jim" Nugent, of Estes Park, from whom she had recently parted with much romantic anguish. The reason for her attraction to the type ought to be obvious. The gentlemanly desperado was a true counterpart to Isabella Bird, the daring lady. Without any question, she saw herself as a female desperado—but a cultured one. For the uncultured kind she had no time at all, and she slips into melodrama when she writes about vigilante violence in Fairplay, which she cannot have personally experienced because the McClung account informs us that the town had recently burned to the ground. Those stories, however, are all told at one remove. Bird's interest was not in others but in herself: she was determined to play out the character of the daring lady. That was what the solo ride was all about. Where were the limits, socially and psychologically, of daring behavior? Could even a woman, if she dared, do anything—and how would she feel about doing it?

Bird tested isolation and risk in the most challenging environment she could find—the Rocky Mountains in winter, which she describes as "Grand! glorious! sublime! but not lovable." She was not afraid. As she wrote at the beginning of the ride: "There are no real difficulties. It is a splendid life for health and enjoyment. All my luggage being in a pack, and my conveyance being a horse, we can go anywhere where we can get food and shelter."[14] However, she pushed her luck. At times she was in pain and genuine danger. More frequently she was simply uncomfortable; much of the ride was unpleasant. But it was worth it. She had challenged herself and fully met the challenge. Isabella Bird's solo ride was indeed the accomplishment of a daring lady, an initiation into an adventurous and celebrated life.

And what of Hester McClung? No public acclaim or fame lay in her future. She lived her life within the family circle, an exemplary maiden aunt. The family traveled and she with it, observant but protected. Throughout the Colorado trip, McClung exerted her best literary efforts to describe what she saw, and she did this increasingly well. She was profoundly affected by her Colorado travels. Although she had neither the temperament nor the financial resources to strike out on her own, she had a glimpse of another world, as this final nostalgic personal description on the eve of their departure shows:

> We left the comfortable wagon from which we had looked out on untold loveliness, and in which during moonlight nights I have lain awake, rather than have the beauty wasted, and traced the net-work of the shadows and aspens cast upon the white cover by the moon's brilliant light, a soft breeze making them as changeable and interesting as the views in a kaliedescope [sic].

Following their Colorado travels, both ladies returned home, Bird to Edinburgh and McClung to Indianapolis. For Bird, however, the Colorado adventure had been decisive, and henceforth her true home would be in foreign lands and strange places, and her persona that of the daring lady. Much more typically, Hester McClung went home and stayed there, and we have no evidence that the Colorado trip made any dramatic change in her life. But it is surely not fanciful to imagine, at some later time, Hester McClung reading Isabella Bird's *A Lady's Life in the Rocky Mountains* and remembering her own free and unfettered life in Colorado.

Notes

1. Isabella Bird, *A Lady's Life in the Rocky Mountains* (Norman: University of Oklahoma Press, 1960).
2. My grandfather, Ernest Merritt, was the "baby" of the Colorado party. He passed on the family copy of the travel letters of "Aunt Hes" to my aunt, Grace Waser, who has kindly given me a copy of them for publication. All quotations from the McClung letters in this article are taken from the family copy.
3. Pat Barr, *A Curious Life for a Lady* (New York: Ballantine Books, 1972), pp. 1-40.
4. Bird, *A Lady's Life*, pp. 138-143.
5. *Ibid.*, p. 142.
6. *Ibid.*, p. 76.
7. Quoted in Barr, *A Curious Life*, p. 35.
8. Bird, *A Lady's Life*, p. 160.
9. *Ibid.*, p. 181.
10. *Ibid.*, p. 182.
11. *Ibid.*, p. 141.
12. *Ibid.*, p. 178.
13. *Ibid.*, p. 184.
14. *Ibid.*, pp. 154-55.

The Ride of Godiva:
Defiant Journeys in 20th-Century
English Women's Plays

Diane F. Gillespie

But I suffer not a woman to teach,
nor to usurp authority over the man, but to be in silence.

—1 Timothy 2:12

Censor the body and you censor breath and speech at the same time.

—Hélène Cixous "The Laugh of the Medusa," in Elaine Marks and
Isabelle de Courtivron, *New French Feminisms*

O NE OF THE quintessential brief journeys in human history is Lady
Godiva's. In *Polyolbion*, his early 17th-century topographical poem
on England, Michael Drayton tells the 11th-century legend contained
in the annals of Coventry:

> . . .Leofric, her lord, yet in base bondage held,
> The people from her marts by tollage who expelled;
> Whose duchess, which desired this tribute to release,
> Their freedom often begged. The duke, to make her cease,
> Told her that if she would his loss so far enforce,
> His will was she should ride stark nak'd upon a horse
> By daylight through the street; which certainly he thought
> In her heroic breast so deeply would have wrought,
> That in her former suit she would have left to deal.
> But that most princely dame, as one devoured with zeal,
> Went on, and by that mean the city clearly freed.[1]

The command that the townspeople go inside, cover their windows and doors, and not look upon Godiva as she passed was violated by a man struck blind for his temerity.

Godiva's ride is worth considering in the context of women and the journey for several reasons. First, while men retain their traditional power over women in many fictional and real women's journeys, Godiva's experience offers a positive paradigm. It is a defiant and independent act within her previously subordinate, powerless relationship with her husband, a relationship that mirrors the hierarchical class structure of her society. Second, as such, the ride is a bid for freedom, power, and respect not only for herself, as in many masculine journey accounts, but also for underprivileged and oppressed groups, especially women and children. Third, although Godiva rides naked, she is not vulnerable to the dangers women ordinarily are taught to fear on the road. Unlike many 19th-century women travelers who donned elaborate, protective costumes,[2] Godiva strips away the trappings of her social role, the clothing and coiffure that symbolize the modesty and chastity of women and thus the private domestic realm they inhabit as silent, submissive possessions of individual men. And fourth, Godiva's verbal protests, her divestiture, and her departure from home effect a kind of rebirth with positive personal as well as communal implications. Having failed to influence her husband by speaking to him privately about the injustices in the kingdom, she mounts a horse and rides out as a visual, public protest in which her unconfined body declares her challenge to the patriarchy. The result of Godiva's ride, however, is not "exclusion *from* society" as Jane McDonnell and Annis Pratt think a woman's "rebirth journey" typically is.[3] Her return home improves both it and the society it mirrors.

While Godiva's story has fascinated many writers, its treatment often bears the marks of the writer's gender.[4] To most of the literary men who retell the story in 19th-century England, for instance, Godiva represents both a revolutionary political ideal and a chaste feminine one; paradoxically they also lavish description upon her naked ride and the long hair that, unbound, partially preserves her modesty. To some of their female successors, however, including forgotten 20th-century playwrights like Olive Popplewell and Clemence Dane (Winifred Ashton), the motivations for and the consequences of Godiva's action are more significant than the ride itself. In their plays, the revolutionary implications of Godiva's behavior clearly link the oppression and liberation of the poor with that of women.

The Godiva plays written by Popplewell and Dane do not contain the only defiant journeys women take in 20th-century British women's drama. They evolve from the revolutionary mood of the turn of the century British women's suffrage movement in which drama, on several levels, played an important role in women's efforts to change the attitudes of their society.[5] Some of the suffrage plays, as well as Cicely Hamilton's *Diana of Dobson's* (1908) and *Phyl* (1911), unintentionally anticipate the way Popplewell and Dane treat the Godiva story. Theater historians searching for precedents for the feminist theater they see arising in both Britain and the United States in the 1960s will find several here.[6] Like contemporary feminist theater, these early 20th-century plays not only give women the central parts and examine their lives and roles in society but also undermine some basic assumptions about the human personality. In feminist drama, as Helene Keyssar notes, "the impetus is not towards self-recognition and revelation of a 'true' self but towards recognition of others and a concomitant transformation of the self and the world."[7] The Godiva plays and the defiant journey motif in early 20th-century women's drama form parts of this pattern. It culminates in Caryl Churchill's *Top Girls* (1982) where, although the transformations are more radical and affect form as well as content, the defiance is muted by the fear that greater freedom and mobility for women may cause them to lose sight of valuable human and communal concerns.

*   *   *

Several literary men of 19th-century England found in Godiva's story the feminine ideal of their own time: the beautiful, innocent, motherly, and giving woman, willing to sacrifice even her maidenly modesty to help others, to be the courageous and justifiable exception that reinforces the rules for acceptable feminine behavior. At a time when women were barred from political activity, these 19th-century English men also made Godiva into a liberal, even a revolutionary political symbol. Defining her concern for the poor as maternal and spiritual, however, they adhered to these and other popular feminine stereotypes.

In Walter Savage Landor's *Imaginary Conversations* (1824-1829), the dialogue between Godiva and Leofric, her husband, portrays him as an insensitive egomaniac. The newly-wed Godiva is persistent, but she is also conventionally modest and flattering in her attempts to persuade him.[8] Leofric, she says, can easily relieve the sufferings of the people because he is "like God." Incensed because his peasants have not paid their taxes, Leofric dismisses Godiva's observation that his tenants are starving. "Must I starve too?" he replies (494). Godiva, however, melted with maternal love, urges her husband to act: "Let not the infants cry for sustenance! The mother of our blessed Lord will hear them; us never, never afterward." Leofric swears that he will save the peasants only when Godiva rides "naked at noontide through the streets" (495). Having identified Godiva's concern with the Virgin Mary's, Landor leaves his heroine struggling to gather the courage to act.

Alfred, Lord Tennyson, after a visit to Coventry in 1840, wrote a poem entitled "Godiva" (1842)[9] in which he also presents her as a predecessor for those of his own age who sympathize with the oppressed poor. Godiva is admirable not because she speaks out, but because she does more than "prate / Of rights and wrongs." Like Landor, Tennyson envisions her moved by the mothers who, with their children, are starving. Unlike Landor, Tennyson tells the rest of the story. Although Godiva commands the people to stay indoors, poets apparently need not respect such injunctions; Tennyson renders his heroine ethereal, yet he verbally relishes the disrobing and riding scenes:

> ...anon she shook her head,
> And showered the rippled ringlets to her knee;
> Unclad herself in haste; adown the stair
> Stole on; and, like a creeping sunbeam, slid
> From pillar unto pillar, until she reached
> The gateway; there she found her palfrey trapt
> In purple blazoned with armorial gold.

In contrast to her lavishly appareled horse, Godiva rides forth dressed only, Tennyson says, in her chastity. Vividly he recreates her mental state as one of extreme sensitivity and timidity in a Coventry filled with eyes. There is no defiance in this naked ride:

> The deep air listened round her as she rode,
> And all the low wind hardly breathed for fear.
> The little wide-mouthed heads upon the spout
> Had cunning eyes to see: the barking cur

> Made her cheek flame: her palfrey's footfall shot
> Light horrors through her pulses: the blind walls
> Were full of chinks and holes; and overhead
> Fantastic gables, crowding, stared: but she
> Not less through all bore up. . . . (174-75)

Ironically, given the way his own eyes linger on the scene he creates, Tennyson describes the punishment meted out to the "one low churl" who peeped, how "his eyes, before they had their will,/ Were shrivelled into darkness in his head,/ And dropt before him" (175-76). Unscathed himself, the poet hurries over the part of the story where Godiva returns, dresses, and meets her husband. She has removed the tax, Tennyson concludes, and "built herself an everlasting name" (176).

Leigh Hunt, who knew Tennyson's poem, retold the Godiva story in his *Tales* (1891).[10] Hunt is more impressed than Tennyson by Godiva's mind, which he describes as "capable of piercing through the clouds of custom, of ignorance, and even of self-interest, and petitioning the petty tyrant to forego" his privilege of taxation (168). Hunt is also more interested than Tennyson in Leofric's imagined reaction. He must have been astonished, Hunt thinks, by Godiva's "intention of acting in a manner contrary to all that was supposed fitting for her sex" and must have been forced to acknowledge "the very beauty of her conduct by its principled excess" (168). Thus Leofric must have been the one to command that the residents of Coventry stay behind closed windows and doors and not look upon his wife, under pain of death.

Like Tennyson, however, Hunt can do what is forbidden: he can turn the eyes of his imagination upon Godiva. In this version, she is set upon her horse and is disrobed before she unbinds her hair. Hunt's use of the passive voice suggests not only the presence of unnamed others (ladies in waiting perhaps) but also Godiva's own sacrificial passivity. The fact that the hair, which as Tennyson says comes "to her knee," does not cover her completely is also highlighted:

> The lady went out at the palace door, was set on horseback, and at the same time divested of her wrapping garment, as if she had been going into a bath; then taking the fillet from her head, she let down her long and lovely tresses, which poured around her body like a veil; and so, with only her white legs remaining conspicuous, took her gentle way through the streets.
>
> What scene can be more touching to the imagination—beauty, modesty, feminine softness, a daring sympathy (168-169).

Hunt, although not to the same degree as Tennyson, takes the fight out of Godiva, less by making her exceedingly timid than by making her passive (however "daring" her sympathy), and then by making her an object of worship. In spite of "her white legs remaining conspicuous" in Hunt's era of long, concealing skirts, he envisions her "riding through the dumb and deserted streets, like an angelic spirit" (169). Oblivious, like Tennyson, to his own poetic license, Hunt objects to "the vulgar use to which . . . some writers" have put the local legend of "peeping Tom." The whole story, he insists, is as "sweetly serious as can be conceived" (169).[11]

Tennyson's and Hunt's versions of Godiva's ride avoid imputations of threatening feminine sensuality and power, but their selection and their descriptions of this portion of the story resonate with the traditional tensions inherent in the imagery. As Elisabeth Gitter points out, "When the powerful woman of the Victorian imagination was an angel, her shining hair was her aureole or bower; when she was demonic, it became a glittering snare, web, or noose."[12] Tennyson and especially Hunt recreate Godiva's hair as angelic aureole rather than as demonic snare. Yet its abundance, even though (or perhaps because) it leaves the skin of her white legs exposed below the knees, also recalls, however inadvertently, the tradition of dangerous feminine sensuality and power that must be tamed by bands of ribbon and concealed by yards of cloth.[13] Indeed, when Orlando shows "an inch or two of calf" beneath her skirt in Virginia Woolf's mock biography, a startled sailor almost falls from the masthead.[14] The image of a naked woman on a horse, however light and easy-gaited a "palfrey" may be, has some of the same ambiguities. Is Godiva a meek hostage (or appendage) of the beast upon which she is set, or does she mount it and, reins in hand, control (or identify with) its power?[15] That Godiva's behavior breaks all the rules of a society in which privileged males possess and dominate less privileged people is easier for Tennyson and Hunt to praise than is any implicit challenge to men's possession of women. Indeed, in their descriptions, they possess her themselves.

*   *   *

The English women dramatists of our century, also drawn to Godiva's story, do not make her representative of any feminine ideal. Drama, in which the visual impact is central, lends itself well to transformations of people's appearances, but the women playwrights do not dwell upon Godiva's hair-veiled, naked ride on horseback. I doubt they feared the censor's blue pencil.[16] They simply exhibit more interest in the relationship between clothing and social role, as well as in what Sandra Gilbert calls the "costumes of the mind."[17] They do see the political implications of Godiva's action, like some of their male predecessors, but they focus on the links between the oppression of women and that of the poor, between the personal relationship of Godiva and her husband and the political hierarchies governing England, and between her ride and the betterment of society. Thus the verbal confrontations of Godiva and Leofric, rather than the ride itself, interest the women playwrights most, and their elaborations of the story are more extensive than the men's.[18]

Olive Popplewell, for example, in *The Ride Through Coventry* (a play published in 1937), adds several characters to the story and complicates the others.[19] One addition is Egberta, Leofric's mother. She is a severe critic of Godiva's kindness to the servants and acts as a mouthpiece for (although hardly a model of) a woman's complete submission to men. "You should have. . .let me bend Godiva's will to better shape before you wed," she chides Leofric early in the play. When he says that he likes "a wench to show some mettle," his mother warns that "the people say Godiva rules in Wessex." Motherhood, Leofric conventionally believes, will solve that problem (6-7).

When we meet Godiva in Popplewell's play she is hardly an admirable character, although her kindness to the servants indicates potential for improvement. Immature and spoiled, she actually says that Leofric should impose an additional tax on the people in order to buy her a new dress, and the prospect of war promises excitement. When Ingrid and Tom, a poor Coventry woman and her son, ask to see Godiva, however, her character develops. Ingrid has seen Godiva looking with pity upon the suffering townspeople and comes to remind her that they are starving. She appeals to Godiva as a woman who also "may bear a son" and, as in the renditions of Landor and Tennyson, Godiva's motherly nature is touched. That, however, is not her only motivation. "Out there in Coventry," Ingrid adds, "the sons of women are not men but beasts of burden, . . .The serfs will give their due to the Earl, willing enough, but he has dragged them from their plough, and made them pay in corn or coin till men who once were free are slaves, broken on the soil—and for what? To build a race of fighting men, all brawn and muscle, who live on us, like lords at ease" (12).

Godiva, who can envision what Ingrid describes, offers her pearls to help relieve Coventry and begs Leofric to repeal the tax. When he refuses, she realizes what none of the male-created Godivas do: "Oh, God! I am less free than any serf!" She goes further. "I will possess myself," she resolves; "I will be free!" (18-19). When Godiva confronts Leofric, he issues the famous challenge, then sits back smugly. "That draws the teeth of little vixens," he concludes; "that will bring my falcon feeding from my hand" (20). Leofric orders all shutters barred but not, as in Hunt's version, because he is impressed by Godiva's daring. "This bargain can harm none but you," she has said, and he acts only to protect his reputation as master both in his house and out of it (20). If he repeals the tax, he can always impose a harsher one later, he and his mother conclude. "This chit must learn humility; a woman's crown," his mother adds (21).

In this play, Godiva's ride occurs off stage. Popplewell presents its psychological and social results. Her treatment of "peeping Tom" is characteristic and, because he and his mother are the serfs whose sufferings we know, complex. Tom is no vulgar voyeur. He says he prayed for the Virgin's blue cloak to cover Godiva and, when he looked, that's what he saw; after such an experience, he does not mind being blind. Godiva, however, convinces him there is much beauty to see in the world, prays for his sight, and it is restored. Presumably because of her intervention, the world Tom sees will be a better one.

The influence Godiva now has on Leofric guarantees a new dispensation. When husband and wife are left alone after her ride, it becomes clear that part of him does admire her courage. Still he says, "I've known some men half kill their wives for less than this." "Did they fear them so much?" she asks astutely. "I have learned that men are often driven to hurt and kill because they fear." Her defiant journey has given her confidence and her words credibility. Although Leofric, still assuming that such power is his, forgives Godiva, she tells him that his behavior has killed her love. Yet just as Godiva grows from a spoiled child to a socially responsible and courageous adult, so Leofric begins to understand what Godiva has said, realizes that he wants her love rather than her submission, and begins to win her respect.

Twenty years later, in 1958, a better-known playwright, Clemence Dane (Winifred Ashton), wrote a radio play called *Scandal at Coventry*.[20] Having done research on the 11th century, Dane incorporates more of the historical context in her version of the story. She immediately establishes Godiva's concern for the poor. Godiva has sold her jewels to pay some of the taxes they owe her husband. Had she known about it, she would also have tried to lift the death taxes levied against a widow who, left without means of supporting herself and her children when her one cow was confiscated, has killed herself. Leofric, in this version, is in part a pawn in a larger historical game. At this time Harthacnut, a Dane, is bleeding the country of its resources; Edward is favored to overthrow him. While Leofric is ready to rise in support of a man who is more concerned about the welfare of the kingdom, he is also a supporter of the law of the land, however harsh. He loves Godiva, but he dislikes her interference on behalf of the poor of Coventry. Such matters, he thinks, are not her concern.

After three successive crop failures and doubled taxes, the suffering people begin to talk of a "riding"–the ancient custom of sending a naked woman on a white horse to the holy Cofa, a heathen god, with an offering. A cross stands where the tree once grew, but confusion remains in everyone's minds between pre-Christian and Christian beliefs. Godiva sympathizes with the people's desire for help. She recognizes that, in her privileged position, she has never had to worry about mere survival. "Stick to your household chores and leave me to govern the Midlands!" Leofric exclaims when she confronts him (22). When she persists he simply forbids her to speak further.

Dane's Godiva, like Popplewell's, confronts her powerlessness. Accepting the low value Leofric places on her counsel, however, she reproaches not him, but herself. She is "dull-minded and weak-willed. Other women use their beauty, or they have devices, or clever tongues; but I, I am nothing and I do nothing. I could help Coventry if I knew how; but–what can I do? I can do nothing" (25). Dane characterizes Godiva as a woman unskilled in the traditional feminine wiles and as one who finds such manipulative methods reprehensible. Yet without such feminine methods she is a cipher. The alternative is direct action, but what action can a dependent, silenced, and powerless woman take? When civil war is averted, however, Godiva tries once more to talk Leofric into concentrating on Coventry's troubles. Thinking he will silence her for good on the subject, he challenges her to ride to Coventry cross. Knowing now that the ride is her only recourse, Godiva orders the people into their houses and proceeds.

While in a radio play the ride could be described easily in words, Dane, like Popplewell, puts her emphasis elsewhere, on the causes and results. Godiva's mother-in-law is scandalized, her husband enraged, the townspeople delighted. The blinding of Thomas in this rendition is viewed both as a possible miracle and as a phenomenon with naturalistic explanations. Although Leofric has to keep his promise, word also comes that the Danish king has died and Edward is king. Leofric therefore will escape punishment for breaking the law. These events, combined with Godiva's empathetic ride, promise a political and economic turn for the better in a society in which men still hold power. The play ends, as it begins, with a song about a lady "upon a white horse." Heard at intervals throughout the production, the song emphasizes Godiva's courage and her enduring fame in the popular imagination.

*   *   *

Many treatments of the journey in 20th-century English women's plays, it is true, do not sound such defiant notes. In some, only men do the traveling.[21] Other women characters might just as well stay at home. Gertrude Vaughan's *The Woman with the Pack*, an unconventional play, contains some conventional characters, like the German tourist who lists his wife and daughter in the visitors' book in a way that offends a character named Philippa Tempest.[22] When she objects, her traditional father rebukes her: "A man, when he travels, does so as the head of his family; if he desires to take his wife and daughter with him—at his own expense, mind—I think he is entitled to describe them as. . .appendages" (30). Occasionally, however, appendages acquit themselves well in foreign countries and save their husbands' lives.[23] More often, fathers send daughters on trips to keep them (often unsuccessfully) out of the way of undesirable suitors.[24] Previous travels of older women to distant places are linked to unsavory pasts.[25] Sometimes, an unattached woman traveler meets an unsuitable man and, although tempted to act unconventionally, fails to do so.[26] Whatever the situation, men (fathers, potential or actual husbands, or, less often, lovers) are central. Unlike the Godiva plays, these plays do not contain men whose characters improve. The inequities of their societies are not altered by the women's travel, nor, usually, does the woman's own situation change.

Several suffrage playwrights, however, depart from the prevailing patterns and use the journey as a symbol of women's changing history.[27] Their plays implicitly follow the pattern of the Godiva story in that the women defy the hierarchical structures in which they are subordinated: on their own behalf, on behalf of others (especially women and children) in similar plights, and on behalf of society as a whole. While these plays involve no symbolic stripping away of clothing, they employ other symbols to help us envision similar positive results. The women's actions, like Godiva's, transform their lives, their homes, and society as a whole.

In *The Woman with the Pack* (1912), for instance, Gertrude Vaughan uses a series of tableaux and scenes to present, through a journeying "everywoman," an overview of half a century of struggle for the vote.[28] The woman's burdens are a child, a lantern, and a cross which turns out to be the loom upon which she weaves – not anything so traditionally practical as clothing – but decorative patterns representing the inner lives of those with whom she identifies. In the first scene she weaves a floral design for young Philippa Tempest whose soul is "like a wild rose-bud," not yet opened (44). Philippa, traveling with her family, struggles by speaking out against the restrictions imposed on her by her parents and society. When she insists that she wants to study law instead of marry, her brother supports her, but her father dismisses her wish as "a fad" (38).

The woman with the pack observes, however, that "The English wild rose-bud will not long resist the sun's kisses" (50). Philippa talks increasingly of her desire to help people. "I see a future with no woman overburdened, no man cruel, no child unhappy," Philippa tells the woman with the pack. She envisions "the women of the future, not slaves in thought, not weighed down by fear of the unknown, women free and strong and happy, with all the gates thrown open so that they may work unfettered. . . . I see men and women working together, equals, and no one asks: 'Is it a man who has done this, or is it a woman,' but 'Is the work worthy' " (55). Like Godiva, Philippa is willing to challenge traditional hierarchies to bring about such a society.

The play reveals the kind of suffering that Philippa, like Godiva, wants to eliminate: that of women and children. Back in London, she leaves her own protected environment and, searching for Fanchette, a serving maid in scene one, visits the Higgses, a poor family in whose house she is reportedly a boarder. The trip is short but, like Godiva's, no less significant. Having read the law for six months, Philippa knows that the unemployed Bill Higgs is right when he says that, legally, he is entitled to hit his wife. She observes Higgs's wife and their children, who are not in school, trying to earn a few pennies by making match-boxes. Philippa also discovers that Fanchette, having lost her job, has had to become a gentleman's mistress to support her mother and herself. Philippa is so appalled that, like Godiva, she begins to act as well as talk; she joins the suffrage women marching on Westminster.

Both Philippa and her brother go to prison for their suffrage activities, a situation, in a different social context, as shocking as Godiva's ride. In both cases people choose to act in ways their society defines as shameful, but they do so defiantly, on behalf of the oppressed groups they represent. Their father is thoroughly offended, but their mother is receptive. Although the family is divided, society clearly is changing. Men as well as women are among those working to improve the opportunities for oppressed groups. In spite of a final tableaux which shows Philippa as Joan of Arc, Vaughan does not want us to view her character as an exceptional woman. In her notes for the production, Vaughan calls Philippa "a typical English girl, vigorous, 'out-of-door,' ambitious, with a saving sense of humour" (92). The suffrage movement and social change in general, in other words, depend upon the participation of ordinary people of both sexes, and the resulting changes in society will benefit ordinary people as well.

Vera Wentworth's *An Allegory* (1913) is more Bunyanesque.[29] Again, however, the journey is a symbol of women's changing history. Wentworth depicts a secular pilgrim's progress as Woman walks wearily and painfully upon the "Road of Progress" leading from the "City of Soul's Bondage" to the "City of Freedom." Impeded, however, by the "Chains of Convention" and blocked by Fear and Prejudice, she ultimately is helped by Courage to overtake Man. This outline sounds unpromising, but some of the verbal confrontations between the characters are effective. Again, Woman has to protest against her oppression. She accuses Courage, for instance, of not responding to her calls. He indicates that he has been accompanying Man, but has now left him: "Courage will not stay with those who love him not, and it did not show a love of Courage to go so far ahead, to leave thee struggling in thy chains." A truly brave man, Courage concludes, would help Woman. Man ultimately returns to travel with Woman; he has missed her "counsel," he says. Men and women, the play indicates, must combine their good qualities in order to reach their goals.

*   *   *

Written around the same time as the suffrage plays, Cicely Hamilton's *Diana of Dobson's* (1908) and *Phyl* (1911) also use the journey as a symbol both of defiance against oppression and of changes in gender roles.[30] While the rebellious journeys of Hamilton's heroines are affected more on their own behalf than on behalf of others, their defiance clearly represents that of whole groups, and their radical alterations in clothing produce some of the same psychological and social results as do Godiva's divestiture and reclothing. Godiva wants to improve the lives of the poor and, in the process, makes her husband attend to their concerns. Hamilton's heroines are at the lower end of the social scale and, outspokenly calling the attention of the wealthy to their plight, re-educate at least the men they marry. Whereas Godiva doffs the rich jewels and garments that mark her privileged social class before she takes her ride, Hamilton's Diana and Phyl find ways to doff the poor and ill-fitting clothing that marks their bondage to exploitative jobs. Knowing their transformations are only temporary, they don the costumes of the wealthy appropriate to their stays in expensive hotels on the continent. After their poverty they revel in the power money provides at the same time as they rail against those who abuse such power. When they have to return to poverty, they take with them the self-confidence, resourcefulness, and understanding engendered by their travels not only through space but also up and down the social ladder.

Hamilton's *Diana of Dobson's* was successfully produced in 1908 in London.[31] The play introduces us to the overworked and underpaid female assistants at Dobson's Drapery Emporium. As Diana bitterly describes their situation, they live in a "stuffy dormitory," governed by "mean little rules," eat inferior food in a "gloomy dining-room," work long hours for a "starvation salary," and have no prospects of better lives, unless they can make good marriages (13). Diana realizes how the owners of Dobson's and similar establishments keep down expenses: "Oh, that's the way to make money," she says in Act II to Sir Jabez Grinley, one of her previous employers, "–to get other people to work for you for as little as they can be got to take, and put the proceeds of their work into your pockets. I sometimes wonder if success is worth buying on those terms" (31). Grinley counters that "sentiment is one thing and business is another." Business, according to him, is "commercial war, in which brains and purses take the place of machine guns and shells" and in which only the fittest survive. Success to Grinley is also a kind of journey, one involving a difficult climb. He is proud to have "had grit and push and pluck enough to raise himself out of the ruck and finish at the top" (32). Hamilton's play challenges this masculine myth.

Diana has "grit and push and pluck" too, but she does not use it to advance herself at the expense of others. She leaves Dobson's, something she is only able to do because she inherits £300. "Girls, have you ever grasped what money really is?" she asks her fellow workers. "It's power! Power to do what you like, to go where you like, to say what you like" (16). As Virginia Woolf says later in *A Room of One's Own* (1929), an independent income enables women to say what they think.[32] Diana, who for six years has been sufficiently polite to survive in her low-paying job, now tells off her supervisor. She also intends to travel and to have "everything that money can buy" if only for one month (16-17). Calling herself Mrs. Massingberd, a widow, she outfits herself in Paris, then goes to the mountains.

Soon out of money, Diana rejects Sir Jabez Grinley's proposal of marriage in spite of his wealth, and, when a young spendthrift named Bretherton proposes, she tells him the truth about her circumstances. He is angry at her deception, but she is angry too. She accuses him of having planned to live on her money when all she would get in return are "proprietary rights in a poor backboneless creature who never did a useful thing in his life" (51-52). If Bretherton had to use his own resources as she has done, he could not survive for six months, Diana says, much less six years (53).

In this play, Cicely Hamilton compares unskilled women who have to earn their livings, not to unskilled male laborers, but to men of the upper classes. She goes further, if only by implication. Aristocratic men like Bretherton are the traditional women in the social family hierarchy; unable or unwilling to support themselves, they are dependent on the income of others and often must marry for financial reasons.[33]

In Act IV we see the result of Diana's trip and of her scornful challenge to Bretherton. Back in London, penniless and unemployed, Diana encounters Bretherton, equally broke, sleeping on a park bench on the Thames Embankment. Muddling through Eton and Oxford, he admits, has not given him the practical skills necessary to earn his living. Like a male Godiva, he has removed the symbols of wealth and privilege and, in response to a challenge, ventured out into a world where he is unprotected. Like Godiva, he will return to his privileged life with a new perspective. His £600 per year income now seems abundant to him, even for two. When he proposes marriage again, Diana accepts. She thus escapes jobs like that at Dobson's, or worse fates.

Although early reviewers liked to call it that, this play is no simple Cinderella story. Diana is not rewarded for being passively beautiful, but for defiantly taking action and speaking her mind. If there is no fairy godmother, neither is there any Shavian Professor Dolittle to form Diana for another version of woman's role. Nor is *Diana of Dobson's* any simple Godiva story. Like Godiva, Diana transforms her appearance and takes a defiant journey, but, reversing the male-female roles, she is the one who challenges Bretherton, a potential rather than actual husband, to change his traditional self-indulgent behavior. When he does, it is she who loses her contempt for his dependence and gains the respect that presumably will result in a marriage of equals. As in the Godiva story, however, self-respect and (although not so prominent as in the Godiva plays) concern for others prove more powerful than money and social position.

Phyl (1911), a lesser-known play by Cicely Hamilton, ends with a similar marriage.[34] Phyl, like Diana, rebels against a demeaning job. Many of the trials of a governess represented in the literature of the previous century re-emerge in this play: rude, spoiled students; boredom and loneliness; poverty, and condescending or abusive employers. Jack Folliott, a young man whom Phyl's employer is trying to snare as a husband for her daughter, befriends Phyl instead. When, as a result, she loses her job, Jack asks Phyl what would make her happy. Freedom from counting every penny and travel, she replies. Finally, she wants to be "with people who like me and are good to me – people who think I matter. . . . Everything I haven't got now – that's my idea of happiness" (60). Jack, who is straightforward and honest as well as willing to exploit the situation, challenges her to travel with him to the continent. While she knows she should be offended, she is not. "I'm sick of the proper attitude," she says frankly. "I seem to have been in it ever since I was born" (62).

Her only reservation is about her conventional sister Cathy, who has sacrificed to raise her after their parents' death. She puts the problem out of her mind, however, until Cathy follows Jack and Phyl to Mentone. Phyl is enjoying her new possessions, clothes that fit, Jack's company, and the travel. As Godiva has had to violate the feminine code of modesty and privacy to achieve her ends, so Phyl has had to violate the related code of chastity. Still, even the arrival of her former employer does not daunt her. She has told the woman off before, does it again, and defends herself equally well to her sister: "The wages of virtue were £20 per year and my keep—and the wages of sin are—this! Give me sin!" (38). When Cathy talks of self-respect Phyl replies, Faust-like, "You never said to yourself, I will have happiness—...if I lose my soul for it!"(41).

Like Godiva and Diana, Phyl is rewarded, not punished, for her presumption. Although Jack receives word that his money is gone, enough is left to give him a new start, if he works to earn his living. The situation brings out the best in both of them. Jack, well aware that Phyl had led a perfectly respectable life before he came along, offers her half of the little money he has left. "I'm not a harpy—a shark," she says, refusing it. "And I'm not a blackguard or a brute," he says (27-28), not wanting to be responsible for sending her to the gutter. Phyl, however, realizes that she cares for Jack, not his money, and he admits that he cares for her too. They decide to marry, go to Australia, and work to support themselves. One defiant journey on Phyl's part, then, a journey away from an exploitative job and conventional notions of respectability, precipitates another, back to a more enlightened respectability and a marriage promising teamwork, instead of dependence.

*   *   *

The defiant journey and the transformations it involves continue to intrigue British women playwrights, although their feminism incorporates experiments with form in addition to those with subject matter, and their conclusions are frequently more enigmatic. In Caryl Churchill's *Top Girls* (1982), for instance, Marlene, promoted to director of Top Girls Employment Agency, invites real and legendary women achievers of the past to join a celebration dinner.[35] Among them are Isabella Bird (1831-1904), a Victorian Scotswoman who traveled extensively during the latter half of her life;[36] Pope Joan, who, so the story goes, disguised herself as a man and, while Pope (854-856), bore a child; Patient Griselda from Chaucer's "The Clerk's Tale"; Lady Nijo (b. 1258), the Japanese Emperor's courtesan who, as a Buddhist nun, traveled about Japan on foot as a penance for her past life; and Dull Gret who, in the Breughel painting, *Dulle Griet*, dons armor with her apron to lead a women's charge against the devils of Hell. Marlene toasts them for coming "a long way. To our courage and the way we changed our lives and our extraordinary achievements" (549). The women's speeches overlap as their diverse life stories emerge piecemeal.

Because Churchill focuses on Joan's problems as Pope and on Lady Nijo's penitence, not on their travels, Isabella Bird is the character of most interest in the context of this essay. She tells, in fragments counterpointed with bits of the other women's stories, how she discovered what she liked to do best. As the daughter of a clergyman, she tried to play the proper role: "Needlework, music, charitable schemes. . .the metaphysical poets and hymnology" (539). A cruise to improve her health had the opposite effect until she fell in love with life on the sea: "I woke up every morning happy, knowing there would be nothing to annoy me. No nervousness. No dressing" (544). No dressing, however, did not mean Godiva-like divestiture. Nor did it mean dressing as a man. When Pope Joan mentions that she left home at age 12 dressed as a boy, both for safety and for access to the library in Athens, Isabella Bird counters, 'I always travelled as a lady, and I repudiated strongly any suggestion in the press that I was other than feminine" (544). At her age and with her appearance, she adds, she did not have to be so concerned about safety, and "Rocky Mountain Jim," in fact, "found it interesting. . .that I could make scones and also lasso cattle" (545).

The joy of traveling, Isabella Bird admits, depended partly upon having her sister Hennie waiting at home for her letters. When Hennie, both audience and alter ego, died, Isabella married a similar person of "sweet character," the doctor who had nursed her sister. Again she tried "very hard to cope with the ordinary drudgery of life" and again coping made her ill. When her husband died, she went to Tibet. "I always felt dull when I was stationary. That's why I could never stay anywhere," she explains (549).

Churchill thus presents Bird's travels as challenges to the traditional feminine role. She also presents Bird as a product of her socialization. She returned from Tibet to Scotland where, "to atone" for her life of "self-gratification," she launched into charitable works and lecturing. "I talked and talked explaining how the East was corrupt and vicious. My travels must do good to someone beside myself. I wore myself out with good causes" (554). In the context of the Godiva story, however, this concern for others is a positive counterpart of the concern for self, a point the first portion of Churchill's play does not develop. Trying to be like her dead sister, this part of the play does stress, again made Bird ill: "It is dangerous to put oneself in depressing circumstances. . . . How can people live in this dim pale island and wear our hideous clothes? I cannot and will not live the life of a lady" (562).

So off she went once more, at the age of 70 and against doctors' orders, to become "the only European woman ever to have seen the Emperor of Morocco." Bird marvels at her achievement: "What lengths to go to for a last chance of joy. I knew my return of vigour was only temporary, but how marvellous while it lasted" (565). With that positive observation, not really characteristic of the other women's stories of struggle, suffering, penance, and punishment, the first scene of the play ends.

At one point in that first scene, Marlene, in spite of her congratulatory toast, asks the assembled women, "Oh God, why are we all so miserable?" (562). The rest of the play has many fewer comic touches but is related to the opening fantasy in that it details Marlene's own achievements. As with the women from history and legend, her success often seems hollow. The actresses playing the women of the past become employees or job seekers in Marlene's Top Girls Agency. To succeed, the women, Marlene in particular, have to become aggressive and competitive like traditional men, and the price they pay is in their thwarted relationships with other people. Preaching a Margaret Thatcher version of Darwin's "survival of the fittest," Marlene abnegates all responsibility for the unsuccessful members of her family: her parents, her sister, even her own daughter. While Isabella Bird's travels constitute the most positive woman's story in *Top Girls*, Caryl Churchill also dramatizes Bird's inner conflicts and puts her achievements in this sobering modern context. As Virginia Woolf had warned in *Three Guineas* (1938), defying the restrictions of the traditional female role should not mean uncritically accepting the traditional masculine one.[37]

* * *

The women who dramatized the Godiva story, those who wrote plays for suffrage movement programs, Cicely Hamilton, and Caryl Churchill all associate women's journeys with psychological and social change. The women at the centers of their plays transform themselves by breaking free of roles that render them silent, submissive, and passive in the face of their own exploitation and that of other groups of people. Becoming active on their own behalf and on behalf of others involves, in most of these plays, speaking out, moving about, and casting off the clothing symbolic of their place in the domestic and related social hierarchy. Whether or not they take up the old costume again, they undermine its power to define them. In doing so they also transform, or anticipate the transformation of the societies around them in the direction of greater fluidity and multiplicity of class and gender designations. During the earlier decades of the century, because of the suffrage movement, the tone is one of exhilaration, even inspiration. Yet when Cicely Hamilton's Diana refuses to improve her situation by exploiting or deceiving others, we are prepared for the kinds of questions Caryl Churchill raises about the nature of change for women. All transformations, in the individual and in society, are not necessarily positive, especially if they involve the total substitution of one restrictive role for another. All women's journeys beyond their traditional roles are not to the City of Freedom unless the abundance of different roles within the individual and within society is recognized and, more important, valued.

Notes

1. Michael Drayton, "The Thirteenth Song," *Poly-Olbion* (1612), reprinted in *Renaissance England: Poetry and Prose from the Reformation to the Restoration*, ed. Roy Lamson and Hallett Smith (New York: W. W. Norton, 1956), 718.
2. See the essay by Birgitta Ingemanson in this volume.
3. Jane McDonnell, " 'Perfect Goodness' or 'The Wider Life': *The Mill on the Floss* as Bildungsroman," *Genre* 15:4 (Winter 1982): 394. McDonnell identifies her views with Pratt's.
4. I use "gender," as Elaine Showalter does, to mean "the social, cultural, and psychological meaning imposed upon biological sexual identity." See "Introduction: The Rise of Gender" in *Speaking of Gender*, ed. Elaine Showalter (New York: Routledge, 1989), 1-2.
5. The Actresses' Franchise League presented dramatic performances as part of the entertainment at suffrage meetings. Actresses, other women writers, and men who supported the movement, wrote the plays. Inez Bensusan, the enthusiastic Australian actress in charge of the AFL's play department, found the necessary writers, performers, and money. To branches of the National Union of Women's Suffrage Societies (NUWSS), she sent plays that emphasized enfranchising women on an equal basis with men and working with men to achieve this end by peaceful, constitutional methods. To the Women's Social and Political Union (WSPU), however, she sent plays advocating more militant tactics. Plays popular with all the suffrage groups avoided the disagreements about methods and focused instead on the inequality of women in English society. See Julie Hollege, *Innocent Flowers: Women in the Edwardian Theatre* (London: Virago, 1981), 60-101, and Dale Spender and Carole Hayman, eds., *How the Vote Was Won and Other Suffragette Plays* (London: Methuen, 1985), 10-13.
6. See, for example, the chapter on "Women Pioneers" in Sue-Ellen Case's *Feminism and Theatre* (New York: Methuen, 1988), and the chapter called "Foothills: Precursors of Feminist Drama" in Helene Keyssar's *Feminist Theatre* (New York: Grove, 1985).
7. Keyssar, *Feminist Theatre*, xiii-xiv. Patricia Waugh in *Feminine Fictions: Revisiting the Postmodern* (London: Routledge, 1989) makes the related point that, in both modern and postmodern fiction by women, "differentiation is not necessarily separateness, distance, and alienation from others, but a form of *connection* to others" (11).
8. Walter Savage Landor, "Leofric and Godiva," *Imaginary Conversations: English Romantic Poetry and Prose*, ed. Russell Noyes (New York: Oxford, 1956), 494-496. Subsequent references appear in the text.
9. Alfred Tennyson, "Godiva," *The Poems of Tennyson*, 3 vols., 2nd ed., ed. Christopher Ricks (Harlow, U.K.: Longman, 1987), 2: 171-176. Subsequent references appear in the text.

10. See *The Poems of Tennyson*, 2: 172. Leigh Hunt, "Godiva," in *Tales by Leigh Hunt*, ed. William Knight (Freeport, N.Y.: Books for Libraries Press, 1971; first published, 1891), 166-170. Subsequent references appear in the text.

11. Another 19th-century treatment of Godiva is Charles Kingsley's novel, *Hereward the Wake: 'Last of the English'* (London: Macmillan, 1866). The hero is one of the children of Godiva. Kingsley briefly imagines Godiva's life after her famous ride in his treatment of her stormy relationship with her son and in her continuing good deeds and saintly reputation, but his focus is on Hereward.

12. Elisabeth G. Gitter, "The Power of Women's Hair in the Victorian Imagination," *PMLA* 99:5 (October 1984): 936.

13. *Ibid.*, 938.

14. Virginia Woolf, *Orlando: A Biography* (New York: Harcourt Brace Jovanovich, 1956; first published, 1928), 157.

15. See Virginia Hyde's discussion of D. H. Lawrence's horsewomen in this volume.

16. From 1843 to 1968 the Lord Chamberlain licensed plays in areas and theaters under his jurisdiction. In the early 20th century, performances of avant-garde plays by theater societies were considered beyond the censor's control. When that loophole was challenged in 1965, accumulated dissatisfaction with the licensing system resulted in its abolition.

17. Sandra Gilbert, in "Costumes of the Mind: Transvestism as Metaphor in Modern Literature," *Critical Inquiry* 7 (Winter 1980): 391-417, contrasts the male modernist view of costume and identity with the female. The women, she says, "not only regard all clothing as costume, they also define all costume," including nakedness, "as false." They believe that "no one, male or female, can or should be confined to a uni-form, a single form or self" (393-394).

18. While journeys can be handled in allegorical or experimental productions, they are not popular on the realistic stage. Playwrights opt for static settings like outdoor scenes or hotel interiors. Pauses in journeys, not the journeys themselves, are what we usually see. Moreover, the difficulties of putting a live horse on the stage in a realistic production of the Godiva story are obvious. The differences between male and female treatments of the story, however, go far beyond the limitations of the dramatic genre.

19. Olive Popplewell, *The Ride Through Coventry: A Play in One Act* (London: H. F. W. Deane, 1937). Subsequent references appear in the text. Not much is known about Olive Popplewell. She wrote two other plays with which I am familiar, *The Pacifist: A Play for Women in One Act* (London: H. F. W. Deane, 1934) and *This Bondage*, in *Five New Full-Length Plays for All-Women Casts*, ed. John Bourne (London: Lovat Dickson and Thompson, 1935). On the basis of these plays, it is clear that Popplewell had a strong political orientation, particularly as politics affect women.

20. Clemence Dane (Winifred Ashton), *Scandal at Coventry: A Short Play in Three Acts* (1958) in *The Collected Plays of Clemence Dane*, vol. 1 (London: Heinemann, 1961). All subsequent references appear in the text. Dane (1887-1953) was one of the better-known early 20th-century British women dramatists. She was also a painter and sculptor, an actress (as Diana Portis), a fiction writer (of novels like *Broome Stages*), and an essayist. Twenty-two of her plays were staged, broadcast, or televised. One of the best known was her first, *A Bill of Divorcement* (1921).

21. In Clemence Dane's *Will Shakespeare: An Invention in Four Acts* (London: Heinemann, 1922; first published, 1921), for example, Anne Hathaway is left behind by her young husband who feels smothered by his life with her in Stratford and wants to go to London.

22. Gertrude Vaughan, *The Woman with the Pack: A Sketch in Four Scenes and Two Tableaux* (London: Ham-Smith, 1912), 30. Subsequent references appear in the text.

23. In *Secrets*, which May Edginton wrote with Rudolf Besier, Mary Carlton elopes with her husband to America. There, shooting a cattle thief who has broken through the door of their cabin, she saves her husband's life.

24. An example is Margaret Kennedy's *Escape Me Never: A Play in Three Acts*, *Seven Plays* (London: Heinemann, 1935).

25. See, for example, B. N. Graham's *Decoy Duck*. It exists in typescript in the Lord Chamberlain's Play collection, vol. 28 (1937) in the British Library, London.

26. An example is C. L. Anthony (Dodie Smith), *Autumn Crocus: A Play in Three Acts* (London: Golancz, 1931). A middle-aged English schoolteacher falls in love with a married innkeeper in Switzerland but, instead of staying near him, she returns to her dull life.

27. Theater historians do discuss the suffrage plays as precedents for the feminist theater of more recent decades, but not in relation to travel. For a discussion of suffrage drama in relation to the movement as a whole, see Hollege, *Innocent Flowers*, 49-101. For brief introductory remarks see Spender and Hayman's *How the Vote Was Won*.

28. Gertrude Vaughan, *The Woman with the Pack: A Sketch in Four Scenes and Two Tableaux* (London: W. J. Ham-Smith, 1912). All references appear in the text.

29. Vera Wentworth, *An Allegory*, in *English Plays* (1913). This volume contains eleven short plays dealing with the subject of votes for women.

30. Cicely Hamilton (Cicely Mary Hammill) (1872-1952) acted in Shaw's *Fanny's First Play* and traveled with touring theater companies, but she is best known for her writing. Of her 20 or so plays, the best remembered are *Diana of Dobson's* (1908), *A Matter of Money* (1913), *The Brave and the Fair* (1920), and *The Old Adam* (1925). Active in the suffrage movement, Hamilton wrote plays for it as well. *How the Vote Was Won* (1910) was frequently produced and well-received. It has been reprinted in Spender and Hayman's collection, *How the Vote Was Won. The Pot and the Kettle* (1909), with Christopher St. John, and *Pageant of Great Women* (London: The Suffrage Shop, 1910), also grow out of this context.

31. Cicely Hamilton, *Diana of Dobson's: A Romantic Comedy in Four Acts* (London: Samuel French, 1925). When the play was produced at the Kingsway Theatre, London, on February 12, 1908, Lena Ashwell played Diana Massingberd, and both her acting and the play itself were enthusiastically reviewed.
32. Virginia Woolf, *A Room of One's Own* (New York: Harcourt Brace Jovanovich, 1957; first published, 1929), 38.
33. Cicely Hamilton makes this point about traditionally trained women in *Marriage as a Trade* (London: Chapman and Hall, 1909) and in a play, *Just to Get Married*, which was produced in 1910 (London: Samuel French, 1914).
34. Cicely Hamilton, *Phyl*, in the Lord Chamberlain's Plays (1911), vol. 24, in the British Library.
35. Caryl Churchill, *Top Girls*, in *Landmarks of Modern British Drama: The Plays of the Seventies* (London: Methuen, 1986), 533-623. All references appear in the text.
36. Churchill acknowledges Pat Barr's book, *A Curious Life for a Lady* (London: Macmillan), as her source of information about Isabella Bird. Churchill altered her source in several ways, however, including her representation of the femininity of Bird's dress. Bird wore a split skirt and rode astride.
37. Virginia Woolf, *Three Guineas* (New York: Harcourt Brace Jovanovich, 1966; first published, 1938), 74-75.

Section II

Gender, Race, and Class

SOJOURNER TRUTH'S famous question "Ain't I a woman?" may indeed have come as a surprise to the white, middle-class women of her time, since the ideologies of race and class are so powerful and intractable that they can override gender. As Cora Kaplan points out, a feminist reading "which privileges gender in isolation from other forms of social determination offers . . . a reading bled dry of its most troubling and contradictory meanings."[1] In women's travel literature, for example, class and race distinctions are extremely common, and no less pronounced for being often unconscious. Many of the white women who have gone to Africa, for example, prefer the plants and animals to the people who live there. Those who do not despise the Africans just as often infantilize and patronize them (Isak Dinesen is a notorious example of the magnanimous European making *grande dame* gestures for "her" natives).

The following four essays explore the connections of gender identity with class and race ideologies. The first, Joan Burbick's "Under the Sign of Gender: Margaret Fuller's *Summer on the Lakes*," describes how Fuller's contact with women of other races and classes gives her glimpses of her own identity as a white, middle-class "lady." Entangled with notions of nature, Fuller's problematic "civilization" gives her power over other women but also limits her personal freedom.

The next two essays, Bonnie Frederick's "Fatal Journeys, Fatal Legends" and Annette White-Parks's "Journey to the Golden Mountain" present sororal complements to the better-known structures of American slave narratives. Slave narratives contain two major journey patterns: the forced journey to hell (the voyage from Africa to the Americas, shuttling between masters, and being sold down the river) and the flight to freedom against great odds. "Fatal Journeys" studies the forced journey to hell, this time from the experience of European women captured by Indians in Argentina and Uruguay. The journeys described here represent painful separations of women from their communities, and result in alienation and longing for home. Their fate is the reverse image of the male journey of triumph in Latin America: the men journey to conquer, while the women journey because they are conquered. "Journey to the Golden Mountain," on the other hand, illustrates the triumphant journey pattern, showing how some Chinese women immigrants, up against great obstacles, could turn into personal triumphs their journeys across an ocean and a cultural divide just as deep. As women they must usually face domination (though of different kinds) from both Anglo men and Chinese men, some of whom collaborate in one form of domination of Chinese women lucrative for both, prostitution-enslavement. Many of the immigrants face great horrors, yet a lucky few are able to escape and shape their lives according to their own will.

The fourth essay, Marina Tolmacheva's "Ibn Battuta on Women's Travel in the Dar al-Islam," reveals a culture that may seem to many readers as a kind of inside-out world, where in the matter of travel, aristocratic and mercantile women's privilege means the right not to be forced along on men's journeys. Women do, however, travel for their own purposes, especially to make the pilgrimage to Mecca. On the other hand, women of less privileged classes must follow along on their husbands' journeys, just as slaves must accompany their masters. This essay is an example of how stereotypes of women's immobility may not stand up to documentary evidence; when the careful historian looks specifically for women's activities, there emerges a picture of women who may be willfully mobile and just as willfully immobile.

Note

1. Cora Kaplan, "Pandora's Box: Subjectivity, Class and Sexuality in Socialist Feminist Criticism," *Feminisms: An Anthology of Literary Theory and Criticism*, ed. Robyn R. Warhol and Diane Price Herndl (New Brunswick, N.J.: Rutgers University Press, 1991): 858.

Under the Sign of Gender:
Margaret Fuller's *Summer on the Lakes*

Joan Burbick

To Euro-American women during the 19th century, the journey to the frontier was not only a geographical passage that beckoned families and individuals, but also a cultural transition in which the meaning of gender could become unsettled. Riddled with the abandoned cultural baggage of east coast parlors—the indispensable pianos and overstuffed settees—the trail west equally upset some women travelers' understanding of what was necessary for their identity as women. The frontier writings of these women as found in travel accounts, settlers' diaries, oral histories, novels, and historical fiction grapple with the everyday effects that a radical shift of environment had on the behaviors and values associated with definitions of women's sphere.[1] Not only do these women's writings describe specific gender issues, they also frequently reveal to what extent gender was inseparable from their particular class and racial beliefs.[2]

In *Summer on the Lakes*, a travel account published in 1844 of a summer trip to the Midwestern frontier, Margaret Fuller describes her reactions to both the landscape and the people as she journeys west. An account woven with quotes, letters, and imagined conversations and lives as well as description, the text periodically questions the meaning of gender and its social construction. Like the writings of other well-educated women of the eastern seaboard and Europe, however, Fuller's reactions to what she sees are an index of the conflicts inherent in separating issues of gender from race and class during the 19th century. In particular, her contacts with other women as sister travelers, frontier settlers, and native peoples elicit descriptions from Fuller that often unintentionally blur the category of gender and, hence, raise questions for the reader about the inseparable relationship of gender to class and race.

An understanding of how Fuller represents issues of gender in *Summer on the Lakes* is important because it precedes her classic work, *Woman in the Nineteenth Century* (1845), in which she argues that gender is a necessary and universal category for the understanding of women's oppression. In contrast to her inspirational polemic of 1845 for women's increasing liberty, her experiences with relationships between women on the frontier significantly thwarted such a focused moral argument and led her into a series of puzzling representations about the meaning of gender. In many ways, Fuller's observations about women on the frontier constantly make the concept of gender multivalent and entropic. This essay explores the rhetorical complexity of Fuller's language about gender, a complexity often unacknowledged by Fuller herself. Later, when writing *Woman in the Nineteenth Century*, Fuller diminishes this rich descriptive complexity of gender language and instead places all women, rich or poor, "red, white, or black," under the sign of gender alone, strengthening for her the moral and practical force of her argument to a predominantly Euro-American audience.

Before focusing on *Summer on the Lakes*, however, the debate about women's writings on the frontier needs some attention since it bears on the continuing use of these writings even today to provide a "moral" vision for the dominant society. The writings of women on the American frontier have become a passionate scholarly pursuit in American history and literature. In an important sense, the retrieval of women's writings directly challenges the canonical works on the West, written and interpreted primarily by men, and acts as a lever to unsettle the standard history and literature of the frontier. One woman historian writes, "As we discover the real lives of western women, we will destroy both the female stereotypes—the lady, the helpmate, and the bad woman—and the male myths of adventure, individualism, and violence."[3] Even further, however, the "rewriting" of the frontier often carries with it the demands of narrative truth, and the utopian desire to have the "real lives" of women unlock the layers of falsification in the historical past, a position that frequently refuses to recognize the representational quality of all narratives of the past and their participation in the language and ideology of their times.

One of the most forceful arguments for an alternative tradition to narratives of heroic male exploration and the scientific accumulation of knowledge on the frontier is Annette Kolodny's, which states that interpreters of the American West need to examine the "unacknowledged fantasies" written by both men and women that drove them either "to desecrate or to preserve the world's last discovered Earthly Paradise."[4] By "unacknowledged fantasies" in general she means the neglected fantasies of primarily Euro-American women migrating to the frontier. By "Earthly Paradise," I assume she means the geographic land mass stretching from the Appalachians to the Pacific Ocean, already settled by widely diverse indigenous peoples, though this last assumption is much more problematic in her study.

To create a space for voices of women on the frontier, Kolodny argues against the figure of the American Adam, claiming that it "excludes women," and instead articulates the female tradition in which "the newly self-conscious American Eve proclaimed a paradise in which the garden and home were one."[5] Convinced that this female fantasy is less violent than the male's, Kolodny also asserts that women were more reluctant to tolerate "the single-minded transformation of nature into wealth without any regard for the inherent beauty of the place."[6] An aesthetic imperative kept in check the violation of the land. She points to Caroline Kirkland in particular as a woman settler who criticized the intense land speculation on the frontier and felt compelled to speak out against the hypocrisies of settlement life.

But in creating this space for women's voices, Kolodny often diminishes the sense of cultural conflict contained in these voices and the way in which women participated in the "settlement" and conquest ideology of the American frontier. To say, as Kolodny does, that "women avoided male anguish at lost Edens and male guilt in the face of the raping of the continent by confining themselves, instead, to the 'innocent...amusement' of a garden's narrow space" is to place women in a garden space uncontaminated by the dominant ideology of their times.[7] Their actions and writings are held apart from sustained cultural analysis; their gardens beyond the already present agriculture of the soil.

Oddly enough, Kolodny sees Fuller as somewhat blinded by her aesthetic need for the landscape as garden. She insists that Fuller "allowed herself to overlook contradictions and inconsistencies" and that her need to find picturesque beauty on the prairie prevented her from grasping the rupture between fantasy and reality that structures much frontier literature.[8] The need to find the garden, for Fuller a fusion of her mother's garden and the serene beauty of the prairie, blocks her from understanding the actual oppressive conditions of women on the frontier. Nonetheless, Kolodny notes that although *Summer on the Lakes* is a flawed text it does anticipate the argument in Fuller's later work, *Women in the Nineteenth Century*, where the universal oppression of women across race and class lines finds expression. Kolodny argues that on the prairie Fuller actually did see, though she refused fully to admit it, how all women, including Native American women, were prevented from inhabiting the paradise of the West.

In my view, the difficulties Fuller faced in finding all women "dispossessed of Eden," that is, oppressed under the sign of gender, are central to her journey account and reveal how problematic it was for Fuller as an observer of women's life under frontier conditions to dismiss the effects of class and race as she found them. New hierarchies emerge on the frontier, not the least of which is the oppression of native women by their Euro-American sisters. Expressions of power and domination take disturbing forms, and women's participation confuses the lines of oppression. Fuller's *Summer on the Lakes* is less a flawed text unable to sweep all under the sign of gender than a narrative of frustration and transient hope, a sober view of frontier life that anticipates her future writings as a journalist and foreign correspondent. The inspired voice of the transcendentalist promoting a moral cause, as in *Woman in the Nineteenth Century*, is only audible in fragments. Instead, when she describes what she observes rather than declares what ought to be, Fuller encounters a world of frustration in which women are separated from each other by class and race; and these demarcations are not trivial—to be swept away by the realization of gender. This frustration is tempered, however, by moments of hope, in that Fuller describes at the end of *Summer on the Lakes* a scene of women talking together, carrying on a conversation in which story telling and gift-giving signify an alternative to frontier violence and exploitation.

Fuller's journey began at Niagara Falls, already a well-established tourist attraction, then continued on to Chicago, the Rock River sections of Illinois, Wisconsin Territory, including Milwaukee, and then on to Mackinaw Island, Sault St. Marie, and home to New England. Armed with a traveling case of self-conscious representations of the landscape, Fuller often finds her expectations of natural beauty fulfilled. At Niagara, for instance, she writes, "I found that drawings, the panorama,

&c. had given me a clear notion of the position and proportions of all objects here; I knew where to look for everything, and everything looked as I thought it would" (p. 4).[9] Except for a fright at the falls in which the much anticipated experience of the sublime is accompanied by the fantasy of a murderous attack by tomahawk-wielding Indians and a few moments of mild disappointment, Fuller begins her travels as the proper tourist, receiving the appropriate, aesthetic "views" of the American landscape.[10]

When she starts to journey away from the acclaimed vista of the falls to the frontier of settlers and native peoples, her ability to find "quiet satisfaction" at the fit between her preconceptions and her experience still remains fairly self-assured. Early on in her travels, near Detroit, Fuller records a detailed story of "moral beauty" that she overheard told by a fellow passenger. This story, a conversation within a conversation, concerns the mother of a passenger who was insulted while traveling by the "ill-bred" wife of a "gentleman." The gentleman married "beneath" his class, a woman "whose coarse and imperious expression showed as low habits of mind as her exaggerated dress and gesture did of education" (p. 20). This fatal error, perhaps partially caused by a momentary passion, was borne by the gentleman as a living form of punishment in the "indecorous" behavior of his wife who drank and insulted his friends in public. Rather than abandon his wife, the suffering gentleman makes "brave atonement" and stays loyal to her no matter how vulgar she becomes. Fuller admits that she is profoundly moved by this story of male fortitude, but the telling of the tale clearly reveals the expectations of class behavior that define a gentleman's wife. An example of the classing of gender, the tale constructs the alignment between gender and class.

Nonetheless, as Fuller journeys onto the prairie, these definitions of the "lady" are precisely what undergo revision. Under the disorienting conditions of the frontier, Fuller, like other eastern seaboard writers, begins to observe the dissolution of the conventional relationship between gender and class. As many critics have shown, the behavior of Euro-American women in the 19th century was molded by the potentially refining expectations of class, that is, bourgeois dreams of elegance in manner, attire, and education or the more republican visions of patriotism, simplicity, and moral truth.[11] Caroline Kirkland's *A New Home—Who'll Follow?* is a dense compendium of the slippages of class behavior as women often leave behind the material culture of their class such as clothing, furniture, and eating utensils and have to "make do" and improvise their household arrangements.[12] Like Kirkland, Fuller attempts to solve the problem of the "lady" by replacing her with the middle-class Yankee girl whose democratic spirit rejects the trappings of affluent fashion, yet maintains her moral vision and does not degenerate to the "ill-bred" behaviors of lower class women. The story on the ship, however, about the disturbing behavior of the "ill-bred" wife is a descriptive residue that Fuller often unselfconsciously articulates in which the categories of judgment for women are bound in fairly conventional class terms.

As *Summer on the Lakes* continues, however, Fuller's expectations about the landscape and the people start to transform. In her travels onto the prairie, in contrast to her experience at Niagara Falls, Fuller rejects the conventional representations of the prairie landscape. Aware of James Fenimore Cooper, who synthesized much previous descriptive material on the prairie when he wrote in the 1820s that "the eye became fatigued with the sameness and chilling dreariness of the landscape,"[13] Fuller nonchalantly disregards the conventions. Instead, Fuller is exhilarated by what she sees and forcefully expresses the need to adjust the eye to a "new form of life" (p. 35). She would climb to the roof of the house where she was staying and contemplate the "lovely, still reception on the earth; no towering mountains, no deep tree-shadows, nothing but plain earth and water bathed in light" (p. 35). Later in the Rock River area of Illinois, she would describe the "sumptuous" beauty of the river valley (p. 51). Tossing away the representation of the prairie landscape as uniformly monotonous, Fuller takes on the challenge of describing what she sees without the reassurance of guidebooks and novels. But if she attempts to move away from conventional descriptions of the landscape, she also begins to revise her perceptions of people on the frontier, in particular the daily life of women.

In a parallel fashion, the women represented on the frontier upset the familiar alignments between class and gender, creating dissonance within hierarchies of "good" and "bad" women. Fuller quickly sees that women on the frontier have to abandon many of the class labels that marked them as "true" women or ladies. Having to stay overnight at a barroom and sleep on a supper table, Fuller notes in a whimsical moment how the Yankee women "made do" and had a good night's sleep while an English woman "sat up all night, wrapped in her blanket-shawl, and with a neat lace cap upon her head; so that she would have looked perfectly the lady, if any one had come in" (p. 41).

But no sooner does Fuller assert the resiliency of Yankee women than she decides that they too are unable to adapt to the conditions of the frontier because of their middle-class values. Fuller perceives these values as so strong that they continually create community and generational conflict. In the towns scattered on the frontier, Fuller sees women either exaggerating their commitment to the roles of domesticity or abandoning them with no alternative roles available. Because domestic labor is intense on the frontier, "ladies, accustomed to a refined neatness, feel that they cannot degrade themselves by its absence, and struggle under every disadvantage to keep up the necessary routine of small arrangements" (p. 61). Alternatively, poor women give up under the pressure and lose their sense of purpose, becoming indolent and slovenly.

The cultural and class meaning of gender is not easily forgotten or transformed by Euro-American women on the frontier. As Fuller remarks, they watch their daughters grow up without the constant reminders of Euro-American conceptions of womanhood, and they worry about their lack of gentility. "If the little girls grow up strong, resolute, able to exert their faculties, their mothers mourn over their want of fashionable delicacy" (p. 62). Fuller in many ways welcomes the change and idealizes to herself the "new woman" who could be born on the frontier, a redeemed "Yankee girl of the prairies." This woman would have the skill both "to make home beautiful and comfortable" as well as the "bodily strength to enjoy plenty of exercise, the woods, and streams" (p. 63). Her culture would be decentered from urban displays of taste, preferring the guitar or flute to the piano, the sounds of her own voice singing with friends to that of the concert hall. Not surprisingly, the "Yankee girl of the prairie" nostalgically resembles the idealized picture of the colonial American woman before the excesses of urban affluence turned her republican simplicity into fashionable excess and display.[14]

The frontier, then, becomes a space where class-bound definitions of gender persist doggedly, but the possibility of their breakage and transformation is imminent. Though interpreted by Fuller as potentially liberating, this breakage offends certain women on the frontier, creating a frightening eclipse of "genteel" behavior, a deterioration of morals, and a loss of control over the next generation of daughters.

In an odd moment, after the discussion of the unfitness of Yankee women on the frontier, Fuller notes that some of the "ladies" that hosted her stay in Oregon, Illinois, found that "after all the pains and plagues of building and settling," a "favorite pastime" was "opening" Indian burial mounds. One of these "ladies" also performed the feat of capturing a deer with her bare hands while moments before she was making bread in her kitchen (p. 66). Fuller does not interpret these moments of violation and violence; they sit in the text without interpretation or comment. Euro-American women do, indeed, act differently under frontier conditions, performing actions totally at variance with the moral strictures usually placed on the actions of "ladies." But this "liberation" leads to the disturbing fact of blood and violence.

The most problematic moments in *Summer on the Lakes*, however, come when Fuller attempts to describe native women. Ironically, her observations of native women are often depicted by critics as the catalyst that finally brought Fuller to an understanding of the oppression of all women. By declaring native women as victims of male privilege, she disclosed the oppressed world of Euro-American women. As Kolodny writes and other feminist critics have observed, "it was only by means of pursuing the Indian woman's status that Fuller came, albeit circuitously, to an understanding of the white woman's as well."[15] But a reading that sees *Summer on the Lakes* as a developmental step toward *Woman in the Nineteenth Century* suppresses more than it reveals.

Painfully, Fuller experiences both the attitudes of native women towards her and the attitudes of her fellow Euro-American women towards them. In her first visit to an Indian encampment on Silver Lake in Wisconsin, where a band of Potawatomis had settled, a storm comes up and the party is forced to seek shelter under the Indian lodges. Here she sees the effects of American settlement in the sickness and starvation in the lodge and the puzzling reactions of the women: "They seemed to think we would not like to touch them: a sick girl in the lodge where I was, persisted in moving so as to give me the dry place; a woman with the sweet melancholy eye of the race, kept off the children and wet dogs from even the hem of my garment" (p. 119). Not clear about the social norms of the lodge, Fuller cannot decide if these attitudes are courteous or a recognition of the sense of repulsion found among the American settlers towards the Indians.

Later, on Mackinaw Island, Fuller witnesses the Chippewa and Ottawa tribes receive their "annual payments from the American government." In a transitional period, these tribes who had been intricately involved in the French and British fur trade since the early 18th century, were by 1843 controlled by the policies of American Indian agencies. Shortly, for some as soon as 12 years later, the pressures of American mining and settlement would eventually bring about their confinement to reservations.[16] Walking amidst the lodges, Fuller describes the "picturesque" quality of Indian life. Focusing on the activities of the women, she notices how they cook outside over small fires, surrounded by the constant sounds of playing children. "Here and there lounged a young girl, with a baby at her back, whose bright eyes glanced, as if born into a world of courage and joy, instead of ignominious servitude and slow decay" (p. 173). Even their labor as women seems for a moment less oppressive. "Some girls were cutting wood, a little way from me, talking and laughing, in the low musical tone, so charming in the Indian women" (p. 173). These scenes of everyday life softened her persistent perception of the native woman as "beast of burden."

In relation to her witnessing the annuity payments and describing the Indian camp, Fuller presents the debates about whether native women were relatively in a better position to their men than Euro-American women were to theirs. Citing such women writers as Mrs. Schoolcraft and Mrs. Grant, Fuller constructs the arguments for presenting native women as more empowered or less empowered than their European and Euro-American "sisters."[17] Importantly, however, the argument is not as concerned with an equal level of oppression, but with who is more or less oppressed, providing additional evidence about the superiority of Euro-American culture. Schoolcraft, who did have sustained contact with native peoples, judges that " 'on account of inevitable causes, the Indian woman is subjected to many hardships of a peculiar nature, yet her position, compared with that of the man, is higher and freer than that of the white woman' " (p. 175). Fuller objects to Schoolcraft's reasoning, and wants to see a more complex picture where there could be both instances of less and more empowerment.

Quoting Anna Grant, who finds a consistent brutality in the position of women among the Mohawks, though tempered when older women are the mothers of warriors, Fuller concludes that Grant is closer to the truth because "she looked more at both sides to find the truth" (p. 178). Given these exceptions, however, Fuller states that "Notwithstanding the homage paid to women, and the consequence allowed her in some cases, it is impossible to look upon the Indian women, without feeling that they *do* occupy a lower place than women among the nations of European civilization" (p. 179). She is willing to admit that native women "may suffer less than their white sisters, who have more aspiration and refinement, with little power of self-sustenance" (p. 179). Ultimately, however, she concludes that "their place is certainly lower, and their share of the human inheritance less" (p. 179). Fuller cannot equate the oppression of native women with the oppression of European or Euro-American women. Oppression must exist, but it must be deeper and more brutal, insuring the hierarchy of the Euro-American over native peoples. Her insight is not that all women are alike, but that in their oppressed position they ironically mark an additional hierarchy of values. The native women's extreme oppression, in one sense, legitimates the inevitability of their demise.

This inevitability Fuller never ceases to accept. Resigning herself, like many other contemporary American intellectuals, to the painful yet unavoidable displacement and defeat of native peoples by Euro-Americans, Fuller urges, however, a cessation to the brutal treatment of Indians by whites. Attacking the hypocrisy of the Christian trader and missionary, she rails against the institutions of business and religion that perpetuate a policy of humiliation and hatred. Fuller also indicates that the separation between white settlers and native peoples exists not only in articulated social structures but also the intimate space of the domestic.

In a moment of irritation, Fuller records the particular animosity she experienced between Euro-American women and Indians. She writes, "I have spoken of the hatred felt by the white man for the Indian: with white women it seems to amount to disgust, to loathing. How I could endure the dirt, the peculiar smell of the Indians, and their dwellings, was a great marvel in the eyes of my lady acquaintance; indeed, I wonder why they did not quite give me up, as they certainly looked on me with great distaste for it" (p. 183). Even in situations of adoption of Indian children by whites, Fuller finds subtle human cruelty. She records that one white woman said, " 'Do what you will for them, they will be ungrateful. The savage cannot be washed out of them. Bring up an Indian child and see if you can attach it to you' " (p. 183). This statement, mixing two cultural attitudes – the need to destroy the "savage" in the child and the need for this newly constructed child to return a "grateful" love to the adoptive parent – indicated to Fuller the extent to which white women participated in a form of domestic brutality toward native peoples. Maternal love, the great fetish of many 19th century American women, was exposed, contaminated, and thereby contained within racial hatred.

In her descriptive writings Fuller records these inconsistencies and ruptures on the frontier but, except for stabbing at Christian hypocrisy, does not draw them together into a coherent critique. Instead, she quotes the lengthy poem *Governor Everett Receiving the Indian Chiefs, November, 1837,* recapitulating the inevitability of conquest, the "vanishing race" motif, and the necessary sorrow at the process. But she leaves gaps throughout her journal account, indicating a sustained sense of conflict. At one point she grasps at amalgamation or intermarriage as the "only true and profound means of civilization," only to declare that those "of mixed blood fade early, and are not generally a fine race. They lose what is best in either type, rather than enhance the value of each, by mingling" (p. 195). Despite these attitudes, she judges past American policy toward native peoples as a sin and entreats "every man and every woman, in their private dealings with the subjugated race" to "avoid all share in embittering, by insult or unfeeling prejudice, the captivity of Israel" (p. 236).

In her final chapter of *Summer on the Lakes*, Fuller, however, does describe a momentary meeting between herself and two other women that seemed to break the demarcations of class and race. Back on board the steamboat headed home, Fuller gets to know two chambermaids, one Dutch the other Indian. Since they both spoke English, they "entertained" Fuller with stories about their lives. The Dutch woman spoke of her love for the improvised "shepherd's dance" that allows the dancers to "invent to the music all kinds of movements, descriptive of things that may happen in the field" (p. 238). The Indian woman told her about her troubles with her estranged husband and how she consistently answered "no" when asked by him if he could live with her again. Fuller is struck by the strange freedom that these women have, and about the Indian woman she writes, "I was pleased by the nonchalance of this woman, and the perfectly national [sic] manner she had preserved after so many years of contact with all kinds of people" (p. 239). Hardly the beast of burden described earlier in *Summer on the Lakes*, this woman's life seems remarkably open to the lived experiences of diverse groups of other people. At the end of the journey Fuller receives gifts from both these women and a sense of affectionate regard pervades their relationships.

In the larger context of the ship, Fuller remains, of course, the only "lady" on board, and these two women remain chambermaids. They have in effect all left the frontier behind and the Dutch and native women have already radically adapted to the demands of the expansionistic American drives onto the frontier. But in these women's discrete lives a conversation and exchange began that seemed qualitatively different from Fuller's other experiences on the frontier. The stories these women tell of their lives alter Fuller's concept of freedom from narrowly conceived gender and class definitions, causing her to reflect more on her own life than on theirs; with their freedom she dreams of her own liberation. Commenting on the native woman's behavior, she writes, "Here she was far freer than she would have been in civilized life" (p. 239). More a reflexive remark about her own sense of restrictions, Fuller immediately laments the lack of freedom she has had as a sojourner; how much she has not been allowed to do or see. Sitting up at night to hear the sound of the approaching rapids as she nears her journey's end, she recognizes the limits a woman of her class has as a traveler:

> . . . I shall not enter into that truly wild and free region; shall not have the canoe voyage, whose daily adventure, with the camping out at night beneath the stars, would have given an interlude of such value to my existence. I shall not see the Pictured Rocks, their chapels and urns. It did not depend on me; it never has, whether such things shall be done or not (pp. 242-243).

No longer a debate over the relative freedom of native versus Euro-American women, Fuller's writing underscores her personal sense of restriction and the sorrow at its impoverishment of her life. In a moment of sadness she even envies the labor of native women in the woods, singing as they gather fuel, and admits that the "burden" of their work ironically places them within the "free woods" (p. 245). The oppressed class of the native woman who had previously marked a deeper victimization now represents a forbidden freedom to wander beyond the gilded cage of "civilization." The native woman as the "other" that Fuller encounters on her journey provides a mirror in which to see herself and the ways in which her gender is constructed by Euro-American middle-class values.[18] In this context, Fuller's desire for liberty finds its most moving expression.

Grasping for the journey that would bring her heightened experiences of pleasure and fear, challenges to the predictable behavior of her life, Fuller does descend down the rapids with "two Indian canoe-men" and in four brief minutes catches a glimpse of what could have been.[19] "I had fancied there was a wall of rock somewhere, where descent would somehow be accomplished, and that there would come some one gasp of terror and delight, some sensation entirely new to me; but I found myself in smooth water, before I had time to feel anything but the buoyant pleasure of being carried so lightly through this surf amid the breakers" (pp. 245-46). Wishing to have "come down twenty times, that I might have had the leisure to realize the pleasure" (p. 246), Fuller recognizes again that "new" sensations are not hers on this journey. Rather than describing the oppression of native women, Fuller has articulated her own.

Like Mariana, whose story interrupts the journey narrative of *Summer on the Lakes* and is embedded in the text as a reminiscence about an old friend, Margaret Fuller confronts the gender restrictions of her own social class. Mariana, a passionate and intellectual woman, confined first to a restrictive boarding school and then an emotionally bankrupt marriage, is fated to become a "solitary and wretched wife" (p. 97), while her husband is off "on excursions and affairs of pleasure" (p. 97). Eventually, she dies in solitude, cut off from human companionship. Defying Mariana's fate through her journey to the prairies, Fuller is nonetheless led to reflect on the continuing entrapment she faces as a Euro-American woman. In this process, the native woman as "other" has provided her with a point of reference to gauge her own liberty.

Almost emblematically, this reflexivity is best represented in an earlier scene at the Chippewa and Ottawa encampment when Fuller attempts to communicate by signs with the native women. Sitting on a canoe at the edge of the lodges, Fuller waits as a native woman comes down and sits beside her. The woman asks to see her parasol, and, after examining it, places it in her baby's hand, looking at Fuller the entire time and mocking her, as Fuller imagines, with a mischievous laugh, "as much to say 'You carry a thing that is only fit for a baby' " (p. 180). How to interpret the woman's laugh? Without a common language, Fuller writes that her "pantomime was very pretty" (p. 180), but its message she interprets as a description about herself. The native woman as "other" becomes the mirror of herself, the child-woman of the 19th century, at once the representative of progressive, republican ideals and the infantilized "lady." Perplexed about meaning, Fuller guesses and records. Without the native woman's voice as a counterpoint to the rich speculations of Fuller's journey, the text displays a rhetorical circularity. The sign of gender keeps pointing inward toward the cultural values of Euro-American women on the frontier. But this inward turning creates the textures of gender that maintain tension with particular historical and cultural conditions, and removes gender from the transcendent and utopian space of universal vision.[20]

As a woman's journey account of a few summer months, *Summer on the Lakes* both implicitly and explicitly questions the construction of gender on the frontier and describes the tentative and paradoxically tenacious hold conventional gender assumptions have once social and economic conditions change. Fuller often inadvertently describes the barriers to placing all women under the sign of gender and the complexities of class and race. Some of these perceptions entail her own story, one of a struggle against middle-class definitions of gender, the other of an attempt to hold onto the republican destiny of American culture and the vision of women within that progressive narrative. In the end, she hints at the communitarian principle of "voluntary association" that needs exporting to the frontier, but quickly adds that "nations" do not abide such human arrangements.

Margaret Fuller's *Summer on the Lakes* does, as Kolodny forcefully argues, expand and revise our sense of the American frontier, but does it reside in the "purer" space of the garden? In significant ways, oppression in *Summer on the Lakes* does not have a clear gender. Fears about the loss of cultural identity on the frontier lead to an infinite play of variations that affect perceptions of race, class, and gender. Hierarchies crisscross the narrative in oblique angles, at one point privileging Euro-American civilization, at the next lamenting entrapment within its gilded cage. Throughout the text, however, the frontier remains both a vision of potential liberation and a fatal limit to freedom. The ethical argument, as appealing as it may be, is precisely the point at which the complexities of gender arise and its contingency with race and class emerge, ultimately preventing the sweet consolation of a "purer" text.

Notes

1. There is no adequate way to acknowledge the immense amount of material presently available on the frontier writings of women. Some helpful materials as starting points are: Susan Armitage and Elizabeth Jameson, eds., *The Women's West* (Norman: University of Oklahoma Press, 1987); Carol Fairbanks, *Prairie Women: Images in American and Canadian Fiction* (New Haven, Conn.: Yale University Press, 1986); John Faragher, *Women and Men on the Overland Trail* (New Haven, Conn.: Yale University Press, 1979); Julie Roy Jeffrey, *Frontier Women: The Trans-Mississippi West, 1840-1880* (New York: Hill and Wang, 1979); Annette Kolodny, *The Land Before Her: Fantasy and Experience of the American Frontiers, 1630-1860* (Chapel Hill: University of North Carolina Press, 1984); Sandra L. Myres, *Westering Women and the Frontier Experience, 1800-1915* (Albuquerque: University of New Mexico Press, 1982); Glenda Riley, *Women and Indians on the Frontier, 1825-1915* (Albuquerque: University of New Mexico Press, 1984) and *The Female Frontier: A Comparative View of Women on the Prairie and the Plains* (Lawrence: University Press of Kansas, 1988); and Lillian Schlissel, *Women's Diaries of the Westward Journey* (New York: Schocken Books, 1982). See in particular the historical fiction of the colonial frontier: Lydia Maria Child, *Hobomok and Other Writings on Indians*, ed. Carolyn L. Karcher (New Brunswick, N. J.: Rutgers University Press, 1986) and Catharine Maria Sedgwick, *Hope Leslie*, ed. Mary Kelley (New Brunswick, N. J.: Rutgers University Press, 1987). Also of interest is the first dime novel by Anne S. Stephens, *Malaeska: The Indian Wife of the White Hunter* (New York: The John Day Company, 1929).

2. My approach to the concept of gender and its relationship to class and race has been influenced by the writings of Michele Barrett, "Ideology and the Cultural Production of Gender," in *Feminist Criticism and Social Change*, ed. Judith Newton and Deborah Rosenfelt (New York: Methuen, 1985), pp. 65-85; Michelle Zimbalist Rosaldo, "The Uses and Abuses of Anthropology: Reflections on Feminism and Cross-Cultural Understanding," *Signs* 5 (1980): 389-417, and with Jane F. Collier, "Politics and Gender in Simple Societies," in *Sexual Meanings: The Cultural Construction of Gender and Sexuality*, ed. Sherry B. Ortner and Harriet Whitehead (New York: Cambridge University Press, 1981), pp. 275-329; Joan Wallach Scott, *Gender and the Politics of History* (New York: Columbia University Press, 1988); and Gayatri Chakravorty Spivak, "Three Women's Texts and a Critique of Imperialism," in *"Race," Writing, and Difference*, ed. Henry Louis Gates, Jr. (Chicago: University of Chicago Press, 1985), pp. 262-280, and *In Other Worlds: Essays in Cultural Politics* (New York: Methuen, 1987). As a result, my method differs from that of Susan J. Rosowski, "Margaret Fuller, an Engendered West, and *Summer on the Lakes*," *Western American Literature* 22 (1990): 125-144, who describes *Summer on the Lakes* as Fuller's "most developed autobiographical account

of personal change," p. 125. Rosowski argues that Fuller "engenders" the narrative by consistent reference to female images and by the end of the travel account addresses a female reader exclusively. The social, economic, and racial tensions within this engendering are not the major focus of her interpretation.

3. Armitage, "Through Women's Eyes: A New View of the West," in *Women's West*, p. 17.
4. Kolodny, *The Land Before Her*, p. xii.
5. *Ibid.*, p. 6.
6. *Ibid.*, p. 7.
7. *Ibid.*, p. 7.
8. *Ibid.*, p. 121.
9. All textual quotes come from S. M. Fuller, *Summer on the Lakes, in 1843* (Boston: Charles C. Little and James Brown; New York: Charles S. Francis and Co., 1844). A later edition edited by Fuller's brother, Arthur Buckminster Fuller, excised sections such as the narrative of Mariana, the translated story of the Seeress of Prevorst, native American myths and sources, as well as various letters and poems. Unfortunately, this edition also did not include the sketches and drawings of Sarah Freeman Clarke who accompanied Fuller on much of the journey. See Arthur Buckminster Fuller's "Preface" in Margaret Fuller Ossoli, *Summer on the Lakes*, ed. Arthur B. Fuller, 2d ed. (1856; reprint, New York: Haskell House Publishers, 1970).
10. See the remarks on Fuller in Elizabeth McKinsey, *Niagara Falls: Icon of the American Sublime* (New York: Cambridge University Press, 1985), pp. 215-222.
11. See in particular, Linda K. Kerber, *Women of the Republic: Intellect and Ideology in Revolutionary America* (New York: W. W. Norton & Co., 1986) and Carroll Smith-Rosenberg, *Disorderly Conduct: Visions of Gender in Victorian America* (New York: Oxford University Press, 1985).
12. [Caroline M. Kirkland], *A New Home—Who'll Follow? Or, Glimpses of Western Life. By Mrs. Mary Clavers. An Actual Settler* (1839; reprint, New York: Garrett Press, 1969).
13. Cooper, *The Prairie: A Tale*, ed. James P. Elliott (Albany: State University of New York Press, 1985), p. 13.
14. Many women reformers were concerned with constructing roles for women that would stand against the fashionable excesses of the times. See in particular the writings of Catharine Beecher and Lydia Maria Child.
15. Kolodny, *The Land Before Her*, p. 127.
16. Edmund Jefferson Danziger, Jr., *The Chippewas of Lake Superior* (Norman: University of Oklahoma Press, 1978), pp. 68-90. See also, Robert M. Utley, *The Indian Frontier of the American West: 1846-1890* (Albuquerque: University of New Mexico Press, 1984) and Ronald N. Satz, *American Indian Policy in the Jacksonian Era* (Lincoln: University of Nebraska Press, 1975).

17. Fuller may be referring to Mary Howard Schoolcraft, the wife and amanuensis of her husband Henry R. Schoolcraft, Indian agent and prolific writer on native customs and myths, who became known for her pro-slavery writings during the 1850s and 60s, but her reference to Mrs. Schoolcraft's premature death raises clear questions about the source. Anna Grant wrote *Memoirs of An American Lady: With Sketches of Manners and Scenes in America, as They existed Previous to the Revolution* (1808 rpt.; Albany, N. Y.: Joel Munsell, 1876). Among others, Fuller also used material on native peoples from the works of James Adair, Jonathan Carver, George Catlin, James Fenimore Cooper, Alexander Henry, Washington Irving, Anna Jameson, Thomas McKenney, and Henry R. Schoolcraft.

18. For discussions about the poetics of ethnography and the reflexive loops that descriptions of the "other" present to the author of such descriptions, see the essays in *Writing Culture: The Poetics and Politics of Ethnography*, ed. James Clifford and George E. Marcus (Berkeley: University of California Press, 1986); and Mary Louise Pratt, "Scratches on the Face of the Country; or, What Mr. Barrow Saw in the Land of the Bushmen," in *"Race," Writing, and Difference*, pp. 138-162.

19. The desire to dispel ennui by travel experiences hence assuring a transformation of subjectivity is crucial to much travel writing by Europeans and Euro-Americans at this time. See in particular Mrs. Jameson, *The Diary of an Ennuyee* (Boston: Houghton, Osgood, and Company, 1879), first published in 1826.

20. For a provocative discussion of the voice at the margin see Gayatri Chakravorty Spivak, "Can the Subaltern Speak?" in *Marxism and the Interpretation of Culture*, ed. Cary Nelson and Lawrence Grossberg (Urbana: University of Illinois Press, 1988).

Fatal Journeys, Fatal Legends: The Journey of the Captive Woman in Argentina and Uruguay

Bonnie Frederick

IN COLONIAL AND 19TH-CENTURY Argentina and Uruguay, Hispanic women being captured by Indians was both fact and cultural nightmare. Thousands of women and children were captured, some to be ransomed, some to become wives and slaves. The horror of this prolonged frontier warfare inspired many oral folkloric tales that circulated among the Hispanic community; out of these came the literary image of the captive woman that forms a recurrent motif in the literature of Argentina and Uruguay. Though literary captivity tales claim historical times and places, a close examination of the stories reveals a folkloric pattern drawn from the tradition of Spanish captivity ballads and Christian saints' tales. However, the captivity story in Hispanic America differs from its Spanish source in an important way: the captive is always a woman, not a man. This gender difference significantly alters the nature of the captive's journey. Her abduction is a forced journey with no return; her destination signifies sexual violation, racial contamination, and the sacrifice of her husband, her children, or her own life. Moreover, because the narrator of her story is male, the captive woman's experience is manipulated to instruct female readers in the limits of their permitted freedom and sexuality.

The captivity tale was already common in the folklore and literature of Spain when the *conquistadores* came to America. Centuries of warfare between the Moors and the Christians in Spain had produced an immense variety of such stories and lore,[1] popularly told in a traditional verse form called the *romance* or ballad.[2] The verse captivity narratives followed a typical journey patter: abduction of a Christian by infidels, imprisonment in hell, sexual threats or temptations, and escape through miraculous intervention. The first and second stages of the journey, the abduction and imprisonment in hell, are seen in this popular captivity story:

Mi padre era de Ronda,	[My father was from Ronda,
y mi madre de Antequera;	and my mother from Antequera;
cativáronme los moros	the Moors captured me
entre la paz y la guerra,	between war and peace,
y lleváronme a vender	and took me to be sold
a Jerez de la Frontera.	at Jerez de la Frontera.
Siete días con sus noches	Seven days with their nights
anduve en almoneda	I was in the slave market;
no hubo moro ni mora	there was neither man nor woman
que por mí diese moneda,	who would give money for me,
si no fuera un moro perro	except a dog of a Moor
que por mí cien doblas diera,	who gave 100 doubloons for me,
y llevárame a su casa,	and took me to his house,
y echárame una cadena.	and put me in chains.
Dábame la vida mala,	He gave me the bad life,
dábame la vida negra,	he gave me the black life,
de día majar esparto,	pounding grass fibers by day,
de noche moler cibera,	and grinding grain by night,
y echóme un freno a la boca,	and he put a bit in my mouth
porque no comiese de ella,	so that I could not eat of it,
mi cabello retorcido,	and he twisted my hair,
y tornóme a la cadena.[3]	and put me back in chains.][4]

The sexual temptations found in the third stage of the captivity ballads are also religious in nature, as can be seen in the captive Jacinto's temptation by the Moorish princess Zaida:

. . .–Mira, cautivo,	[. . ."Look, captive,
Si tú olvidas a tu Dios	If you will forget your God
Y sigues la ley que sigo	And follow the law that I follow
De mi profeta Mahoma,	From my prophet Mohammed,
Tú te casarás conmigo,	You could marry me,
Gozarás muchas riquezas,	You would enjoy great riches,
Y tendrás muchos cautivos. . .	And you would have many captives. . ."
–¿Cómo quieres que yo olvide	"How can you ask me to forget
A un Dios de gracia infinito,	A God of infinite grace,
A un Dios que por su bondad	A God who through his goodness

Quiso y por su amor divino	And divine love wants
Redimirme con su sangre	To redeem me with his blood
Por librarme del abismo?[5]	And deliver me from the abyss?"]

The captivity ballads usually end with a rescue that is attributed to divine favor and the direct result of prayer:

Desque en salvo nos fallamos,	[From the time we were saved,
fuimos besando la tierra:	we kept kissing the ground:
mil gracias a Jesús dimos	we gave a thousand thanks to Jesus
y a María, madre nuestra,	and to Mary, our mother,
que romper del cautiverio	who made the chains
quisieron nuestras cadenas.[6]	of our captivity break.]

By telling the story in religious terms, the captivity narrative is elevated to moral as well as historical-national status; the tales of captivity become a kind of popular hagiography, teaching proper behavior and beliefs through the example of courage under duress.

The tradition of captivity stories flourished during the age of discovery and conquest; for example, Miguel de Cervantes (who had suffered five years of Moorish captivity himself) wrote various captivity stories, such as the one in *Don Quijote* (volume I, chapters 39-41). Spanish soldiers brought this powerful tradition to America.[7] They imposed the vocabulary, imagery, and ideology of the struggle between the Moors and the Christians on the Argentine experience.[8] They described the Indian with the vocabulary previously used to describe the Moorish infidel, and the American desert was transformed into hell. This vocabulary was so pervasive that even the Indians adopted the Spanish custom of referring to the Europeans as "Christians" rather than "Spaniards" or "whites." Various Spanish solders suffered captivity in the New World and wrote about it; for example, *El cautiverio feliz* [*The Fortunate Captivity*] by Francisco Núñez de Pineda y Bascuñán describes his seven months' captivity in 1629. Its basic structure, not surprisingly, is the traditional pattern of abduction by infidels, imprisonment in hell, sexual temptation, and escape through miraculous intervention. His captivity was "fortunate" or "happy" (*feliz* carries both meanings) because he still exercised his will even during captivity. Though tempted, he rejected the Indian women offered to him and insisted on wearing the European clothes he had been captured in, which maintained his outward identity of a Christian. Moreover, he was rescued, and lived to tell about his captivity and his salvation.

When the captive was a woman, however, she could not exercise her will in the same way; there was very little she could do to defend herself against the threat of rape or forced marriage. Writers who believed that the Indians should be wiped out for the good of the Christian nation exploited her sexual vulnerability. This ideological subtext can already be seen in the earliest Argentine captivity tale, told in *La Argentina* (1612) by Ruy Díaz de Guzmán. He relates that in 1532 a Spanish Woman, Lucía Miranda, comes to the New World with her husband, Sebastián Hurtado. Two Indian brothers, Mangoré and Siripo, see her and fall in love with her. Lucía, however, remains faithful to her husband. The Indians then attack the Spanish garrison and overcome them; in the fighting, Mangoré is killed and Lucía and Sebastián taken prisoner. Siripo takes Lucía as his wife. Giving in to her pleas, he allows Sebastián to live, provided that he take an Indian wife. Lucía and Sebastián cannot hide their love for long, however, and they are denounced to Siripo. He orders a martyr's death for them both: Lucía to be burned to death and Sebastián shot with arrows. They both die calling on the mercy of God, thus "es de creer que marido y mujer están gozando de su santa gloria."[9] [It is supposed that both husband and wife are enjoying holy glory.]

There is little reason to believe that the story of Lucía Miranda is factual. Efforts to find historical proof have failed, and the story itself is suspiciously reminiscent of saints' tales, which were so widely known on all levels of Hispanic society that they functioned as both secular and religious folklore. It cannot be accident, for example, that Lucía is burnt after refusing sexual transgression, as was the saint of the same name. Similarly, St. Sebastian was a Roman soldier condemned to death by being shot with arrows, as is the hero of the Lucía Miranda legend; St. Sebastian's gory statue was—and is—a common sight in Hispanic churches. Yet in spite of its fictional-folkloric nature, the story of Lucía Miranda so captured the attention of 19th-century writers that it repeatedly surfaced in popular works.[10]

The first female captivity tale already contains the altered journey pattern of the captive woman that will be imitated in other works. Later writers followed Díaz de Guzmán's lead in retaining the opening elements of the captive's journey from the Spanish tradition. However, because the captive is a woman, the final element of the traditional pattern—escape through miraculous intervention—is changed. Instead, death (of a husband, a child, or the captive herself) becomes the ultimate destination in the captive woman's journey. This altered pattern can be seen in four works that still hold honored places in the literary canon of Argentina and Uruguay: *La cautiva* (1837) by Esteban Echeverría; *La vuelta de Martín Fierro* (1879) by José Hernández; *Tabaré* (1888) by Juan Zorrilla de San Martín; and "Marta Riquelme" (1902) by the Anglo-Argentine William Henry Hudson.

All those tales begin by identifying the captive woman as an angel — Marta in the story "Marta Riquelme," María in *La cautiva*, and Blanca in *Tabaré* — while also describing her abductors as devils. The most extreme description is the one found in *Tabaré*: Blanca is as pure (and European) as her name implies, "con sus estrellas en los ojos,/ sus alas invisibles en la espalda"[11] [with stars in her eyes,/ Invisible wings on her shoulders.] The captives' angelic beauty is paralleled by their bravery, which is also a divine gift. For example, the captive in *La vuelta de Martín Fierro* saves Fierro's life, an act that he attributes to God's special aid to women:

¡Bendito Dios podoroso!	[Blessed be Almighty God!
¿Quién te puede comprender?	Who can understand your ways?
cuando a una débil muger	You gave at that time,
le diste en esa ocasión	to a weak woman
la juerza que en un varón	strength such as maybe
tal vez no pudiera haber. . .	even a man would not have had. . .
Ausilio tan generoso	This help so generous
me libertó del apuro;	freed me from that tight spot.
si no es ella, de siguro	If it weren't for her, the Indian
que el indio me sacrifica,	would have slaughtered me for sure
y mi valor se duplica	and her noble example
con un ejemplo tan puro.[12]	made me twice as brave and strong.]

María in *La cautiva* is also brave and strong. She kills the Indian who captured her, talks her husband Brian into escaping, and survives longer than he does in the desert. Brian too gains strength from María's courage. He has told her to leave him to die, but she refuses:

Huyamos, mi Brian, huyamos;	[Flee with me, Brian, flee;
que en el áspero camino	on the hard road ahead
mi brazo, y poder divino	my arm and my divine strength
te servirán de sostén.	will sustain you.
—Tu valor me infunde fuerza,	—Your courage gives me strength
y de la fortuna adversa,	and I only want to share with
amor, gloria o agonía	you, María, adverse destiny,
participar con María	love, glory, or death.
yo quiero. ¡Huyamos! ven, ven—[13]	Let us flee, come, come—]

The Indians are set in contrast to these angelic and divinely brave women; here is how Echeverría describes the demonic Indian camp at night:

Noche es el vasto horizonte,	[Night is the vast horizon,
noche el aire, cielo y tierra.	night the air, sky and earth.
Parece haber apiñado	The prince of darkness
el genio de las tinieblas,	seems to have gathered
para algún misterio inmundo,	for some obscene ceremony
sobre la llanura inmensa,	on the immense plain
la lobreguez del abismo	the blackness of the abyss
donde inalterable reina.	where he eternally reigns.
Sólo inquietos divagando,	Only unquiet spirits roam
por entre las sombras negras,	among the black shadows,
los espíritus foletos	the flames of lost souls
con viva luz reverberan,	shimmer with light,
se disipan, reaparecen,	dissipate, reappear,
vienen, van, se alejan	come, go, become distant,
mientras el insecto chilla,	while insects buzz,
y en fachinales o cuevas	and in caves and marshes
los nocturnos animales	the nocturnal animals
con triste aullido se quejan.[14]	complain with sad cries.]

By living in this demonic region and imprisoning angelic women, the Indians become less than human, even animalistic. David Haberly points out that this rejection of the Indians' human nature has its origins in the ideology and vocabulary of the Moorish-Christian struggle in Spain.[15] That being an Indian meant being non-human can clearly be seen in the description of the half-breed Tabaré: "Esa línea es charrúa; esa otra...humana."[16] [That line is Charrua; that other...human.] Hudson's narrator also uses Marta Riquelme's angelic appearance to imply the inferior appearance of the Indian women:

> Marta was the loveliest being I had ever beheld; though in this matter my opinion may be biased, for I only saw her side by side with the dark-skinned coarse-haired Indian women, and compared with their faces of ignoble type Marta's was like that of an angel.[17]

The polarity of angel/devil is found in many 19th-century works, especially those written during Romanticism. In the case of the captive women, however, angelic beauty and virtue have an added role. They help establish what Joyce Williams and Karen Holmes call the "good rape," that is, the rape that is regarded by society as an act of unprovoked violence against a woman whose own behavior is above reproach.[18] The fact that so many of these heroines are married (María, Marta, the mother in *Martín Fierro*) should be understood as another gesture of unimpeachable respectability. These women must conform to the ideal of respectable femininity if they are to escape the blame that is attached to the rape victim suspected of complicity. Their victimization must be complete and unquestioned in order to provoke unsceptical outrage in the reader. Similarly, by this standard, the Indians must be portrayed as inhumanly cruel and incapable of honorable behavior.

The influence of this respectable feminine ideal can be seen in how the women's bravery is limited. In spite of claims of divine strength, these women are actually helpless and unable to survive on their own. For example, the bravery of the mother that Martín Fierro praises is only of brief duration; she is unable to prevent her child's death, and once she pulls the Indian off Fierro, she does not act again. Marta Riquelme tries to escape on her own, but her escape is an impulse with no plan or provision, so she is quickly recaptured. Even María, who has just killed two Indians and released Brian, praises Brian's bravery at the expense of her own: "De la amada patria nuestra/escudo fuerte es tu diestra,/ y, ¿qué vale una mujer?"[19] [Your right arm is the strong shield of our beloved nation, but of what worth is a woman?] Brian, however, is unable to help María, and they both die. Even when the captive women seek male helpers, the men are unsuccessful (as in the case of *La cautiva*), unable to save the children (as in *La vuelta de Martín Fierro* and "Marta Riquelme"), or lose their own lives (as in the Lucía Miranda legend and *Tabaré*).

Another indication of the women's helplessness is that they all weep at great length. Though they shed tears at various stages in the narrative, the most important scene is the death of their children at the hands of the Indians. Marta Riquelme, for example, first loses her child by her Spanish husband Cosme, then later loses her Indian child as the price of her escape, a price that later haunts her: ". . .through many days of scorching heat and many night of weary travel she was always piteously pleading for her lost child—always seeming to hear it crying to save it from destruction."[20] The mother of Tabaré is pictured as crying in every scene; in the 13 pages that relate her captivity, there are 24 mentions of tears. Her weeping is even reflected in nature, as when she bids farewell to her baby:

> La madre lo estrechó, dejó en su frente
> Una lágrima inmensa, en ella un beso,

Y se acostó a morir. Lloró la selva,
Y, al entreabrirse, sonreía el cielo.[21]

[The mother laid him down; she left on his forehead
an immense tear and a kiss,
and then she lay down to die. The forest wept,
and upon taking her in, the heavens smiled.]

The tears and helplessness of the captive women emphasize the danger of this stage in their forced journey: imprisoned in the hell that is home to their infidel captors, the captives now face the threat of sexual violation. Unlike male captives, they are not permitted sexual temptation (with one exception which will be examined later). The sexual danger in the female narrative changes the traditional male captivity pattern from a triumphant escape against great odds to a fatal pattern of contamination and expulsion. By changing the gender of the captive, the ideological system is changed as well.

In the ideology of captivity narratives, a society's integrity is more threatened by rape committed by the enemy during warfare than it is by rape committed by one of its own members. As Susan Brownmiller points out, wartime rape is more than the act of an unbalanced individual: "rape by a conquering soldier destroys all remaining illusions of power and property for men of the defeated side. The body of the raped woman becomes a ceremonial battleground, a parade ground for the victor's trooping of the colors."[22] It is no accident, for example, that the folkloric-historical image of conquered Mexico, La Malinche, is a woman, and that she is despised for having been violated and bearing a *mestizo* (half-breed) child.[23] Whether she actually suffers rape or not, the captive woman is regarded with that curious ambivalence with which society views rape victims—victims, yes, but somehow contaminated. She is forced to pay for her captivity by the death of a loved one, by her own death, or by being rejected by Spanish society. There is, for example, that discordant scene in *La cautiva*, when Brian rejects María after she sets him free:

ya no eres digna de mí.	[You are no longer worthy of me.
Del salvaje la torpeza	The lewdness of the savage
habrá ajado la pureza	must have ruined the purity
de tu honor, y mancillado	of your honor, and stained
tu cuerpo santificado	your body that was sanctified
por mi cariño y amor;	by my love and affection;
ya no me es dado quererte—.[24]	I can no longer love you—.]

María reassures him that she killed her captor before rape could occur. Brian accepts her word and only then do they prepare to escape. Brian's rejection of María is very briefly told in a poem that did not mind lingering on other topics for pages. Yet this is an important scene; it interrupts their tearful embraces, their reuniting after terrible separation. María managed the impossible: escaping rape. Yet that is not enough. She must face the rejection of her husband, endure great suffering in the wilderness, lose her husband and child, and finally die.

Marta Riquelme's rape is told through the fate of her long, golden hair, a traditional symbol of female sexuality.[25] (In this case, her blond coloring also affirms that she is of Spanish, not Indian, descent.) When Marta is first taken captive, she tries unsuccessfully to escape. As punishment, her Indian captor cuts off her hair and makes it into a belt; the narrator calls it "a golden trophy which doubtless won him great honor and distinction amongst his fellow-savages."[26] When Marta returns to her village, the priest immediately sees that "her head, bowed down with sorrow and despair, was divested of that golden crown which had been her chief ornament."[27] He mentions several times that her hair is now coarsened by the sun; that is, the narrator blames the very elements of the desert for participating in this symbolic rape. Finally, rejected by her husband and gossiped about by the villagers, Marta becomes insane and is magically transformed into a *kakuy*, a bird with sad cries that the villagers consider the animal form of an *ánima en pena* [soul in torment]. Significantly, her metamorphosis begins with her short hair rising up into a bird-like crest.[28] Marta's long hair, tears, and sexual defilement are all reminiscent of that favorite of Hispanic good woman/bad woman ambivalence, Mary Magdalene.

If society's attitude toward the captive woman is at best ambivalent, its attitude toward her half-Indian children is straightforward rejection. The mother's love for her *mestizo* children is viewed as a kind of betrayal of Spanish society even if she has remained loyally resistant to the Indian father. This rejection is an important element in the poem *Tabaré*. Tabaré, the half-Indian hero of the poem, is described as a conflicting mixture of races and thus natures:

> ¡Extraño ser! ¿Qué raza da sus líneas
>   A ese organismo esbelto?
> Hay en su cráneo hogar para la idea,
> Hay espacio en su frente para el genio.
> Esa línea es charrúa; esa otra...humana.
>   Ese mirar es tierno...

¿No hay, en el fondo de esos ojos claros,
Un ser oculto con los ojos negros?[29]

[Strange being! What race gives its lines
        to that slender body?
There is in his brain a home for thought,
There is room in his forehead for intelligence.
That line is Charrúa; that other. . .is human.
        That gaze is gentle. . .
Could there be, behind those blue eyes,
a hidden being with dark eyes?]

Later, he is called "el indio imposible, el extranjero,/ El salvaje con lágrimas. . ."[30] [the impossible Indian, the stranger,/ the savage with tears]. Tabaré's fate is sealed when he meets Blanca, the pure and innocent Spanish woman. She is attracted to him and secures his release after he is taken prisoner. Then Blanca herself is captured in a raid; her brother searches for her after the raid: "Y no está muerta. . . ni siquiera muerta!"[31] [And she is not dead. . .not even dead!] Tabaré finally denies his Indian allegiance by saving Blanca from Yamandú, her captor. The rescue scene is charged with sexual imagery; for example, Blanca (who happened to be captured wearing only a filmy nightgown) lies on a "lecho de hojas"[32] [a bed of leaves; *lecho* implies a marriage bed]. The narrator uses only two synonyms for her name: *la española* and *la virgen*. At the end of her journey, there is death, but not her own. Instead, Tabaré dies. This could be simply a case of the hero's fatal destiny, of course. However, there is another reason as well for his death: alive, Tabaré threatened Blanca's Spanish purity, though not by rape. Indeed, perhaps the only fate worse for Blanca than rape by Yamandú is a willing sexual union with the *mestizo* Tabaré. While a male captive is permitted sexual attraction to infidel women, the female captive is forbidden sexual temptation. In the dedication that the author of *Tabaré* wrote to his wife, he makes this racial imperative clear. She has shown sympathy for Tabaré and antipathy for the Spanish soldier who kills him:

Si a ti se te hubiera dado a elegir el desenlace de mi poema, yo bien sé cual hubieras elegido. ¡No podía ser! No: tu idea era imposible. Blanca—tu raza, nuestra raza— ha quedado viva sobre el cadáver del charrúa.[33]

[If you had been given the choice of how to end my poem, I know very well how you would have chosen. It could not be! No, your idea was impossible. Blanca—your race, our race—, has remained alive over the cadaver of the Charrúa.]

This statement is interesting not only for its clear racism, but also because his wife needed to be reminded of the message of the text: a Spanish woman is forbidden to love an Indian.

The attitudes portrayed in these literary works also appear in non-literary sources. For example, Lucio Mansilla's *Una excursión a los indios ranqueles* is full of references to captives, who by the 1870s numbered about 600-800 among the eight to ten thousand Ranqueles.[34] There is little question that Mansilla was horrified and disgusted by the rape of the captives, and he repeated his admiration for the women "que se negaron a dejarse envilecer, cuyo cuerpo prefirió el martirio a entregarse de buena voluntad"[35] [who refused to let themselves be degraded, whose body preferred martyrdom to willing surrender]. The most telling episode occurs when Mansilla meets Fermina Zárate, taken captive at the age of 20 and mother of three children by the *cacique* Ramón. Ramón tells Mansilla that she has his permission to return to her family:

> Doña Fermina le miró con una expresión indefinible, con una mezcla de cariño y de horror, de un modo que sólo una mujer observadora y penetrante habría podido comprender, y contestó:—Señor Ramón es buen hombre. ¡Ojalá todos fueran como él! Menos sufrirían las cautivas. Yo, ¡para qué me he de quejar! Dios sabrá lo que ha hecho. Y esto diciendo se echó a llorar sin recatarse.[36]

> [Doña Fermina looked at him with an indecipherable expression, with a mixture of affection and horror, in a way that only an observant and perceptive woman could have understood, and answered: "Sir, Ramón is a good man. If only all men were like him! The captives would suffer less. As for me, what do I have to complain about! God will know what he has done." And saying this she began to cry openly.]

When Mansilla is alone with Zárate, she explains that indeed she can leave, but she would have to leave her children behind, which she refuses to do. Mansilla is silently repulsed. He cannot understand that she would grieve for her *mestizo* children: "no me resolvía decirle: Déjelos usted; son el fruto de la violencia"[37] [I couldn't bring myself to tell her: Leave them, they are the fruit of violence]. Zárate then explains to Mansilla her realization that Spanish society is now closed to her:

Además, señor, ¿qué vida sería la mía entre los cristianos después de tantos años que falto de mi pueblo? Yo era joven y buena moza cuando me cautivaron. Y ahora ya se ve, estoy vieja. Parezco cristiana, porque Ramón me permite vestirme como ellas, pero vivo como india; y francamente, me parece que soy más india que cristiana, aunque creo en Dios, como que todos los días le encomiendo mis hijos y mi familia.[38]

[Besides, sir, what would my life be like among the Christians after being away so long from my people? I was young and pretty when they captured me. And now, as you can see, I am old. I appear Christian, because Ramón permits me to dress like Christian women, but I live like an Indian, and frankly, it seems to me that I am more Indian than Christian, even though I believe in God, so that every day I commend to him my children and my family.]

Zárate's sad story is known to us because Mansilla reports it, but she does not write of it herself. Unlike North America, Hispanic America does not have a body of memoirs written by the captive women themselves. In part, this is due to the more widespread illiteracy on the Hispanic frontier. Many women in North America could read and write (at least to some degree) due to the Protestant mandate to read the Bible in order to secure one's own salvation. Though often primitive and sporadic, schooling did exist on the North American frontier. Hispanic women generally did not have this opportunity, especially those who lived in rural areas. There were few *cautivas* who could have written their own story even if they had wanted to. But judging from Fermina Zárate's comments, few would have wanted to submit themselves to such public examination. Therefore, the only versions of the captive experience that survive are the oral and literary tales, which were written almost exclusively by men.[39]

That the captive woman's experience is framed in a male voice is an important aspect to consider. Travel literature of all sorts, even the literature of the forced journey, is usually a very personal genre: the narrative "I" is assumed to be autobiographical, though of course autobiography is also a kind of fiction. The sights and experiences of the journey are filtered through a personal vision, and the pleasure of the text depends not on the events themselves, but on the charm of the personal filter. Narrative filters, however, also impose an ideological interpretation on the text. In the case of the captive women's stories examined here, the ideological filter is one of national destiny: the Indian must be eliminated in order to achieve the Hispanic national goals. This call for genocide is justified by portraying the Indians as savage animals who rape and kill white women. During the 1880s such genocide was in fact carried out.

The male narrative contains another message as well, this one encoded in the tragic fate of the female characters. The traditional miracle of escape does not occur for them (María, for example, dies at the end of *La cautiva*) or, if it does occur, carries a terrible price (as in *La vuelta de Martín Fierro,* when the mother is saved because her attacker slips on the blood of her slain child). By departing from the folkloric pattern, the narrators encode an ideological message to women, warning them against venturing into the desert and prohibiting relations with Indian men. (There is, of course, no such warning for Hispanic men, though Indian women also suffered slavery, rape, and death at the hands of Christian soldiers.) As Zorrilla's response to his wife indicates, the ideal of Hispanic womanhood demands the subjugation and death of the Indian, and Hispanic women are wrong to sympathize with the Indians.

The captivity stories thus serve a didactic purpose, purveying a code of social values deemed necessary for national survival. This is especially true of the works published during the actual time of war and captivity; Echeverría, for example, is said to have been inspired to write *La cautiva* (1837) by meeting a woman whose husband had been killed in an Indian raid. Yet it is also true of works such as *Tabaré* and "Marta Riquelme" (1902), written after the Indians had been virtually wiped out and the danger of captivity past. Evidently, the captive women symbolized something more than a historical reality. They became ritual victims, expelled in order to retain national/racial purity. The fact that the words studied here continue to be read as part of the established literary canon in Argentina and Uruguay is evidence of the enduring power of the image of captive woman.

The fatal journey of the captive women is the ironic inversion of the triumphant journey paradigm of the male travelers to Latin America. The *conquistadores* also encounter hostile Indians and an unwelcoming natural environment, but they successfully do battle with their enemies. Their journey also had religious meaning, because they both conquer and convert in the name of God and Christianity. Though faced with suffering, defeats, and loss of companions, the Spanish eventually triumph over the obstacles, a success attributed to God's special favor and mercy. The chronicles of the conquest are ultimately a genre of optimism, as are the captivity ballads and saints' stories, because they end with salvation. The woman's journey into captivity, however, is shaped by the gender of the captive. Unarmed and unschooled in combat, she is unable to overcome her enemies or her environment. She is vulnerable to rape and forced marriage, both victim of and justification for a war of genocide. The forced journey of the deceptive woman in Latin America is structured around a clash of opposing cultures, played out in terms of sexual violation. By crossing into alien cultural and sexual territory — however unwillingly — the woman is denied the journey home.

Notes

1. George Camamis, *Estudios sobre el cautiverio en el Siglo de Oro* (Madrid: Gredos, 1977). An interesting study of documents relating to actual captivities is by Juan Martínez Ruíz, "Cautivos precervantinos, cara y cruz del cautiverio," *Revista de Filología Española* 50 (1967): 203-56.
2. C. Colin Smith, ed., *Spanish Ballads* (Oxford: Pergamon, 1964), 1-42; and David William Foster, *The Early Spanish Ballad* (New York: Twayne, c. 1971).
3. Fernando José Wolf and Conrado Hofmann, eds., "131: Romance que dice: Mi padre era de Ronda," in *Primavera y flor de romances* (Berlin: Asher, 1856), reprinted in Marcelino Menéndez y Pelayo, ed., *Antología de poetas líricos castellanos* vol. 8, 9 (Madrid: Perlado, Páez y ca., 1914) 8: 245-46.
4. All English translations are mine, except for the passages from *La vuelta de Martín Fierro* which are by C. E. Ward.
5. Agustín Durán, ed., *Romancero general* (Madrid: Biblioteca de Autores Españoles, 1926) 16: 295.
6. Luis Santullo, ed., *Romancero español* (Madrid: Aquilar, 1968), 813.
7. Ismael Moya, ed., *Romancero* (Buenos Aires: Imprenta de la Universidad, 1941).
8. David Haberly, "Captives and Infidels: The Figure of the *Cautiva* in Argentine Literature," *The America Hispanist* 4 (October 1978): 11-12.
9. Ruy Díaz de Guzmán, *La Argentina* (Buenos Aires: Espasa-Calpe, 1945), 61.
10. Myron Lichtblau, "El tema de Lucía Miranda en la novel argentina," *Armas y Letras* 2, 1 (1959): 23-31.
11. Juan Zorrilla de San Martín, *Tabaré* (Buenos Aires: Estrada, 1944), 132.
12. José Hernández, *El gaucho Martín Fierro*, trans. C. E. Ward (Albany: State University of New York Press, 1967), 260. This edition includes both *El gaucho Martín Fierro* and its sequel *La vuelta de Martín Fierro*.
13. Esteban Echeverría, *La cautiva. El matadero* (Buenos Aires: Kapelusz, 1965), 24-5.

14. *Ibid.*, 9.
15. Haberly, "Captives and Infidels," 11. Also see Dorothy McMahon, "The Indian in Romantic Literature of the Argentine," *Modern Philology* 56, 1 (August 1958): 17-23.
16. Zorilla, *Tabaré*, 90.
17. William Henry Hudson, "Marta Riquelme," in *El Ombú* (New York: AMS Press, 1968), 150.
18. Joyce E. Williams and Karen A. Holmes, *The Second Assault: Rape and Public Attitudes* (Westport, Conn.: Greenwood Press, 1981), 125-30. The chilling phrase "the good rape" is used in courthouse slang in the U. S., according to Williams and Holmes. They report that they have heard prosecuters "state publicly that they cannot take rape cases because they are not 'good cases' (meaning that the victim's behavior and/or reputation are not above reproach) and juries will not convict" (18). The components of a "good rape" are: "the assailant was a stranger; the victim's activity/behavior was not in question; a weapon was involved; [and] the victim was injured" (128).
19. Echeverría, *La cautiva*, 25.
20. Hudson, "Marta Riquelme," 158.
21. Zorrilla, *Tabaré*, 20.
22. Susan Brownmiller, *Against Our Will: Men, Women, and Rape* (New York: Simon and Schuster, 1975), 38.
23. Octavio Paz, *The Labyrinth of Solitude,* trans. Lysander Kemp (New York: Grove Press, 1961), 85-7.
24. Echeverría, *La cautiva*, 23.
25. Elizabeth G. Gitter, "The Power of Women's Hair in the Victorian Imagination," *PMLA* 99 (October 1984): 936-54.
26. Hudson, "Marta Riquelme," 156.
27. *Ibid.*, 159.
28. *Ibid.*, 165-66.
29. Zorrilla, *Tabaré*, 90.
30. *Ibid.*, 205
31. *Ibid.*, 184
32. *Ibid.*, 193.
33. *Ibid.*, 34.
34. Lucio Mansilla, *Una excursión a los indios ranqueles* (Mexico City: Fondo de Cultura Económica, 1947), 392-93.
35. *Ibid.*, 228-29.
36. *Ibid.*, 369.
37. *Ibid.*, 370.
38. *Ibid.*
39. Three Argentine women – Rosa Guerra, Eduarda Mansilla de García, and Celestina Funes – wrote about the Lucía Miranda legend during the 1800s, though their works have not been conserved in the literary canon. Their versions will be included in my longer study, *The Needle and the Pen: Women Writers of the Argentine Generation of 1880*, in preparation.

Journey to the Golden Mountain: Chinese Immigrant Women[1]

Annette White-Parks

WHEN JONE HO LEONG'S uncle returned to China in 1940 and complained about how hard he had been made to work in the United States, his niece replied: "OK—you can come back here to stay and send us—the women—over there. We'll see how we can make out in the Golden Mountain."[2] Though her words were spoken almost a century after the California gold rush prompted the first Chinese migrations to North America, Jone Ho Leong spoke for many women who were part of those journeys.

Women from China were as eager to travel to the American West as were immigrants—both male and female—from other parts of the globe. Many 19th-century women managed to do it, under varying circumstances: independently, making their own ways; as wives, in response to Chinese husbands who had migrated first and were partly established; and as captive slaves or prostitutes. The first Chinese women immigrants traveled to North America during the same period as the first Chinese immigrant men, namely in the 1840s and 1850s. However different the travels of Chinese women and men were, though, a common thread unites those of the women: female immigrants faced formidable odds that continually worked to deny them the journey, odds that they, alone or in concert, attempted to defy. This essay will focus on selected examples from both history and literature to demonstrate how Chinese women travelers persisted in maintaining their personal and cultural autonomy, whatever the hardships. The stories of the Anglo-Chinese writer Sui Sin Far/Edith Maude Eaton (1865-1914), the first known author to deal with the perspectives of Chinese immigrant women to North America in fiction, will be viewed, in particular.

Chinese tradition may have dictated that no "decent" woman might travel,[3] yet Judy Yung clearly shows Chinese immigrant women on the Western frontier as early as Chinese men. The first recorded of these, Marie Seise, stepped off a ship named *The Eagle* in San Francisco in 1848 as the servant of a family of traders, the Gillespies of New York. Lest her journey sound trivial, it is worth emphasizing the route Marie traversed before meeting the Gillespies: she ran away from her parents in China to avoid being sold, worked as a servant in Macao, married a Portuguese sailor, and moved as a servant with another family to the Sandwich Islands after the sailor deserted her.[4] Marie was obviously determined, at whatever expense, to chart her own course. Nor was she alone. Another "China Mary"—a generic name, Yung explains, ascribed to many Chinese immigrant women by their new frontier neighbors[5]—ran away from her home in China when she was nine, made her way to Canada by age thirteen, outlived three husbands, and then moved to Sitka, Alaska, where she survived as a fisherwoman, hunter and prospector, restaurant keeper, nurse, laundress, and official matron of the Sitka federal jail. Yet another, Ah Yuen, similarly outlived three husbands and was said to have been "the toast of her countrymen"[6] in the Wyoming mining and railroad camps where she cooked during Pony Express days. Another woman to reckon with, Mary Tape, sailed from Shanghai with missionaries at age 11, then survived independently in California, working as an interpreter and contractor of labor, teaching herself photography and telegraphy. When the San Francisco Board of Education tried to bar Tape's daughter from public schools, Tape took the case to court and won.[7]

To appreciate the odds these independent women faced, we need to look at the positions traditionally assigned to Chinese women in both China and the United States in the mid-19th century. Amy Ling notes that Confucius classified women "with slaves and small humans," and further cites that "a code governing the behavior and training of women, called the Three Obediences and Four Virtues, was promulgated by imperial decree throughout China and remained continuously effective...until the early twentieth century."[8] Basically, this code decreed that a woman must "obey her father before marriage, her husband after marriage, and her oldest son after her husband's death"—all roles of subordination sanctioned by conventions so ancient that to defy them was to challenge the sacred.

When the injunction is added that no "decent" woman of the Chinese upper or middle class could travel even to a shop in the village without escort and covered face, it becomes obvious that a decision to cross the Pacific would have taken some courage. Yet the protection the woman in traditional China gained in return for her obedience was often analogous to the "protection" Sojourner Truth expressed for the African-American woman. In the words of the narrator to Maxine Hong Kingston's *Woman Warrior,* "girls are maggots in the rice"– if the need arose, they could be sold. Such a transaction forced many Chinese females into journeys of which the old doctrine took no account.[9]

Added to her continued subordination by gender in the North American culture, the Chinese immigrant woman also faced, on the western side of the waters, hostile immigration laws and dehumanizing stereotypes imposed by the Westerners on all Chinese. The writer Sui Sin Far, meeting an editor who did not know her mother was of Chinese descent, was told, "I cannot reconcile myself to the fact that the Chinese are humans like ourselves; their faces seem so utterly void of expression that I cannot help but doubt."[10] The life of Marie Seise highlights the incongruity between this stereotype and the all-too-human reality of women's actual lives. So does the attitude Sui Sin Far confronted when she was advised that "to succeed in literature in America I should dress in Chinese costume, carry a fan in my hand, wear a pair of scarlet beaded slippers, live in New York, and come of high birth."[11] The posed China doll Sui Sin Far was invited to emulate reflected a popular conception of both the Chinese noblewoman and the successful courtesan, and hearkened back to the days when entrepreneurs and exhibitors brought Chinese women to the United States. Like a doll, a woman named Pwan Yekoo was displayed at Barnum's Chinese Museum in 1850, eating with chopsticks, playing Chinese musical instruments, and twinkling her tiny "fairy feet (only two and a half inches long)."[12] But as historian Lucie Cheng Hirata shows, in reality most Chinese immigrant women in the 19th century were working class wage earners and wives. Besides cooking, cleaning, and making clothing and shoes for her own family, the immigrant woman – in common with most other pioneer females of America's West – usually also sewed, cooked, and cleaned for others, did laundry and gardened.[13] Quock Jung Mey's mother sailed to Monterey, California, where she gave birth to her daughter in 1859 and worked throughout her life baiting fishing hooks, processing each day's catch, and gathering seaweed.[14] The doll-like stereotype, then, served to establish distance between white Americans and their new countrywomen, substituting a fantasy of the "exotic Oriental" for knowledge based on contact with flesh and blood Chinese Americans on a daily basis. Ultimately, the racist assumptions about the Chinese as "other" that underlie this stereotype would lead to contentions that the Chinese were unassimilable aliens and help to justify discriminatory legislation.

If the fantasy in fan and beaded slippers had any relevance to actual Chinese immigrant women, it was to the wives of Chinatown merchants who, Hirata points out, customarily enjoyed more luxurious accommodations (if often less freedom) than their working class sisters.[15] Not unlike other Victorian middle class women, the well-to-do Chinese merchant's wife often lived in a comfortably furnished apartment, occupied her days with bits of cooking and needlework, and broke the routine with afternoon teas and chats with her friends when, as Sui Sin Far put it in an 1897 article, "there is such a clattering of tongues one would almost think they were American women."[16] Such lifestyles were rare, however, applying in the late 19th century to no more than one percent of Chinese American women.[17]

In the first years of the gold rush many immigrant Chinese women were brought to North America to serve as slaves and prostitutes for men of every racial descent, on a Western frontier where few women of any race existed and where Chinese male immigrants, forbidden by miscegenation laws to marry or mix sexually with white women, experienced increased sexual pressure. In 1882 the United States government enacted the Chinese Exclusion Act, which prevented all Chinese women, except the wives (or wives to be) of Chinese American merchants, from entering as legal migrants. The value of the wife of a merchant thus stood very high, by a measure that parallels in some ways, yet differs profoundly, from the value of women prostitutes during the earlier years.[18] Merchants' wives were brought to North America to begin raising families, implicitly making possible the establishment of permanent communities in the new world—a "threat" to the European-based cultures of Canada and the United States that later exclusionary legislation in both countries would attempt to eliminate.[19]

One similarity between prostitutes and merchants' wives as travelers, however, is that the woman seldom made the decision to migrate herself. The Chinatown wife, too, was often shipped across the Pacific in response to male needs. Moreover, as depicted in the fiction of Sui Sin Far, these wives had their own difficulties. In Sui Sin Far's story "The Americanization of Pau Tsu" (1912), for example, the Chinese woman Pau Tsu is betrothed to Lin Fo before he leaves China, then waits at the home of his parents to be sent to him "in a few years' time."[20] When Pau Tsu arrives in San Francisco and Lin Fo takes his bride to the Chinatown apartments that he has "furnished in American style," Pau Tsu declares her own preference by bringing out the furnishings she has carried over the Pacific, transforming "the American flat into an Oriental bower." Thus begins a conflict that rages throughout the story, as Lin Fo tells Pau Tsu to eat with a fork and she mourns for her chopsticks, as he buys her elegant western style dresses that she refuses to wear. The climax comes when Pau Tsu gets sick and her husband sends for a male Anglo-American doctor, before whom Pau Tsu's breast is exposed and "the modesty of generations of maternal ancestors was crucified." Determined to maintain her cultural identity, Pau Tsu flees from Lin Fo, moving with her maid A-Toy into the home of "a woman learned in herb lore."

The shock of transition between cultures is a constant issue in Sui Sin Far's stories of Chinese immigrant brides. From the moment that Pau Lin, heroine of "The Wisdom of the New" (1912), arrives in a steamer at the San Francisco docks and meets Wou Sankwei, the husband she wed in China seven years before, the distance between the Americanized husband and the wife who stayed behind to care for his aging parents and raise their child yawns wider than geography. Not only does Sankwei have to ask the ship's officer to point out his wife and son before he can recognize her "as his," but he also arrives with two white women, for whom Pau Lin felt "a suspicion natural to one who had come from a land where friendship between a man and woman is almost unknown."[21] These women are customers and informal patrons of Sankwei, who has become a successful Chinatown bookkeeper, but as one of the women sketches the couple's six-year-old son Yen—though Pau Lin decorously "keeps a quiet tongue in the presence of her man"—her resentment simmers inwardly like a bed of banked coals. As her husband increasingly takes their son out, leaving Pau Lin to her housekeeping, the bewildered and lonely new immigrant spends "most of her time in the society of one or the other of the neighboring merchants' wives."

One source of courage for women who travel, especially under pioneering conditions, has always been other women; in this, the Chinese immigrant woman of any class was no exception. On the night that little Yen comes home speaking English, Pau Lin burns the boy's hand in reprisal and, after Sankwei retaliates by taking Yen out to supper and a show, Pau Lin's frustration is eased by the circle of women that Sui Sin Far gathers around her. "You did perfectly right. . . . Had I again a son to rear, I should see to it that he followed not after the white people," old Sien Lau leans over her balcony to say to Pau Lin. "One needs not be born here to be made a fool of," Pau Tsu adds in the voice of experience. "In this country, she is most happy who has no child," Lae Choo interjects, resting her elbow upon the shoulder of Sien Lau.

Other heroines in Sui Sin Far stories demonstrate that the external reticence of these merchants' wives, who undertook their journeys at the decree of their husbands, should never be mistaken for passivity. Beneath their acquiescence to duty a cautiously held rebellion finds its own outlets, rising to its most intense when their children and Chinese cultural identities are threatened. The climax in "The Wisdom of the New" is foreshadowed on the night Sankwei tells Pau Lin that in the morning Yen will begin attending an American school. At early dawn the father hears a strange noise, goes into Yen's room, and finds him dead, poisoned by his mother. If it seems a monstrous act, we must pause and consider Pau Lin's expressed motive: " 'He is saved,' smiled she, 'from the Wisdom of the New.' " We have seen the mother's love and despair the night she lifts the sleeping Yen from his bed and rocks him, "crooning and crying." In the aftermath of a second baby's death, she again holds her first son and vows: "Sooner would I, O heart of my heart, that the light of thine eyes were also quenched, than that thou shouldst be contaminated with the wisdom of the new." And on the eve of Yen's death, she tells the boy that his feet are to his "spirit as the cocoon to the butterfly." Like the black mother in Toni Morrison's *Beloved* who kills her infant daughter to save her from slavery, Pau Lin sacrifices her child's body to save his soul—in her definition, the Chinese heritage that her husband's enthusiasm for western culture threatens to eradicate.

Rarely is a married woman depicted by Sui Sin Far who is not cradling a baby or child as she exercises passionate vigilance against forces ever poised to take that treasure from her. The importance of children, suggests Gail Nomura, is that in a situation where all other family has been left behind, a baby is a treasure, a start of the new.[22] Inversely, through the generational lifelines they offer, children are also a link with the past and home culture. In fact, one major reason a man traditionally married before leaving China was in the hope that his wife would bear him a son and thus assure his enduring position in the land he was leaving. Either way the child represents more than itself: it represents cultural continuity.

Sui Sin Far's story "In the Land of the Free" shows the damage that child theft can inflict: not just loss of the child, but, more far-reaching, loss of the child's culture.[23] This story opens with Lae Choo completing her voyage from China back to San Francisco, where her home was already established with her husband, Hom Hing, before Lae Choo sailed back to China to give birth and take care of Hom Hing's aging parents. The ship pulls into the dock where the father is waiting, and Lae Choo presents their son to Hom Hing, who lifts him up joyously. At this moment a customs officer steps in between, asking for the child's papers. When papers cannot be produced, The Little One is physically confiscated. The couple spends 10 months of their life, all of Hom Hing's money, and Lae Choo's family jewels getting him back. Furthermore, when Lae Choo walks into the mission nursery to pick up her baby she finds not The Little One she remembers, but a boy dressed "in blue cotton overalls and white soled shoes," who — when his mother reaches for him — hides "in the folds of the white woman's skirt." A close look at the story's details shows that Lae Choo sensed this danger from the beginning and did everything in her power to prevent it from happening. When the officer first reaches out for her child on the docks, Hom Hing is holding him. " 'No, you not take him; he my son, too,' " Lae Choo cries in heroic defiance, grabbing her child back. It is Hom Hing who is persuaded that: " 'Tis the law,' " convincing his wife to hand him the baby who he, in turn, "delivered. . .to the first officer." Why does Lae Choo "yield" the boy? Because, the story's narrator reveals, she is "accustomed to obedience." That she is not docile, however, Lae Choo has already proved by defying the officer. " 'You, too,' " she says to her husband accusingly, as the couple walk to their apartment above Hom Hing's Chinatown grocery, minus their child.

In Sui Sin Far's stories, the environments in which women travel are dangerous, fraught with restrictive conventions from one culture and hostile laws in the other. Taking a decisive course of action is often not easy for these women, but take action they do, even in the direst of circumstances. Fin Fan, of "The Prize China Baby," experiences the dual position of being both a slave and the wife of the Chinatown merchant, Chung Kee, to whom she is sold. She has a daughter who is her "one gleam of sunshine."[24] Mindful of the fact that Chung Kee does not want the baby because it takes too much of Fin Fan's time from winding tobacco leaves in his factory, Fin Fan gets up very early and goes to bed very late, trying to make as much money as she did before having the baby so Chung Kee will not get rid of it. Hearing of a "Chinese baby show" being staged by Presbyterians, Fin Fan rolls her baby into her shawl and slips out, hoping that if the child wins a prize, its father will value it. While they are out, the father makes arrangements to sell the baby—it may be significant that she is a girl. In one of Sui Sin Far's multi-layered ironies, Fin Fan thwarts his plans when she and her daughter are run down by a butcher's cart on the way home and "her head fell back beside the prize baby's—hers forever." Fin Fan does keep her baby, though not in the way she or Sui Sin Far's reading audience might have intended.

Death obviously is not defeat in either of the stories cited above, but a stand that, in the minds of the individuals taking it, seems less horrific than alternatives when they are pressed to the wall. Sometimes rewards come in the future, bringing resolution from pain. Within context, Pau Lin's act is successful for, with the death of his son, Sankwei finally comprehends his wife's desperation and returns with her to China, symbolically healing the split in their family and restoring cultural continuity. In similar spirit does Lin Fo of "The Americanization of Pau Tsu" locate his wife Pau Tsu, vowing, "I will not care if she never speaks an American word, and I will take her for a trip to China, so that our son may be born in the country that Heaven loves." Both women thus successfully resist the journey into assimilation by white North America, choosing instead to make a turn back to their cultural roots.

The journey of the enslaved prostitute was the most difficult circumstance for the Chinese woman traveler to overcome, partly because the patriarchal traditions in both Europe and China blamed a woman for her own victimization and judged her responsible for a situation over which she often had no control. Two incompatible images coalesce in the stereotype of the prostitute: in the one, she wears the scarlet beaded slippers and carries the fan we have seen in the portrait with which Sui Sin Far was presented; in the other, she is pressed against the bars of a small cage labeled "crib," face emptied of hope.[25] The reality of her story is often that she was torn from home soil and enslaved, to lead a fragmentary and short-lived existence helping her captors get rich.

An alternate perspective is suggested by Lucie Cheng Hirata, who regards the first five years of the California gold rush, 1849-1854, as a period of "free competition"[26] during which Chinese women, in common with prostitutes from other countries, saw the Golden Mountain as opportunity and migrated under individual initiative. The legendary Ah-Choi, also known as A-Toy, came to San Francisco and rose to be belle of the city; she earned enough in two years to open her own brothel, which attracted lines of men a block long who, it was claimed, would pay a full ounce of gold simply to look on her face.[27] Another woman, Lai Chow, started her career as one among two dozen 12 year olds, all shipped from China in crates labeled "dishware"; Lai Chow grew up to smuggle in her own "girls."[28] Hirata cites a bestselling novel in China that interpreted the capitalistic aims of such travelers through the character of a Cantonese prostitute who, after seven years in California where she had gone with her "American paramour," returned to Hong Kong with $16,300, "married a Chinese laborer," and opened an import store.[29] Similarly, in her short story "Lin John," Sui Sin Far portrays a Chinese prostitute who is happy with her lot and resists her brother's efforts to "rescue" her because she prefers the material rewards of her work to his goals of returning her to China for "respectability in marriage."[30] However, the era of free competition was short-lived for, by the mid-1850s, entrepreneurs represented by both white America and the six companies of Chinatown had caught the rich scent of money and taken over, giving rise to a slave trade intricately organized across the Pacific.[31]

Writer John Gardner once suggested that there are only two plots in literature: a person takes a journey, or a stranger comes to town.[32] For the Chinese woman who came up against the horrors of slavery, these two plots were allied—in her case, it was the "stranger" who initiated the journey. In the negotiations that prepared for her trip, a young Chinese female could move from "decent" woman to prostitute in the time it took a procurer to strike a bargain, usually with the girl's parents. A number of stories are told about such metamorphoses. Sometimes the capture came via coercion, as in the case of Lalu Nathoy

who had been her father's "treasure"– his "thousand pieces of gold"[33]–
until the moment when a bandit threatened the father, threw two bags
of soybean seed at his feet as payment, and rode off with the captive
Lalu. Sometimes it was managed with sweet talk, as when the mother
of Wong Ah So was promised that the $450 she was paid for her daugh-
ter would continue to draw dividends through the rich months ahead,
from the earnings Wong Ah So would be sending back "as an entertainer at Chinese banquets."[34] Such ruses became even more devious
when the bargainer was a returned immigrant from the family's own
village, someone whom they well knew and trusted. Victorian
melodrama has nothing on the pathos of some of these actual cases.
There was Ah Yee, "a refined, sensitive little creature" of dead father
and poor mother whom the "dashing young adventurer" Jeah Sing Fong
married, telling her that her troubles were over. He escorted his new
bride to the Golden Gate Hotel on a honeymoon, then turned her over
to King Fah, the female brothel keeper who paid the nuptial pair a welcome home visit and procured Ah Yee as a prostitute.[35]

These stories make it clear that the stereotype categorizing all
enslaved females as coming from the lowest socio-economic classes
in China was simply not true. Jean Ying, for example, was the kidnapped
"daughter of a well-to-do Canton manufacturer."[36] Nor is it accurate to
generalize them as "women." Recalling Lai Chow, who at age 12 was
packed in a dish crate along with other stolen girls, we recognize that
many were barely adolescents. An even more extreme case is the baby
girl brought to the United States by a "grandmother" who had purchased
the baby for $10 in China and planned to raise her as an investment
in future merchandise.[37] For merchandise, in actuality, is what the enslaved female became during the course of her journey.

A method that superficially sounds more legitimate was the "contract," similar to indentured servitude except that the women whose
lives were, quite literally, being laid on the line could neither read nor
write. They "signed" not with a name but with a thumbprint affixed
at the bottom of the document after the deal had been settled.[38] Simple purchase was frequent. Hirata tells of an old woman servant in
California who had been resold four times, the first at age seven when
her way of fighting against banishment from home and family was to
cry and hide under the bed.[39] If all else failed, there was kidnapping;
for instance, the woman who was invited by a man to tour a steamer

anchored at the dock in Shanghai, then found herself sailing across the Pacific in the bottom of the coal bucket into which he pushed her.[40]

The usual attitude in the United States was to fault the Chinese exclusively for this trade in female slavery. But one would have to seek far to find a more mutually cooperative Chinese-American venture in the 19th century than the enslavement of these Chinese women. Historian Dorothy Gray describes the dual responsibility:

> The system had its roots in the culture of the homeland China where prostitution and slavery were open practices. But in America the slave system of prostitution contravened the most essential aspect of law and was possible only through the continued connivance of American officials who amassed fortunes in graft.[41]

This point again illustrates how the immigrating woman was often caught between the repressive aspects of her traditional culture and the unbridled exploitation of the new capitalism.

A normal passage from China to North America's West Coast took one to two months,[42] but the clandestine traveler might find herself diverted through Mexico or Canada. Lai Chow, of Nell Kimball's autobiography, tells of bringing her cargo in through Canadian ports, then on to San Francisco by coach. Sometimes the entry was managed in the same manner used by George Sand to gain access to Paris streets late at night—through disguise as a man. Sui Sin Far's "Smuggling of Wah To," though not a slave incident, narrates the attempted migration of a young Chinese "male" who jumps into the river to avoid police while crossing the Canadian border. The body, when retrieved, turns out to be female.[43] On the American side of the border the enslaved woman's immediate destination was customarily San Francisco, where she was held in a kind of underground warehouse termed a "barracoon."[44] There—unless a purchase had been made in advance—she was put up for bid. Her purchaser might be, as in the case of the fictional Fin Fan in Sui Sin Far's "A Prize China Baby," a Chinatown merchant seeking a slave wife. It might be the owner of a local brothel (distinguished by Yung as either "high class" or "inferior den"). It might be, as in the case of Lalu Nathoy (who became Polly Bemis), a saloon-keeper from an Idaho mining camp, a transaction causing her journey to swerve from urban to rural. Although Lalu/Polly personally led a long life, Yung notes that "prostitutes could meet with no worse fate than to be banished to the mining camps, where they led lives as harsh as they were short."

Altogether, evidence indicates that the enslavement of Chinese immigrant women was the most widely known secret in the American West in the mid-19th century. In the same era that Lincoln signed the Emancipation Proclamation to free black slaves in the Confederacy, Gray estimates that several thousand Chinese females a year were being smuggled through San Francisco's immigrant station to be sold into slavery. Public knowledge of the slave trade was such that, in 1869, the *San Francisco Chronicle* could report the arrival of a ship from China in this manner:

> The particular fine portions of the cargo, the fresh and pretty females who come from the interior are used to fill special orders from wealthy merchants and prosperous tradesmen. A very considerable portion are sent into the interior. . . in answer to demands from well-to-do miners and successful vegetable producers.[45]

Well into the 20th century, newspapers sported headlines such as "Woman Tells of Traffic in Slave Girls," and novels with titles like *Chop Suey Lady* enjoyed popular sales.[46] Epithets of "frail, childlike creatures" with "exotic dress and features" reduced human individuals to romantic figments who could be slipped by not only customs officials, but also the democratic ideals of the United States nation.[47]

Responses of these Chinese female travelers to their predicaments were as varied as their constrained circumstances permitted. When learning that her role as a San Francisco "entertainer" was a euphemism for prostitution, Wong Ah So turned inward, resigning herself to accept her condition with dutiful recitations of "stories of Chinese children renowned for their piety," promising her mother to "return to China and become a Buddhist nun" when she had earned enough money.[48] One Idaho China Annie (a generic name like China Mary) chose a more aggressive method, running off with her lover to Boise where they were married and won out over Annie's former owner in court after he sued her for "stealing herself."[49] Others who broke for freedom took a real risk by going to law enforcement officials, for—from the "Chinatown Specials" to San Francisco's city hall—many were on the Tong's payroll.[50]

Protestant mission houses, opening on the edges of Chinatowns during the Progressive Era, offered another option for these women. Launching what was as close to an anti-slavery reform movement as the West would experience, the Christian missions had a historical connection with China. Frank Chin refers to the "almost fifty years of travel books on China written by Chinese missionaries and 'world travelers' who cited missionaries as authorities on China."[51] Missionaries coming from China frequently brought converts back, and those in American Chinatowns, as noted by Yung, "proved to be a vital link" in joining homebound immigrant wives, such as the fictional Pau Lin and Pau Tsu, to a world outside their small flats.[52]

Margaret Culberston, director of the Presbyterian Chinese Mission later to achieve fame as San Francisco's Cameron House, issued a challenge in regard to prostituted immigrant women: "Cannot anyone suggest a plan to remedy this evil?"[53] Writers of purple prose, both in fiction and daily newspapers, were fond of scenes in which runaway women slaves fell at the feet of white policemen, begging for help. The lawmen, if they did not hand the women back to the "highbinders" (the term for men sent to retrieve runaway prostitutes), usually passed them along to the Presbyterian mission. This was especially true after the arrival of Donaldina Cameron, who set about to free enslaved Chinatown women with a fervor causing Gray to term her "the most active and daring freedom fighter in the history of the West."[54] Known by the Tongs as "the White Devil," Donaldina staged constant raids, using methods that created episodes in the journeys of Chinese immigrant women that resemble the pages of Gothic fiction:

> If a word that the White Devil was coming preceded the raid, the slaver would try to smuggle the girl away through the dark, narrow alleys of Chinatown. Sometimes girls were hurried away over the rooftops. But Donaldina was quick in pursuit and in time developed an instinct for where the quarry might emerge and stationed a policeman or assistants from the refuge to watch the possible exit.[55]

Though Donaldina is generally credited with being something of a redeemer, the women she "rescued" did not necessarily see her this way. Wong Ah So, for example, had been told by her owner that Donaldina "was in the habit of draining blood from the arteries of newly 'captured' girls and drinking it to keep up her own vitality."[56] Yet because she was "tired" and "sick," the young woman broke through her fears and went to the mission where she subsequently "reformed" and married with the missionaries' blessing. Thus she followed the pattern Peggy Pascoe describes, exchanging "prostitution for marriage,"[57] a choice that often replaced one form of servitude for another. The price of such "rescue work" is frequently dramatized by Sui Sin Far through mission woman characters who continually attempt to lure Chinese children away from their home culture, a fiction grounded in historical records through which Pascoe shows how Christian missionaries brought female children they termed "neglected or abused" into their homes, raising them and gaining control over the next generation by arranging their marriages to Chinese immigrant men who were converted Christians. A twist on this motif appears in the short story "Pat and Pan," in which the mission woman Anna Harrison arranges for a little white boy to be taken away from the Chinese American family with whom the boy's dying mother has left him to be raised, and placed with a White American family.[58]

It is interesting to contrast the fate of the city voyager Wong Ah So with that of the rural Lalu Nathoy. Stolen from her father in exchange for two bags of soybean seed and bought in San Francisco by an Idaho saloon keeper, Lalu was later won in a poker game by Charlie Bemis, who gave her freedom. She went on to marry Charlie, eventually to bury him, and finally to inherit the mining claim they had worked together. Thus Lalu Nathoy became Polly Bemis, probably the first Chinese immigrant woman actually to own her personal patch of the Golden Mountain. Should her journey be viewed within the pattern of slave prostitution? Of marriage? Of legendary Wild West success?

As this example shows, categories for Chinese immigrant women cannot be rigidly prescribed. Among the many such women who defied stereotypes we would have to go far to find one more determined to write her own journey than Sui Sin Far herself, whose mother made her way to North America via missionary training in England and marriage to an English trader in Shanghai. Sui Sin Far fought for personal survival against racism, invalidism, sexism, and poverty while growing up in England, New York, and Montréal as one of 14 siblings. She also battled for her parents, brothers, and sisters against the severe prejudices they encountered wherever they roamed. As an adult she continued the struggle: from Montréal to the West Indies, from Seattle to Boston, up and down the Pacific Coast, working as a stenographer and reporter, writing copy for the railroads to pay for her travels, living wherever she could earn her way to continue writing the stories about Chinese immigrants to North America to which she had committed her brief life to telling. Arriving in San Francisco "so reduced by another attack of rheumatic fever that I only weigh eighty four pounds," Sui Sin Far typed correspondence for a railway agency at five dollars a month, yet remained "hopeful that the sale of a story or newspaper article may add to my income."[59] Viewed with caution by her mother's people because she looked European and could not speak the "mother tongue," scorned by her father's when they learned she was one of "the 'brown people' of the earth," she continued to defend her right simply to *be* in either arena. And somehow she survived and kept writing, enriching those of us who want to learn about Chinese immigrant women nearly a century later with accounts of journeys we might otherwise never experience.

This brief survey of the travels of real and fictional 19th-century Chinese immigrant women shows these women's determination to maintain personal and cultural autonomy, whatever the odds. I do not attempt to claim that Chinese immigrant women did not suffer oppression, or that they were always able to overcome it. It is obvious, first, that they came up against as many difficulties as did other pioneer women and, second, that these difficulties were multiplied because they were of Chinese descent in a racist society during an era of extreme xenophobia. Nevertheless, the above examples clearly demonstrate that the stamina and ingenuity of these Chinese women travelers were vital ingredients in the creation of an emerging Chinese American — and, indeed, American — culture. Thus, when Jone Ho Leong offered to "see how we [women] make out in the Golden Mountain" in 1940, we must view her anticipated journey not as a first or rare undertaking but in the context of the century of Chinese women immigrants to North America who had dared it before.[60]

Notes

1. I would like to thank the members of the Women in Literature Research Collective at Washington State University who have provided hours of support and editing help on this manuscript.
2. Jone Ho Leong, *Bitter Melon: Stories from the Last Rural Chinese Town in America,* ed. Jeff Gillenkirk and James Motlow (Seattle: University of Washington Press, 1987), 101.
3. Lucie Cheng Hirata, "Free, Indentured, Enslaved: Chinese Prostitutes in Nineteenth-Century America," *Signs* 5:1 (1979): 6-19.
4. Judy Yung, *Chinese Women in America* (Seattle: University of Washington Press, 1986), 14.
5. *Ibid.*, 25.
6. *Ibid.*
7. *Ibid.*, 30.

8. Amy Ling, *Between Worlds: Women Writers of Chinese Ancestry* (New York: Pergamon Press, 1990), 3. Ling further writes that "The authorship of this oppressive code has been attributed to Ban Tso (A. D. 43?-A. D. 115?), a highly educated woman."

9. Maxine Hong Kingston, *The Woman Warrior: Memoirs of a Girlhood Among Ghosts* (New York: Alfred A. Knopf, 1977); and Amy Ling, *Between Worlds* both explore the low status assigned to daughters relative to sons in traditional China.

10. Sui Sin Far, "Leaves from the Mental Portfolio of an Eurasian," *Independent* 66: 3138 (21 January 1909): 129.

11. Sui Sin Far, "Leaves," 131.

12. *Ibid.*

13. Hirata, "Chinese Immigrant Women in Nineteenth-Century California," *Women of America: A History*, ed. Carol Ruth Berkin and Mary Beth Norton (Boston: Houghton Mifflin, 1979), 222-244.

14. Yung, *Chinese Women in America*, 15.

15. Hirata, "Chinese Immigrant Women," 238.

16. "Chinese Women in America," *The Land of Sunshine* 6:2 (January 1897): 62.

17. Hirata, "Chinese Immigrant Women," 224-227.

18. In "Free, Indentured, Enslaved," Hirata thoroughly examines this subject.

19. The first major anti-Chinese legislation in the U. S. was the Exclusion Act of 1882, which excluded all Chinese women, except wives of merchants, from legally entering the U. S. Discriminatory legislation in Canada took the form of singling out Chinese immigrants to pay "head taxes"; these began in 1896 at $10 and were increased regularly until by 1904 they had reached their peak of $500.

20. "The Americanization of Pau Tsu," *Mrs. Spring Fragrance* (Chicago: A. C. McClurg & Co., 1912), 144-161.

21. "The Wisdom of the New," in *Mrs. Spring Fragrance*, 47-84.

22. Interview by the author, Washington State University, Pullman, Wash., February 1987.

23. "In the Land of the Free," *Independent* 67:3170 (2 September, 1909): 504-508.

24. "Prize China Baby," in *Mrs. Spring Fragrance*, 214-219.

25. Yung describes the crib as a "small cubicle." No larger than a small closet, the crib had bars on the windows, from behind which prostitutes "hawked their trade to passersby" (23).

26. This category is from Hirata, "Free, Indentured, Enslaved," which details in-depth experiences of prostitutes, both free and enslaved.

27. Yung, *Chinese Women in America*, 14.

28. Dorothy Gray, *Women of the West* (Millbrae, Cal.: Les Femmes, 1976), 68-69. See also Nell Kimball's autobiography, *The Life of an American Madam* (New York: Macmillan, 1970).

29. Hirata, "Chinese Immigrant Women," 4.

30. *Land of Sunshine* 10:2 (January 1899): 225-228.

31. Hirata, "Free, Indentured, Enslaved," 8. The precise date set by Hirata for the end of "Free Competition" is 1853, at which time her designated "Period of Organized Trade" began, lasting until 1925.
32. Mary Morris, "Hers," *New York Times*, 30 April 1987, p. 18.
33. The complete story of Lalu Nathoy, later known as Polly Bemis, is told by Ruthanne Lum McCunn in *A Thousand Pieces of Gold* (New York: Dell Publishing Co., 1981).
34. Peggy Pascoe, *Relations of Rescue: The Search for Female Moral Authority in the American West, 1874-1939* (New York: Oxford University Press, 1990).
35. Hirata, "Chinese Immigrant Women," 7, quoted in Charles Shepherd, "Chinese Girl Slavery in America," *Missionary Review* 46 (1923): 893-895.
36. Richard H. Dillon, *The Hatchet Men: The Story of the Tong Wars in San Francisco's Chinatown* (New York: Coward-McCann, Inc., 1962), 237.
37. Gray, *Women of the West*, 71.
38. Hirata, "Free, Indentured, Enslaved," 9.
39. Hirata, "Chinese Immigrant Women," 17.
40. Hirata, "Free, Indentured, Enslaved," 12.
41. Gray, *Women of the West*, 72.
42. Yung, *Chinese Women in America*, 17.
43. "The Smuggling of Wah To," in *Mrs. Spring Fragrance*, 185-193.
44. Hirata, "Free, Indentured, Enslaved," 13.
45. As cited by Stephen Longstreet, *The Wilder Shore: A Gala Social History of San Francisco's Sinners and Spenders, 1849-1906* (Garden City, N. Y.: Doubleday, 1968), 160-161.
46. William Purviance Fenn, "Ah Sin and His Brethren in American Literature" (unpublished Ph.D. diss., State University of Iowa, 1932), 109.
47. Gray, *Women of the West*, 71.
48. Pascoe, *Relations of Rescue*, 6.
49. Yung, *Chinese Women in America*, 19.
50. As asserted by both Gray, *Women of the West*, and Dillon, *The Hatchet Men*.
51. Frank Chin, et al., eds., *Aiiieeeee!: An Anthology of Asian American Writers* (New York: Anchor Books, 1975), xiii.
52. Yung, *Chinese Women in America*, 30.
53. Dillon, *The Hatchet Men*, 225.
54. Gray, *Women of the West*, 68.
55. *Ibid.*, 70.
56. Pascoe, *Relations of Rescue*, 1.
57. *Ibid.*, 11.
58. "Pat and Pan," in *Mrs. Spring Fragrance*, 333-344.
59. Sui Sin Far, "Leaves," 130.
60. Ruthanne Lum McCunn, *Chinese American Portraits, Personal Histories 1828-1988* (San Francisco: Chronicle Books, 1988) documents many more journeys of Chinese immigrants to North America.

Ibn Battuta on Women's Travel in the Dar al-Islam

Marina A. Tolmacheva

STUDIES OF ISLAMIC culture have not explored the subject of travel by medieval women. It has been recently noted that, in general, "the role of travel in Muslim societies and in Islamic doctrine is not a topic which has been systematically explored by historians or social scientists."[1] The few studies undertaken on travel by modern Islamic women have focused on religious pilgrimage or journeys to the West; legal aspects of travel have not been addressed at all. Yet the issue of women's spatial mobility under Islam is sufficiently important to studies of both gender and modernization that a widely read work on male-female relations in modern Muslim society defines itself as "a book about sexual space boundaries."[2]

In the current sweep of reaction against social freedoms gained by contemporary Muslim women in some areas of life, tradition-inspired restrictions on women's public life and physical mobility play such an important role that it may be difficult to imagine pre-modern women of the Abode of Islam leading a life not subject to strict confinement. In addition, the Western stereotype of the heavily veiled, male-dominated Muslim female becomes overlaid and complicated by Western preconceptions concerning female travel. Yet a simple consideration of the long tradition of nomadic lifestyle historically prominent among Islamic societies reveals that these stereotypes are not merely simplistic but erroneous. The reality, when explored in historical perspective and with due attention to evidence, is complex. Although travel by Muslims was common, travel *per se* was not assigned positive value even for males. Discomfort, invasion of privacy, and physical dangers concomitant with travel were given serious consideration both socially and legally. It was well known, for example, that pilgrim caravans were in constant danger of attack by Bedouins. Travel by women was legally subject to control by males; the woman's safety and that of her children were of paramount concern.[3] Recent scholarship has shown that seclusion, too, was legitimized under the *Sharia* (Holy Law) as a positive value.[4] Nevertheless, it is not difficult to discover in medieval sources evidence of physical mobility and travel by Islamic women or women residing in areas governed by Islamic law. To provide examples of these phenomena I have chosen to focus on the eyewitness testimony of the Arab traveler of North African origin Abu 'Abdallah Muhammad ibn 'Abdallah al-Lawati al-Tanji, better known to the West as Ibn Battuta (1304-1377).

The greatest traveler of the Middle Ages, Ibn Battuta traveled about three times as far as Marco Polo[5] and left an extensive and invaluable record of visits to numerous places in Africa, Asia, and Europe. Still not fully available in English,[6] Ibn Battuta dictated this account to a secretary in 1355-56 in Fez (Morocco). The resulting book *Tuhfat al-nuzzar fi ghara'ib al-amsar wa 'aja'ib al-asfar* ("Gift to those eager to observe the wonders of cities and marvels of journeys," commonly referred to as *Travels*) is a straightforward narrative, distinguished by literary qualities that make it an outstanding example of *Rihla*, the genre of Arab travel literature.[7] What makes Ibn Battuta's book an important source on women's travel is the fortuitous combination in his character of a lively interest in all aspects of travel with an acknowledged enjoyment of keeping company with women. Ibn Battuta was an unusually self-aware traveler: the subject of travel led him to inquire about itineraries, transport, seasons, and schedules. He decided early on never to travel by the same road twice if he could help it,[8] and so observed the terrain, economy, and population from diverse routes. He traveled by camel, horse, mule, litter, wagon and boat, never failing to describe the mode of transportation for himself, his companions, and his hosts.

It is important that his are the observations of an expert witness: Ibn Battuta had received training as a legal scholar in the Maliki school[9] of Islamic law and served as a judge on several occasions. It is all the more significant then, that very few of his remarks are openly critical or disparaging of women or of society's "permissiveness" in regard to their social manner or mobility in public space. A few practices are judged "bad," and unclothed bodies of Indian or African women[10] or competitive bargaining for jewelry by Turkish women in Tabriz[11] scandalize him. But much more often, Ibn Battuta uses restrained words like "interesting" or "strange" in reference to local custom, or gushes compliments to women's "extraordinary" or "surpassing" beauty, physical grace, modesty, virtue, hospitality, generosity, and so on.

As a source, the *Travels* reflect Ibn Battuta's foremost interest in the people of the Muslim world, with whom he shared the civilization of Islam, whose values he was taught and legally trained to uphold. Ross E. Dunn has recently argued that in his devotion to travel and persistence in exploring the *Dar al-Islam*,[12] the Muslim cosmopolite approached the world not as discrete societies but as a global community whose men and women "shared not merely his doctrinal beliefs and religious rituals, but his moral values, his social ideals, his everyday manners."[13] But the Dar al-Islam included more than Muslims. Christians, Jews, and Zoroastrians were legally allowed to maintain their faith and customs, and in the fringe areas—Africa, India, Southeast Asia—animistic religions, Hinduism and Buddhism, were tolerated out of necessity. On the whole, Ibn Battuta's tales are remarkably free of religious prejudice, although not of all Islamic sensibilities.

Ibn Battuta provides evidence of widespread physical mobility among women of the realm of Islam. Ibn Battuta had first-hand encounters mostly with three social classes of women: slave girls; daughters of his learned friends, colleagues, and patrons in the service; and—at the top of society—queens and princesses. Public and private lives are of equal interest to Ibn Battuta: the traveler describes distinctive features of their clothing, ornaments, hair styles, public behaviour, social position, and family roles. He particularly delights in noting piety (e.g., among Meccan women) and Islamic education (among the girls of South India[14] or in regard to his own slave girls or wives.[15]) On a more pragmatic level, he discusses sexual customs of the places, comments on the possibilities of contracting a marriage, and, importantly for this essay, inquires into the social norm regarding women's travel away from home.

Ibn Battuta's undisguised interest in the "fair sex," according to one commentator, makes the *Travels* a virtual encyclopedia on women of the Orient.[16] Obviously, he considered information about women of interest to his readers, the majority of whom, it may be safely presumed, were male. Since restriction of women to the private domain did exist, it seems relevant to emphasize that our source gained much information first-hand: in the course of his travels Ibn Battuta repeatedly married and divorced, and fathered several children. It may seem strange to a careful reader that the women of his own family figure only marginally in his account, but Ibn Battuta's casual references to his wives testify not to callousness but to good Islamic manners of social and emotional restraint; occasionally, a fond reminiscence of a wife left behind or a preference for a particular slave girl slip in. Gentle fondness and warm feeling for his mother and daughters (one of whom he buried in India) are apparent.[17] Physical cruelty to women caused him to faint, as when he witnessed the Hindu ritual of the widow's self-immolation on the husband's funeral pyre.[18]

It is a different matter that Ibn Battuta's family life cannot be characterized as "stable." Marriage and divorce are the part of the Islamic social system that differs most dramatically from the Western norm: polygamy, although infrequent in practice, is allowed under Islamic law, and in the days of slavery a man could have an unlimited number of concubines. The ease of divorce for men made the system "admirably suited to a roving life,"[19] and Ibn Battuta chronicles his divorces along the route, making it clear that the urge or imperative to travel often caused them.

Below, Ibn Battuta's information on travel opportunities open to Muslim women and the circumstances of their journeys is arranged according to categories of motivation (or lack of such) for permissible travel, with reference to mode of travel and transportation, and to the women's social and cultural background. The attempt here is not to plot out the geography of women's journeys, even when on Ibn Battuta's route,[20] but rather to explore the range of women's spatial mobility as recorded by a legally minded witness who, in the role of spouse or owner, sometimes himself became a prime cause of the women's travel. The effort is directed at exploring the historical patterns of medieval Muslim women's journeys and redefining our own notions of female travel.

Brides, Wives, and Slaves

The stereotype of female journey occasioned by male mobility[21] is sustained in part by some phenomena observed or experienced by Ibn Battuta. The most prominent among these is the bridal journey. In the patriarchal, patrilocal Arab society women had to move to the site of their marriage covenant and, at the direction of their father or (male) guardian, travel, if need be, to their marital residence. Such was the case of Ibn Battuta's first two marriages:

> I had made a contract of marriage at Safaqus (Sfax, in Tunisia) with the daughter of one of the Syndics at Tunis, and she was conducted to me at Atrabulus (Tripoli, in Libya). I then left Atrabulus, at the end of the month of Muharram of the year [seven hundred and] twenty-six (January 1326) taking my wife with me. . .to Qubbat Sallam. There we were overtaken by the body of the caravan who had stayed behind at Atrabulus, and I became involved in a dispute with my father-in-law which made it necessary for me to separate from his daughter. I then married the daughter of a *talib* (doctor of religion) of Fez, and when she was conducted to me at Qasr al-Za'afiya I gave a wedding feast, at which I detained the caravan for a whole day, and entertained them all.[22]

Several of the princesses and queens encountered by Ibn Battuta are foreign to the lands where they reign: Turkish women from Khorasan (eastern Iran) he met in India and Central Asia, possibly even Indonesia, and the Greek princess in the Golden Horde on the Volga. Their bridal journeys have to remain presumed since Ibn Battuta only chronicles their sojourn in a foreign country.

Women sometimes bitterly resented the need to travel occasioned by marriage, and their complaints reflect their relative lack of choice in the matter. Wives who accompanied their husbands on pilgrimage could find themselves settled there among the "sojourners" who devoted their time to pious study and exercise. Among such travelers to Mecca who settled there was Shihab al-Din al-Nuwairi (d. 1336-37). He came from Upper Egypt and married the daughter of the Qadi (Muslim judge) Najm al-Din al-Tabari, who "stayed with him for some years and traveled with him to al-Madina the Illustrious, accompanied by her brother," before being divorced.[23] To some women, travel might be a threatening experience, objected to and even resisted, as in the case of Tash Khatun, the widow of the governor of Shiraz. She and her children were arrested by the new governor with the intention of carrying them off to Iraq. By rousing the public to her defense at the very moment of transportation, Tash Khatun managed to escape deportation, imprisonment, and probable death.[24] In another instance, Ibn Battuta mentions that after the fall of the above-mentioned Chingizid Tarmashirin in 1334-35, his son Bashay Ughli fled, "together with his sister and her husband Firuz, to the King of India."[25]

On the frontier of the Dar al-Islam, Ibn Battuta reports on wives traveling with their husbands to distant state functions, as in the case of Mongol rulers among whom, by the mid-14th century, many professed Islam.[26] In relating some of the regulations of the "Great Yasa" of Chingiz Khan he reports, correctly, that "one of its prescriptions is that they shall assemble on one day in each year, which they call the *tuy* (meaning the day of the banquet). The descendants of Tankiz and the amirs come from all quarters, and the khatuns (princely women) and superior officers of the army also attend." Two years after Ibn Battuta's arrival in India (i.e., approximately in 1336), such a meeting was held "in the most remote part of [Sultan Tarmashirin's] territories, adjoining China."[27]

Since the Turkish, Turco-Mongolian, and Turkmenian houses ruled over the large parts of Asia visited by Ibn Battuta, the Turkish custom of moving camp affected even the highest-born women. After leaving the Golden Horde Khan Uzbek in Astrakhan on the Volga, Ibn Battuta traveled all the way to Constantinople before returning to find out that the Khan "had moved and had settled at the capital of his kingdom, so we traveled [to it] for three nights on the river Itil [Volga] and its joining waters, which were frozen over. . . [on the fourth day] we reached the city of al-Sara, known also as Sara Baraka, which is the capital of the Sultan Uzbak."[28] (In contrast, the nomadic lifestyle of the Arab tribes is only fleetingly alluded to by Ibn Battuta.)

And finally, besides the free women forced to abandon or move home by family or political pressures, there was a large group of women whose will and considerations had nothing or little to do with their physical mobility: slaves. Although Islam prescribes gentle treatment of slaves, and slave women in particular could achieve comfort and influence as concubines, their choice of destination and domicile was made for them by their masters, and before being sold, by their captors. (Islam prohibited enslavement of Muslims, but slaves who converted to Islam were not automatically enfranchised.)

In Ibn Battuta's lifetime Islam was undergoing a major expansion,[29] a situation that affected the movement of slaves, and Ibn Battuta mentions holy war as a common occurrence in Africa, India, and southeast Asia. The Turkish-Byzantine warfare, on which Ibn Battuta is silent, also was a constant factor at this time, affecting some of the areas he visited. From the frontier areas captive women would be moved to slave markets in the interior and then disperse all over the Dar al-Islam.

During Ibn Battuta's stay in India, "some captives taken from the infidels" arrived, and he was sent ten "girls" whom he distributed among his companions and retainers.[30] On his last, homeward journey in 1353, Ibn Battuta left Mali for Morocco "with a large caravan which included six hundred women slaves."[31] On a journey along the Niger, going by boat from Timbuctu, he met an Arab slave girl from Damascus[32] and in Khansa (Hangchow, in China) the amir's slaves included Muslim cooks as well as musicians and singers who entertained guests in Arabic and Persian.[33] Here he also encountered Jews, Christians, sun-worshipping Turks, and Muslims among the free population, largely merchants— but as we shall see this does not automatically imply a corresponding presence of free Muslim women in their midst.

The Wives Who Would Not Travel

Although movement abroad and access to travel could be controlled, the right of travel as such was not denied women. Yet so many women did not choose to travel that a second pattern, very different from the one sketched above, must be noted. This pattern also challenges the stereotype of the passive shut-in, because staying at home resulted from considered rejection of the option of travel.

In contradistinction to brides traveling to their grooms and wives accompanying their husbands, Ibn Battuta tells of women who did not leave their country or home town to follow their wandering husbands, as evidently he felt they should: his reaction is annoyance and hurt surprise. For instance, in Zabid, an important and wealthy town he visited in Yemen, women earned his praise along with frustration:

> For all we have said of their exceeding beauty they are virtuous and possessed of excellent qualities. They show a predilection for foreigners, and do not refuse to marry them, as the women in our country do. When a woman's husband wishes to travel she goes out with him and bids him farewell, and if they have a child, it is she who takes care of it and supplies its wants until the father returns. While he is absent she demands nothing from him for maintenance or clothing or anything else, and while he stays with her she is content with very little for upkeep and clothing. But the women never leave their own towns, and none of them would consent to do so, however much she were offered.[34]

In China, women could but were not compelled to follow Muslim men traveling abroad, even if they had been sold to them as slaves.[35]

In the Maldive Islands, the ease of Islamic marriage and divorce resulted, conveniently for travelers, in a practice reminiscent of temporary marriage (allowed in Shi'ite but not in Sunnite law):

> It is easy to get married in these islands on account of the smallness of the dowries [rather, dower, payable in Islam by the husband to the bride] and the pleasure of their women's society. When ships arrive, the crew marry wives, and when they are about to sail they divorce them. It is really a sort of temporary marriage. The women never leave their country.[36]

The women who chose not to travel, or returned home while allowed by law or expected by their husbands to join them on a journey, figure prominently in Ibn Battuta's discussion of womenfolk. Among the stories of wives reluctant to leave parental surroundings, a particularly telling case involves Ibn Battuta's own wife, one of several he married during his eight-year stay in India.

Although he left several other wives behind earlier – one in Damascus and two on this very occasion of Ibn Battuta's departure from the increasingly hostile court at Mahal (in the Maldives) – this woman, related to the royal minister, had originally sailed away with her husband. On reaching another island "my wife was attacked by severe pains and wished to go back, so I divorced her and left her there, sending word to that effect to the Wazir, because she was the mother of his son's wife."[37] Ibn Battuta's compliance with the wife's wish and his concern over her future comfort are apparently dictated by local custom and political concern. Importantly, divorce as a result of one party's travel is clearly perceived in the narrative as a deserving deed rather than an act of abandonment. While Ibn Battuta's wife had no control over his departure, he, in turn, seemed to have no power or wish to force unwanted mobility on her.

The Women Who Chose to Travel

The third pattern, that of women's travel by choice rather than necessity, highlights journeys sanctioned by religion and approved socially. Despite assigning seclusion the value of propriety and prestige, in one respect Islam adopted, from the start, an ancient Arabian custom that offered women an opportunity to travel. The pilgrimage to the Ka'ba sanctuary in Mecca is incumbent on all adult Muslims regardless of sex as long as they can afford it. Modified for women believers by the clause requiring male protection,[38] the *hajj* (pilgrimage) early on brought out numbers of female worshippers sufficient to necessitate reserving one entrance into the sacred area especially for women,[39] as well as scheduling certain days for exclusive women's attendance at the shrine.[40] That *hajj* was important to women beyond the personal performance of a required duty was testified to by women of wealth and high status as early as the eighth century. A pilgrim road from Kufa had been provided with wells, pools, and resting stations by Zubayda, wife and cousin of the famous Harun al-Rashid (786-809). Ibn Battuta in fact traveled parts of the road that became known as Darb Zubayda.[41] In Ibn Battutta's own time a highly placed woman of Mamluk Egypt, Sitt Hadaq, whose visit to Mecca in 1328 is noted by him,[42] commemorated her return from the pilgrimage by erecting a mosque in Cairo.[43]

Meccan women expressed their piety by coming out to perform the circuit of the Ka'ba on Thursday evenings. The women's circumambulation of the Ka'ba was routed "at the outer edge of the pavement."[44] They "come in their finest apparel, and the sanctuary is saturated with the smell of their perfume. When one of these women goes away, the odour of the perfume clings as an effluvium to the place after she has gone." During the ritual no veil is worn over the face, and so Ibn Battuta is able to add to this picture of pious promenade his admiration for the Meccan women's "rare and surpassing beauty."[45]

The spiritual experience of pilgrimage[46] was augmented for some women by intellectual opportunities. In Damascus Ibn Battuta met a woman nicknamed "the goal of the world's travel" who herself traveled extensively in the Near East, undoubtedly including visits to Mecca and Medina, both important centers of religious learning, since she was sought after as a teacher of Holy Tradition. She was the pious woman Shaykh Zainab (1248-1339), daughter of Kamal al-Din Ahmad ibn 'Abd al-Rahim ibn 'Abd al-Wahid ibn Ahmad al-Maqdisi.[47] Her experience stands out because she had poor eyesight and never married but defied her handicap and single state to achieve celebrity. Of course such travel motivated by personal preference was beyond the possibilities of commoners: another blind woman who occasionally accompanied her son's campaigns was the mother of the sultan of Delhi, Makhduma Jahan ("Mistress of the World").[48] It is also possible that being single, at least among the high-born, actually facilitated women's mobility abroad. In India, Ibn Battuta learned the story of a woman who came to rule Delhi. Upon the death of Sultan Shams al-Din

(1210-1235), his daughter Radiya engineered her own election as queen and showed considerable nonconformity. Unmarried, "she held sovereign rule for four years (1236-1240) and used to ride abroad just like the men, carrying bow and quiver and *qurban*, and without veiling her face."[49] (She was later deposed in favor of her younger brother and forced to marry.)

Status and wealth together afforded women means of secure and comfortable travel and even enabled them to serve as patronesses of pilgrims and travelers. On a trip between Mosul and Baghdad, Ibn Battuta joined a returning pilgrim caravan with what a century earlier would have been a princess of the blood:

> Among them was a pious woman devotee called the Sitt Zahida, a descendant of the Caliphs, who had gone on pilgrimage many times and used to fast assiduously. I saluted her and placed myself under her protection. She had with her a troop of poor brethren [i.e. mystics who were in her service]. On this journey she died (God have mercy on her); her death took place at Zarud and she was buried there.[50]

"A descendant of the caliphs" here undoubtedly refers to the Abbasid caliphs, overthrown in 1258 by the Mongols.[51] While the episode is typical of Ibn Battuta's solicitation of favors from persons of high status and influence, his placing himself under a woman's protection when en route deserves our special attention. He found himself in a similar situation in the Golden Horde and on the journey to Constantinople, where he was under the protection of Khan Uzbek's third and fourth wives. Moreover, in reporting travel customs in West Africa, he notes that no caravan can travel through the land of the Bardama (Bergdama) Berbers "without a guarantee of their protection, and for this purpose a woman's guarantee is of more value than a man's."[52]

The Third Khatun's Journey

A journey which required considerable determination and planning from its initiator (and of which Ibn Battuta left us an impression-filled, detailed account) is that of Khatun Bayalun, the third wife of Khan Uzbek of the Golden Horde (1313-1341). This journey took Bayalun and Ibn Battuta all the way across the southern Russian steppe and the Balkans, from Astrakhan to Constantinople.[53] Ibn Battuta had found himself in the Golden Horde after traveling northward from Syria and Asia Minor.

Arriving in camp, he was placed in a hilltop tent with a flag exhibited in front to publicize his arrival. The fourth wife of the Khan Uzbek inquired about the newcomer and gave orders that Ibn Battuta be taken under her protection.[54] In the camp he had ample opportunity to observe the travel and public behavior of the wives, sisters, and female servants of the Khan. Social relations within the camp environment are sketched as open and casual. In the case of a later Muslim author it has been suggested that his frankness and a willingness to discuss women may have "derived in some measure from his experience in the Turko-Mongol *ordu*, the relatively fluid, unstructured society."[55] It may also be suspected that on occasion Ibn Battuta's readiness to praise and overlook insufficient Islamic conformity (such as absence of veiling among the Turkish women, which greatly struck him)[56] grew in direct proportion to the favors received from the royal ladies.

The trip to Constantinople was initiated by the third Khatun, by birth a Greek and an orthodox Christian, who apparently converted to Islam in connection with her marriage: the Mongol rulers of the Golden Horde and their cousins Ilkhanids of Iran adopted Islam in the late 13th century. The subject of travel was brought up upon reaching Astrakhan, after a protracted camping journey through the Crimea and northern Caucasus. The Khatun is identified by Ibn Battuta as "the daughter of the king of the Greeks," despite her Mongol name Bayalun. The timing was occasioned by her pregnancy: she "begged of the sultan to permit her to visit her father, that she might give birth to her child in the latter's residence, and then return to him."[57]

The journey involved elaborate farewell ceremonies and an impressive train that included only part of her slaves, servants, and chattels, as she had to leave most of her slave girls and baggage in her husband's camp.[58] The calendar, if precisely remembered by the narrator, breaks into two stages of 29 and 22 days, divided at the frontier Greek fortress of Mahtuli. The detailed route of the journey, performed probably in July-September of 1332, is impossible to reconstruct;[59] hospitality gifts delivered from the countryside relieved the hardship of travel. Inside the Turkish territory these were delivered to the Khatun as the spouse of a Mongol ruler; on the Greek side she was greeted as the Byzantine emperor's daughter.[60]

After crossing into Greek territory, her Mongol escort turned back, the mobile mosque was left behind and Muslim prayer discontinued. The princess resumed such Christian practices as drinking wine and eating pork. The rich outfit of the princess's horse is described and reminds the reader that inside the Greek territory wagons had to be left behind "because of the roughness of the country and mountains."[61] The magnificence of the princess's reception by her family prior to entry into Constantinople[62] probably made it easy to forget the 5,000 Turkish horsemen, 500 troops and servants, 400 wagons, and hundreds of oxen and camels left behind.

It soon became apparent to Ibn Battuta, whom the journey provided with a unique (for a non-captive Muslim) opportunity to visit the capital of eastern Christendom, that the declared purpose of the Khatun's visit had been a pretext, that "she professed her father's religion and wished to remain with him."[63] In fact, the journey begins to look like a flight home, away from the steppe and the semi-nomadic existence that even queens had to endure among the Turks, away from the faith of Islam and the concomitant cultural, social, and dietary norm. Rather than being a simple family reunion, the apparent flight assumes a particular significance as an act of escaping from Muslim and Turkish values, especially in light of the Byzantine-Turkish struggle that characterized the period in Asia Minor and which was bound to end, in 1453, with the fall of Constantinople to Ottoman Turks. Even here, however, our traveler remains non-judgmental and praises the generosity of the princess in extending her protection during his sight-seeing and in bestowing gifts upon him and her Islamic retinue, who are dismissed from her service.

The homeward journey of the Greek princess represents a deeply personal move toward change, a challenging step of a meaningful and decisive nature. It would be very tempting to imagine the third Khatun as a heroine severing ties with a distasteful environment, putting distance between her past life and her native Constantinople. The princess's courage in traveling home across distances and frontiers is impressive by any standards, although the psychological import of her journey may seem less daring to the modern critic: seemingly nonconformist, she moves "merely" from one male-controlled milieu (virilocal) to another (patrilocal).[64] She abandons Muslim conventions while resuming Christian ones. Ibn Battuta never mentions her again, and the story seems complete. However, the princess did go back; her return journey unrecorded, her presence is noted in the Golden Horde in 1341.[65] Therefore her boldness in reassuming a Christian lifestyle may be judged all the more highly because she acted in front of Muslim witnesses and in the face of eventual return to the Islamized household of her Mongol husband.

Travel Under Islamic Law

Significantly, while the former action breaks Islamic rules for the faithful, the journey itself does not. Travel, particularly travel for profit, is sanctioned by Islamic law without limitation as to time or purpose,[66] although pilgrimage is deemed to be particularly rewarding. Travel in company is to be preferred, and one should share provisions generously with fellow-travelers, give alms before departure, and bring back gifts to the family.[67]

The Muslim husband's authority over his wife's movement extends first of all to the dwelling: if the woman leaves the house unauthorized, her maintenance may be suspended.[68] But while a man may prevent his wife from showing herself in public, clauses in her marriage contract may allow a woman considerable freedom of movement.[69] Visiting parents may be a specific stipulation of the contract, although refusing visitation would be considered boorish even without one. On the evidence of Ibn Battuta, the Greek princess had sought, and obtained, her husband's permission to travel.

Distance of projected travel may be of legal import: according to some authorities, while the husband may prevent the wife's parents from residing with her, he may not prohibit her from visiting them, nor stop them from visiting her once a week (and other relations once a year). Clearly, such frequency of visitation may only be practicable within a reasonable distance between two sites of residence. Day trips or moving between town and surrounding country are not considered travel, and for the most part not subject to restriction.[70] (The weekly excursions of the women of Zabid seem to fall into this category.) On the other hand, a distance involving lengthy absence and breach of privacy imposed certain other limitations: according to the Prophetic Tradition, "no woman shall travel more than three days and three nights, unless accompanied by her husband or her [male] relation."[71] Interestingly, another woman is not, by law, a suitable companion, even if she is a relative.[72] In his story, Ibn Battuta recounts finding women alone in their homes or camp sites, but women whom he encountered en route seem to have had at least one male servant accompanying them, and the cortège of the Byzantine princess included numerous men (and women) owned or hired by her. From the Islamic point of view, the distant and socially inferior position of these companions is legally irrelevant: a woman may travel accompanied by a male only if he is a relation in the degree prohibited for marriage[73] or her slave (which would also make marriage impossible). On the other hand, a husband with several wives may not be free in his choice of the one to accompany him and, according to the Prophetic precedent, is expected to draw lots.[74]

The woman's choice not to leave her home town or country is a right protected on the grounds that travel exposes her to hazards and possible injury; so although a wife is required by the tradition to reside in her husband's permanent home, he is not entitled to carry her away until she has been paid her dower in full. Even then some authorities prevent his doing so against the wife's will. We saw that women who enjoyed the protection and support of their families could refuse to travel even at the price of a broken marriage. Considering Ibn Battuta's divorces in light of a woman's desire to stay in, or return to, her native city (as in the case of his Maldive wives), it may be said that divorce granted by the departing husband was actually beneficial to the woman, who herself could initiate divorce only in very few instances severely circumscribed by law.

Ensuring privacy is the man's responsibility. On sea voyages, Ibn Battuta had to search for ship cabins suitable for his party. Considerations of safety are paramount, and the wife may refuse to accompany her husband on the account of safety for herself and her children. Should she find herself a captive outside the Dar al-Islam, the husband is discouraged from reclaiming her if the infidel spouse has provided safe accommodations.[75] The hardships of travel are considered by law so grave that even a servant (a hired free person) cannot be compelled to follow the master on a journey unless the service is stipulated in the contract. In case of a divorce, the wife is allowed to return to her native city or the place where her marriage contract was executed. However, a place of casual residence (such as the stages of a journey where Ibn Battuta's first marriages were contracted) does not constitute a home.[76] A married woman who becomes divorced or widowed on a journey is subject to a number of restrictions dependent on test of pregnancy and expectations of inheritance, pointing once again to the weight of economic considerations.

These latter resurface in the case of the least questionable journey of all—the pilgrimage to Mecca. Women desirous of pilgrimage
are required by some, although not all, legal authorities to travel under male protection. However, if they should travel without their husbands (who are normally required by law to support them), they are
not entitled to maintenance for the duration of their absence.[77] The
women pilgrims of Ibn Battuta's acquaintance may be presumed possessed of means, even when he fails to mention their economic circumstances, since sufficient health and money are the only two
preconditions for going on pilgrimage.[78] Curiously, the only instance
in which Ibn Battuta reports of a woman's inability to travel refers to
a West African *qadi* forbidden by the Sultan to go on pilgrimage with
a female companion.[79]

*   *   *

It is instructive that the variety of modes and motivations of these journeys does not surprise Ibn Battuta. The contrast between apparent
access to travel in the Middle Ages and enforced immobility of women
in modern times is striking. The question that inevitably arises—when,
why, and how did the change occur?—cannot be fully answered here.
Of course, the majority of women (and men) did not travel centuries
ago; however, when some did, the Dar al-Islam, although divided, did
not impose on them the constraints of contemporary border regimes
throughout the territory equivalent to 44 countries crossed by Ibn Battuta. Furthermore, some of Ibn Battuta's examples belong among the
nomads compelled to migrate *en masse* by their lifestyle; others come
from frontier areas where Islam was weakly enforced against local custom. Within the pattern conforming to Islamic norm, the two criteria
determining public acceptance of women's travel are the perceived need
and status.

It is clear that high status, whether generated by piety, career,
or birth, played an important sanctioning role in initiating, commanding, or acceding to travel. It would be, however, incorrect to suppose
that higher status always offered women more freedom: during the Middle Ages religious authorities increasingly enforced seclusion and especially emphasized it for noble women. By contrast, seclusion and
veiling were not required for slaves. Paradoxically, that left free, high-
born women more constricted in their social and creative activities,

while slave women could leave the house, visit shops and markets, and show their faces to men openly and without opprobrium.[80] In addition to attitudes facilitating slave women's physical mobility, it appears that the free wives' ability to resist travel stood in the way of lasting marital affection and even served to promote closer personal attachment of men to more dependent females.

As soon as he was able to afford it, Ibn Battuta himself resorted to the company of slave girls for more constant companionship than wives provided. He mentions acquiring a Greek slave girl in Ephesus and another one named Marguerite in Balikasri (Asia Minor).[81] On the journey from Bukhara to Samarkand in Central Asia one of his slave girls gave birth to a daughter;[82] both later accompanied Ibn Battuta to India where the daughter died. After the birth of a master's child, especially male, the woman was customarily kept on and could not be sold or given away. At her master's death, if still a slave, she usually gained personal freedom. In this instance, the mother of Ibn Battuta's child was apparently intended to accompany her master on an embassy to China in 1349. Trouble prevented Ibn Battuta from ever completing that mission, and at Calicut, attempting to sail from the port, he and his slaves were separated, the women eventually seized by the ruler of Sumatra.[83] Persisting in his often dangerous quest, Ibn Battuta later sailed to Ma'bar (Coromandel) and survived a shipwreck in which he put the safety of his free male companions and the two slave girls who were with him ahead of his own, offering them the use of a raft. We learn that both parties were rescued and Ibn Battuta was (temporarily) reunited with his concubines.[84]

It follows from these examples that slave women, unlike wives, found themselves exposed considerably more frequently to physical dangers of travel such as shipwrecks, pirate attacks, and rape. The tradeoff, if such it was, came in the form of their master's affection and concern. While some of Ibn Battuta's wives are remembered by him as pious or generously lacking in jealousy, it is his slave to whom he unabashedly refers as "the one I love."

Notes

The work on this paper was supported in part by a grant from the Washington State University Graduate School. The author gratefully acknowledges the assistance of Dagmar Weiler.

1. Dale F. Eickelmann and James Piscatori, eds., *Muslim Travellers: Pilgrimage, Migration and the Religious Imagination* (London: Routledge; Berkeley: University of California Press, 1990), p. xvi.

2. Fatima Mernissi, *Beyond the Veil: Male-Female Dynamics in Modern Muslim Society*, Revised Ed. (Bloomington and Indianapolis: Indiana University Press, 1987), p. xv.

3. *Shorter Encyclopaedia of Islam*, s.v. "Hadjdj," by H. A. R. Gibb and J. H. Kramers. Joseph Schacht, *An Introduction to Islamic Law* (Oxford: Clarendon Press, 1964), pp. 166-168; Jamal J. Nasir, *The Status of Women Under Islamic Law and Under Modern Islamic Legislation* (London; Boston: Graham & Trotman, 1990), pp. 62-64.

4. See Leila Ahmed, "Women and the Advent of Islam," *Signs: Journal of Women in Culture and Society*, 77/4 (1986): 665-691. On the subject of legal interpretation of seclusion see *Encyclopedia of Islam*, s.v. "Hidjab," by F. Chelhod. For historical approaches to gender boundaries in the Middle East see Nikki R. Keddie and Beth Baron, eds., *Women in Middle Eastern History: Shifting Boundaries in Sex and Gender* (New Haven: Yale University Press, 1992). On the origins of doctrinal attitudes to gender see Leila Ahmed, *Women and Gender in Islam* (New Haven: Yale University Press, 1992).

5. H. Yule's estimate is 75,000 miles, quoted by H. A. R. Gibb, ed., in Ibn Battuta, *Travels in Asia and Africa, 1325-1354* (London: Routledge & Kegan Paul, 1983), p. 9. Ross E. Dunn, *The Adventures of Ibn Battuta, a Muslim Traveler of the 14th Century* (Berkeley: University of California Press, 1986), p. 3 has 73,000 miles. Mahdi Husain, *The Rehla of Ibn Battuta* (Baroda: Oriental Institute, 1976), suggests 77,640 miles, and Thomas J. Abercrombie 75,000 miles: "Ibn Battuta, Prince of Travelers," *National Geographic*, 180/6 (1991): p. 8.

6. The most complete but unfinished English version is by H. A. R. Gibb, *The Travels of Ibn Battuta A. D. 1325-1354*, 3 vols. (Cambridge: Hakluyt Society, 1958-1971). The final (fourth) volume is in preparation by C. F. Beckingham. The best edition of the Arabic text is by C. Defrémèry and B. R. Sanguinetti, *Voyages d'Ibn Battuta*, 4 vols. (Paris, 1953-58).

7. In general, very little has been written about Arab travel literature as distinct from geographical literature. For a useful discussion of this distinction see Mary B. Campbell, *The Witness and the Other World: Exotic European Travel Writing, 400-1600* (Ithaca and London: Cornell University Press, 1988), ch. 1. On the travel genre in general, see the pioneering work by Maria Kowalska, *Sredniowieczna arabska literatura podró" nicza* (Warszawa-Krakow, 1973). The *rihla* literature gained special prominence

in the Maghreb; consult M. B. A. Benchekroun, *La vie intellectuelle maro-caine sous les Mérinides et les Wattasides* (Rabat, 1974). On different types of *rihla* see Abderrahmane El Moudden, "The Ambivalence of *rihla*: Community Integration and Self-definition in Moroccan Travel Accounts, 1300-1800," in Eickelman and Piscatori, *Muslim Travellers*, ch. 4.

8. Ibn Battuta, *Travels*, p. 5.
9. In Sunnite Islam there are four schools of law (*madhhab*): Hanafi, common among the Turks, in the Fertile Crescent, and in India; Maliki, spread mainly in the Muslim West; ShariXi, dominant in Egypt and Syria and also found in India and Indonesia; and Hanbali, now found mostly in Arabia. ShiXa Islam developed its own law systems, and Ibn Battuta occasionally displays his animosity toward it.
10. In India, as appointed guardian of Muslim law (*qadi*), Ibn Battuta "tried to make the women to wear clothes, but...could not manage that." See Ibn Battuta, *Travels*, p. 250. About West Africa he writes, "Among their bad qualities are the following. The women servants, slave girls, and young girls go about in front of everyone naked, without a stitch of clothing on them. Women go into the sultan's presence naked and without coverings, and his daughters also go about naked." See Ibn Battuta, *Travels*, p. 330.
11. Gibb, *Travels of Ibn Battuta*, 2: 345.
12. In Islam, a legal category of territory in which the law of Islam prevails, "the Abode of Islam." The opposite is *Dar al-Harb* "The Abode of War," or territory under perpetual threat of the holy war aimed at conversion and control.
13. Dunn, *Adventures of Ibn Battuta*, p. 7.
14. Gibb, *Travels of Ibn Battuta*, 1: 216; Ibn Battuta, *Travels*, p. 230.
15. Gibb, *Travels of Ibn Battuta*, 3: 719.
16. Georgii Vasil'evich Miloslavskii, *Ibn Battuta* (Moscow, Russia: Mysl', 1974), p. 49.
17. Gibb, *Travels of Ibn Battuta*, 1: 8; 3: 555, 740; Ibn Battuta, *Travels*, pp. 266, 306. James T. Monroe offers a concise explanation of such reticence: "for a medieval Muslim, family ties were sacred, and...it was not considered polite to mention one's womenfolk without adding the formula *hasha-ka* 'pardon me for mentioning the subject.' " *Risalat at-tawabi` wa-z-zawabi`. The Treatise of Familiar Spirits and Demons by Abu `Amir ibn Shuhaid al-Ashja`i al-Andalusi* (Los Angeles: University of California, 1971), p. 9.
18. Gibb, *Travels of Ibn Battuta*, 3: 614-616. This provides a meaningful contrast to the reaction of a 17th-century European traveler who, in a detached manner, comments on the victim's gratitude for "the fame which I should carry of her to my own country." *Travels of Pietro della Valle in India*, edited and translated by Edward Grey (New York: Hakluyt Society, 1892), vol. 2, p. 33.
19. Gibb, *Travels of Ibn Battuta*, p. 29.

20. For a brief summary of the route see *Encyclopedia of Islam*, s. v. "Ibn Battuta," by André Miquel. Consult also maps in Gibb, *Travels of Ibn Battuta*, and Dunn, *Adventures of Ibn Battuta*.

21. Most recently upheld by Eric J. Leed in his *The Mind of the Traveler: From Gilgamesh to Global Tourism* (New York: Basic Books, 1991), ch. 8.

22. Gibb, *Travels of Ibn Battuta*, 1:17-18. This marriage is interpreted by Leed as a mere travel accommodation: "A fellow traveler went as far as to provide him [Ibn Battuta] with a wife." Leed, *The Mind of the Traveler*, p. 233.

23. Gibb, *Travels of Ibn Battuta*, 1: 219.

24. *Ibid.*, 2: 307.

25. *Ibid.*, 3: 562.

26. For a classic study of the Mongol impact upon Islam consult Bertold Spuler, *The Muslim World*, Part II, "The Mongol Period" (Leiden: Brill, 1960).

27. Gibb, *Travels of Ibn Battuta*, 3: 560-561. Tarmashirin was the ruler of the Chagatay *ulus* of the Mongol Empire, which included Central Asia and Western Siberia. For a recent overview of the Mongol state see David Morgan, *The Mongols* (London: Blackwell, 1986). On the *Yasa* see G. Vernadsky, "The Scope and Contents of Chingis Khan's *Yasa*," *Harvard Journal of Asiatic Studies*, 3 (1938): 337-360.

28. Gibb, *Travels of Ibn Battuta*, 2: 515. Saray Berke, not far from today's Volgograd, was probably founded by Berke Khan (1255-67). Uzbek (zbek, Oz Beg) was the Khan of the Kipchak *ulus* of the Mongol Empire, known in Europe as the Golden Horde.

29. On this subject see Marshall G. S. Hodgson, *The Venture of Islam* (Chicago: University of Chicago Press, 1974), Vol. 2, Book Four, Ch. IV.

30. Gibb, *Travels of Ibn Battuta*, 3: 741.

31. Ibn Battuta, *Travels*, p. 337.

32. *Ibid.*, p. 334.

33. *Ibid.*, p. 293.

34. *Ibid.*, p. 108.

35. *Ibid.*, p. 286.

36. *Ibid.*, p. 244.

37. *Ibid.*, p. 253.

38. On *hajj* requirements and regulations see *The Encyclopedia of Islam*, 2nd ed., s. v. "Hadjdj," by A. F. Wensinck.

39. Gibb, *Travels of Ibn Battuta*, 1: 169 (on the authority of 'Umar ibn al-Khattab, the second caliph of Islam).

40. Ibn Jubayr, *The Travels of Ibn Jubayr*, trans. R. F. C. Broadhurst (London: Johnathan Cape, 1952), p. 137.

41. Gibb, *Travels of Ibn Battuta*, 1: 243, and note 215. Zubayda reportedly gave away to a pilgrim crowd 54 million silver *dirhams* on the occasion of her own first pilgrimage. Abd al-Kareem al-Heitty, "The Contrasting Spheres of Free Women and *jawari* in the Literary Life of the Early 'Abbasid Caliphate," *Al-Masaq, Studia Arabo-Islamica Mediterranea*, vol. 3 (1990), note 18.

42. Gibb, *Travels of Ibn Battuta*, 2: 357 and note 302. Ibn Battuta calls her the nurse of the Egyptian sultan al-Malik al-Nasir, while Gibb identifies her as the controller of his harem.

43. Caroline Williams, "Mosque of Sitt Hadaq: Female Patronage in Medieval Cairo," paper presented at the 22nd Annual Meeting of the Middle East Studies Association (Beverly Hills, California, 1988). The woman was also celebrated for charitable generosity during the pilgrimage. See Gibb, *Travels of Ibn Battuta*, 3: 357.

44. Gibb, *Travels of Ibn Battuta*, 1: 199.

45. *Ibid.*, 1: 216.

46. For a case study of spiritual and social significance of local pilgrimage in modern times see Nancy Trapper, "*Ziyaret*: Gender, Movement, and Exchange in a Turkish Community," in Eickelman and Piscatori, *Muslim Travellers*, ch. 12.

47. Gibb, *Travels of Ibn Battuta*, 1: 157 and note 337. Such women were part of a medieval tradition: a century earlier, a woman referred to as "learned teacher" was depicted as instructor in Baghdad in a manuscript illumination by al-Wasiti (1236).

48. Gibb, *Travels of Ibn Battuta*, 3: 736.

49. *Ibid.*, 3: 631. An overview of this period is provided in Peter Jackson, "The Mongols and India (1221-1351)" (Ph.D. dissertation, Cambridge University, 1977). See also his article, "The Mongols and the Delhi Sultanate in the Reign of Muhammad Tughlugh (1325-51)," *Central Asiatic Journal*, 19 (1975): 128-143. Quoted in Dunn, *Adventures of Ibn Battuta*, p. 181.

50. Gibb, *Travels of Ibn Battuta*, 2:355.

51. Some women of the 'Abbasid family had enormous political influence: Zaynab bint Sulayman reportedly counseled the first seven 'Abbasid caliphs, whose combined reigns span 750-833. See al-Heitty, "Contrasting Spheres of Free Women," p. 33.

52. Ibn Battuta, *Travels*, p. 64.

53. See description of this journey in Gibb, *Travels of Ibn Battuta*, 2: 497-514. The state of the Byzantine Empire at the time is described in D. M. Nicol, *The Last Centuries of Byzantium, 1261-1453* (London, 1972); on Ibn Battuta's knowledge of Byzantium see, e. g., J. Ebersolt, *Constantinople byzantine et les voyageurs du Levant* (Paris, 1918), and Mehmet Izzeddin, "Ibn Battouta et la topographie byzantine," *Actes du VI Congrs international des tudes byzantines*, vol. 2 (Paris, 1951), pp. 191-196.

54. Gibb, *Travels of Ibn Battuta*, 2: 482.

55. Stephen Frederick Dale, "Steppe Humanism: the Autobiographical Writings of Zahir al-Din Muhammad Babur, 1483-1530," *International Journal of Middle East Studies*, 22/1 (1990): p. 51.

56. So that he repeats the information on several occasions, e. g., Gibb, *Travels of Ibn Battuta*, 2: 416, 481.

57. *Ibid.*, 2: 437.

58. *Ibid.*, 2: 498.

59. *Ibid.*, 2: 500, note 313; see also Dunn, *Adventures of Ibn Battuta*, pp. 170-171.

60. Gibb notes that in Byzantine sources there is no record of the marriage of a daughter of Andronicus III, reigning at the time, to a Khan of the Golden Horde; see Ibn Battuta, *Travels*, p. 357. However, several dynastic marriages with Turkish or Mongol princes took place in the 13th and 14th centuries; see Dunn, *Adventures of Ibn Battuta*, p. 169. Two instances involved bastard daughters; an illegitimate daughter of Andronicus II was married to the ruler of Thessaly. See John M. Sharp, ed., *The Catalan Chronicle of Francisco de Moncada,* Frances Hernández, trans. (El Paso: Texas Western Press, 1975), p. 209.

61. Gibb, *Travels of Ibn Battuta*, 2: 501.

62. *Ibid.*, 2: 502-504.

63. *Ibid.*, 2: 514.

64. Ameliorated in the Turco-Mongol environment by the fact that, in contrast with palace establishments in Arab countries, within the Khan's camp "the favorite wife has the allotment and disposal of a man's wives, keeping back or giving him whichever of them she pleases." E. Denison Ross, ed., *The Tarikh-i-Rashidi of Mirza Muhammad Haidar, Dughlat. A History of the Moghuls of Central Asia.* (Patna, India: Academia Asiatica, 1973), p. 6. The Mongol custom regarding imperial women before conversion to Islam is described in Ann K. S. Lambton, *Continuity and Change in Medieval Persia* (Albany, New York: State University of New York Press, 1988), ch. 8.

65. By Gregory Akindynos in a letter to a Byzantine monk. R. J. Loenertz, "Dix-huit lettres de Grégoire Acindyne, analysées et datées," *Orientalia Christiana Periodica* 23 (1957): 123-124; quoted in Dunn, *Adventures of Ibn Battuta*, p. 180. See also Gibb, *Travels of Ibn Battuta*, 2: 488, note 273.

66. The sacred Tradition, having the strength of sanction in Islamic law, quotes the Prophet Muhammad as saying, "Travel so that you may remain hale and hearty. Travel so that you may derive benefit and get a windfall." *Islam – A Code of Social Life* (New York: Islamic Seminary Publications, 1985), p. 94.

67. *Islam – A Code of Social Life,* pp. 94-98.

68. Schacht, *Introduction to Islamic Law*, p. 168.

69. John L. Esposito, *Women in Muslim Family Law* (Syracuse, N. Y.: Syracuse University Press, 1982), p. 23.

70. Charles Hamilton, *The Hedaya* or Guide; a Commentary on the Mussulman Laws (Lahore: Premier Book House, 1975), p. 134.

71. Hamilton, *Heydaya*, p. 600.

72. *Ibid.*, p. 705.

73. *Ibid.*, p. 705.

74. This is the outcome of stipulated equality among the wives. Mernissi, *Beyond the Veil*, p. 117.

75. Majid Khadduri, *The Islamic Law of Nations: Shaybani's Siyar* (Baltimore: Johns Hopkins Press, 1966), pp. 136-138.

76. Hamilton, *Heydaya*, pp. 55, 140, 506.
77. The logic operating here considers the husband responsible for the wife's maintenance only while she is available for the performance of marital duties. The responsibility also ceases if she is abducted. Schacht, *Introduction to Islamic Law*, p. 168.
78. Arthur Percival Newton, ed., *Travel and Travellers of the Middle Ages* (Freeport, New York: Books For Libraries Press, 1967), p. 91.
79. Ibn Battuta, *Travels*, p. 321. Ibn Battuta is scandalized by the behavior of this judge who breaks the Islamic law by consorting openly with a woman who is neither his wife nor slave. It is possible that the restriction arose from the incompatibility of the intended journey (religious pilgrimage, for the duration of which pious behavior is expected) with the Islamic ban on fornication.
80. al-Heitty, "Contrasting Spheres of Free Women," p. 40.
81. Gibb, *Travels of Ibn Battuta*, 2: 445, 449.
82. *Ibid.*, 3: 555-556. Ibn Battuta was originally informed that the child was male and learned the truth only a week later. Instead of resentment, however, he believed that the girl brought him good fortune.
83. Ibn Battuta, *Travels*, p. 240.
84. *Ibid.*, pp. 261-262.

Section III

Women and Traditions of Narrative

T HE FOLLOWING ESSAYS suggest that women's experiences cannot be made to fit traditional narrative molds originally meant for male heroes; in order to narrate the adventures of a female hero, the narrative pattern must be reconfigured. Perhaps the most powerful and enduring pattern of journey narrative is the quest, and the first three essays explore the feminization of the quest by three very different authors. The fourth essay looks at the journey westward, a pattern so ingrained in the psyche of the United States that mobility is the essence of the American character, according to Frederick Jackson Turner. For the women studied here, however, mobility has become wandering; they leave their home behind rather than seek a new one.

Theoretically, either a man or a woman may go on a quest in the pattern described by Joseph Campbell: separation from society, initiation through a decisive struggle, and a return home with a "boon" of illumination within the self and for society. In practice, however, Campbell's model is insufficient, requiring radical readjustment when the quester is a woman, as the following essays on works by John Bunyan, D. H. Lawrence, and Margaret Atwood document. Both Campbell and Northrop Frye imply a male quester who struggles to gain the "other portion" of himself, thus uniting the male and female within himself and reentering his community in triumph. However, the female quester, says Annis V. Pratt, often cannot return to society; in her encounter with her unconscious she must face and reverse her own internalized patriarchal stereotypes, thus placing herself at odds with the very society of the "fathers" that Campbell's quester ultimately reenters.

The quest in Biblical tradition requires special mention here because it is among the sources informing the accounts by Campbell and Frye and is a well-known influence on both Bunyan and Lawrence. The "journey" from the loss of Eden to the Celestial City follows the outline of separation, initiation, and return as the soul seeks its original wholeness. In "On the Road Again: Class and Gender in *The Pilgrim's Progress*," Louise Schleiner deals with the allegorical journey of John Bunyan's *Pilgrim's Progress*, Part II, which brings the pilgrim's wife Christiana to salvation. Both parts of the work are, of course, based on the Biblical metaphor of life as a journey, but Schleiner shows that Bunyan presents two modes of traveling to heaven—modes that were conditioned, for him and his readers, not only by religious considerations but also by issues of class and gender. Part I is a working-class male rewriting of aristocratic male questing, while Part II is a homologous rewriting of the male heaven quest into androgyny. Virginia Hyde's essay, "Into the Undiscovered Land: D. H. Lawrence's Women Questers," shows that Lawrence's female travelers do not entirely follow the quest "monomyth" as defined by Campbell; instead, they meet some of the criteria for female quests in works by women authors.

The third essay, Susanna Finnell's "Unwriting the Quest: Margaret Atwood's Fiction and *The Handmaid's Tale*," shows that Atwood's heroine longs for a quest she can never undertake. Finnell uses Robert Scholes's criticism and Northrop Frye's criteria for epic and romance activities as points of departure to reveal how Atwood's novel does not follow the male-centered pattern but presents instead a negative quest or anti-quest.

Our studies suggest that something in the nature of Western narrativity (and social reality) has tended to exclude women from the tradition of the successful quest. Christian's pilgrim journey to heaven becomes a different and compensatory affair when it is Christiana who journeys there. Lawrence's sleek, powerful women riders incur disaster or voluntary (and desired) exile. Atwood's parodic inversion of the quest as narrative paradigm—the tale of a heroine trying to flee along a "frailroad" to a future framed out of existence by scholarly interpretive textualizing—shows most clearly the drastic alteration of the quest archetype that occurs when an attempt is made to center a female perspective within it; only in this novel's writerly/readerly dimension is there a possibility of success.

Finally, Sheila O'Brien's "*Housekeeping* in the Western Tradition" addresses the powerful myth of the West in the United States and its connections to lone wanderers or wandering pairs in a hierarchical relationship (Huck/Jim, Lone Ranger/Tonto, etc.). O'Brien proposes a double heritage for *Housekeeping*: masculine journey works such as *The Deerslayer* and feminine journey tales such as *A Narrative of the Captivity and Restauration of Mrs. Mary Rowlandson.* From this dual tradition, *Housekeeping* synthesizes a new pattern of women who wander rather than travel while maintaining a nonhierarchical relationship.

Gendered Journeys in *The Faerie Queene* and *Pilgrim's Progress*

Louise Schleiner

The place of ideology. . .takes the form of the **antinomy:** *what can in [social interaction] be resolved only through the intervention of praxis here comes before the purely contemplative mind as logical scandal or double bind, . . .the conceptually paradoxical, that which cannot be unknotted by the operation of pure thought, and which must therefore generate a whole more properly narrative apparatus—the text itself—to square its circles and to dispel, through narrative movement, its intolerable closure. Such a distinction posit[s] a system of antinomies as the symptomatic expressions. . .of something quite different, namely a social contradiction.*

Frederic Jameson, *The Political Unconscious: Narrative as a Socially Symbolic Act*, 82-83

IN JOHN BUNYAN'S *Pilgrim's Progress*, a book so formative for subsequent Anglo-American culture that it commonly stood beside the Bible on sparse bookshelves, Part II consists of a female pilgrimage along the same Way traveled by the representative plain-man's hero of Part I. This two-part structure invites study that will accommodate multiple perspectives, and I will examine it through an analytical model combining feminist and culturally semiotic descriptions with Bunyan's own theological terms. I will argue that Bunyan, as a working-class preacher writing Christian's male journey in Part I, took over elements of Edmund Spenser's journeying, aristocratic Redcrosse Knight of *The Faerie Queene*, Book I, in a revisionist way, and that Bunyan then analogously recast his own male journey-fiction of Part I to invent the female journey of Part II.[1] The contradictions of power vs. weakness, and initiative vs. determinism, laid down the lines along which he spun out, in turn, his two stories.

Christian of *Pilgrim's Progress*, Part I, is part of a line of allegorical figures standing for "every Christian," stretching from the metaphoric warfaring believer of Ephesians 6 (with the helmet of salvation, shield of faith, sword of the spirit, etc.) through the late classical figures of Prudentius and the medieval Everyman to Renaissance allegorical-pilgrims such as Spenser's Redcrosse Knight and that of Guillaume Deguileville's *Pelerinage de la vie humaine*. Before Bunyan it was assumed in such fictions that a distinctly male figure could stand for everyone. Why did Bunyan, after his Christian's journey, add a wife-and-children pilgrimage just as long as Part I? This innovation might show something new about his and his audience's gender concepts. It might seem to signal a new respect for women, and perhaps in something of his eventual cultural impact, it does. But *The Pilgrim's Progress* in its own time was no trumpet call for the cause of women. It reinforces the Puritan idea, well explained from its Pauline origins by Margaret Thickstun, of woman as spiritually secondary to and dependent on man. Further, a possible new respect for women has little if anything to do with Bunyan's particular way of evolving Part II out of Part I.

The obvious reasons for a sequel no doubt partly motivated him (Van Dyke, 187): that imitators were stealing the story and that (having written one sequel on an anti-Christian, Mr. Badman) Bunyan was uneasy about leaving Christian's initially rebellious wife and children finally abandoned, even though his desertion of them was based on a clear gospel imperative ("If any man come to me and hate not his. . .wife and children, he cannot be my disciple"–Luke 14:26). Perhaps too, Bunyan's evolving novelistic gift for portraying personalities eventually gave him ideas for women pilgrims.

But my argument will propose a more fundamental reason for the sequel. In the course of posing its two propositions I must use certain concepts of Jameson's semiotic Marxism (antinomy and homology in a dialectic or contestive sense – see note 8 and the epigraph above), and study closely the theological problematics linking Bunyan's Parts I and II, namely his treatment of the doctrine of predestination within the very archetype of personal strength and enterprise, the quest.[2] As briefly noted already, my two propositions are 1) that Part I rewrites a paradigm of aristocratic quest romance into a version enacting a working-class male appropriation of religious-ideological validity from debunked representations of the moneyed classes (e.g. Sir Worldly Wiseman, Sir Having Greedy, the evil Cities the pilgrims leave, and the merchants of Vanity Fair), and 2) that Part II is then a necessary shoring up or (homologous) rearticulation of that structure, generated from within Part I, namely a male appropriation of religious-ideological validity from femaleness, defined as valorized weakness and submissiveness. The paradox or antinomy of strength through weakness had to be celebrated in this grand Calvinist tale of struggling forward in macho fashion with one's uttermost might, sword often drawn, toward the goal of leaving everything up to God.[3] Bunyan's treatment of gender does not merely reportray the Puritan doctrine of women's alleged dependence and subservience, but rather in original ways interacts with—indeed shapes—his treatment of class identity, through a theology of "female" weakness as an essential element of the adjusted right spiritual strength for all pilgrims:[4]

> . . .what my first Pilgrim left concealed,
> Thou my brave second Pilgrim, hast revealed;
> What Christian left locked up, and went his way,
> Sweet Christiana opens with her key (Bunyan, 151).[5]

In Part I a certain uneasiness has haunted the fringes of many passages, namely the sense that a heaven-quest of heroic action is radically incompatible with the predestinarian view of all human action as utterly worthless for attaining salvation. A resolution of the problem might seem to be that in Bunyan's allegory heaven equals not salvation *per se* but the knowledge of one's own salvation, and thus one can seek it through good works, the signs of election (Walch, 93). But this epistemological heaven remains only half of Bunyan's construct, for he is having heaven both ways: the City over the river is indeed bliss itself, as well as the knowledge of one's entry there. The pilgrims may or may not feel assurance of salvation at a given time along the Way, and most of their struggles must be experienced—by both characters and readers—as "real" efforts toward sanctification, not as ticket searches.

The conventional Marxist (base and super-structure) view of predestination (Engels 22: 300) is that it legitimized the individual's experience, in capitalist economies, of finding that financial success bore no relation to one's abilities and efforts but was an arbitrary boon of market forces: thus it mythologized an economic phenomenon. That view, however, tells us little about what a group of non-investors like the Baptist tinker Bunyan and his pre-Restoration sectaries found in the doctrine of predestination.[6] The conflict between Bunyan's theology and his fiction does not mean that he erred in using this story pattern; on the contrary, in the sense of the epigraph quote from Jameson above and in accord with recent, more flexible modes of Marxist analysis, he chose it exactly in order to work with and live out a central "antinomy" of the class-specific Dissenter experience of his own milieu: that of claiming a high spiritual status as "chosen" people while being a dominated wage-earner class. The paradox or antinomy that cannot be resolved through abstract thought has spun out a narrative – a quest journey to heaven. The antinomy is, theologically, assurance of election vs. "shame" (the shame of emotionalistic working-class religion); ideologically it is economic subjugation vs. the wealth of an exalted self-concept; narratively it is Christian's "scroll"-ticket to heaven (acquired early in his journey) vs. the recurrent demolitions of confidence and ego strength that he experiences along the Way.

The long-buried paradox at the allegory's root surfaces in the lengthy passage where Christian and Hopeful, near their journey's end and having suffered and learned much, discuss the disturbing case of the pilgrim Little-Faith, an opposite to the martyred Faithful in terms of assertiveness. Little-Faith has, by life's pains and blows, been "robbed of his money," i.e. stripped of all exuberance, assertiveness, and self-confidence enabling accomplishment. Yet safe within Bunyan's allegorical principle that pilgrims cannot be spiritually ruined on the Way unless they consent to the temptations represented by their attackers, Little-Faith stumbles on in a state of miserable dependency, a burden to his fellow pilgrims but clinging to his small pearl of Faith. Christian and Hopeful suppose, almost ruefully, that he will enter heaven just as they hope to. Their alarming, not quite explicit but clear realization is that Little-Faith may be theologically quite as good a model for pilgrimage as Christian, if not indeed a better one, because he is entirely dependent on divine grace.

The first response to the realization is the verses admonishing Little-Faith and his ilk to have more faith, which will be better than achieved victories. But what should be the meaning of "more" and "less" as applied to faith, if so "little" is enough for salvation? Some different grid from this of quantity, some more appealing version of weakness and dependency than this of Little-Faith, is clearly needed. Thus Bunyan will write Part II as a homologous rewriting of Part I because he continues on a further (though already introduced) level, to work with a set of related antinomies. But first let us consider how Part I itself was already a rewriting.

The Pilgrim's Progress vs. Aristocratic
Theological Quest Romance:
Part I as the First "Rewriting"

Bunyan had written Part I, I propose, as a rewriting of the aristocratic theological quest romance paradigm into a working-class male quest for religious validation.[7] As Jameson notes, during the English revolutionary period "the various classes and class fractions. . . articulated their ideological struggles through the shared medium of a religious master code" (88). Bunyan's first "rewriting," to contest class domination, must be analyzed before we can see concretely what he then did with gender as a further system of domination in Christiana's journey of Part II.

Certain methodological points must first be clarified. I do not agree with Jameson and other Marxists that gender oppression is only a function of class oppression under a surviving archaic mode of production subordinating women's labor to men's (Jameson, 99-100; 204). Rather I posit that structures of gender domination have analytically independent status for textual study, though in social practice they are always complexly interacting with other domination structures, namely those of age status, class, race, and ethnicity. Thus feminist analysis should include attention to these other structures or systems of domination, or we may be scrutinizing too narrowly to achieve any accurate account of the functioning of gender concepts. While at times dominated groups may simply be oppressed two or more times over (as women, as blacks, as workers, etc.), there are also, in the workings of systems of domination and in individuals' tapping of them, interactive patterns of displacement, replication, intensification, repression, inversion, and compensation, across the grids of age status, gender, class, race, and ethnicity.[8] Such patterns cannot be discerned if one is looking at only one grid. For 17th-century England, a largely homogeneous society in racial and ethnic terms, we can concentrate on gender and class, noting also at times how the youth-age opposition may reflect or supply some of their patterns of represented domination.[9]

That Bunyan's Christian is a working-class or plain-man's hero has been often remarked but little studied (though see Cantarow and the

Bunyan issue of *ZAA*, 1979). The relatively scant emphasis on this point is probably explained by the fact that the book was early embraced not so much by working-class as by middle-class or mobile merchant-class readers (Walch, 198), eager to see Christian (who is upwardly mobile quite literally) as a universally valid figure. Their easy identification with him will be understandable after a few reflections on Bunyan's milieu.

When Apollyon the dragon, Lord of Christian's home city of Destruction, declares that no ruler willingly gives up his laborers and demands to know why Christian is traitorously emigrating, he replies that Apollyon's wages and benefits are too poor to live on and that he is merely doing what other "considerate persons" do in such cases, looking to "better" himself. He has been portrayed as a town dwelling wage-earner: Worldly Wiseman offers him a job and rented house in his company town of Morality (18), in an episode where Christian consistently calls Wiseman "sir" and "you" (formal second person) while being called "good fellow" and "thee." When Faithful enters the story as a temperamental variant of Christian, the pilgrims' class identity becomes a little more diversified. For Faithful, the tempter equivalent to Worldly Wiseman has been one "Adam the First" (the unregenerate "old Adam" given a royal title), who offers Faithful wages and not merely a rented house, but rather the chance to marry his daughters (all three!) and become his heir (62). Walch characterizes the composite class identification of the pilgrims as that of a mix of wage earners and small scale producer-marketers ("Lohn-arbeitern und kleine Warenproduzenten," 202 – Bunyan was a pot maker/repairman), between whom no clear status line could be drawn. In other words, their class-identification straddles the line between the outmoded and diminishing class of independent small producer-marketers and the emerging one of modern wage-earners. In Bunyan's England this mix of people hoped for upward mobility into such positions as that of a prosperous innkeeper or skilled "master" of a large shop, who would rely on "factors" (middle men) to market his products. To later bourgeois readers and American colonists, aspiring in their own terms to upward mobility, the particular economic features of this outdated mix were probably unclear, but it suggested an ethos of hard work and hope for betterment into which they could easily read their own situation.

Bunyan's contextual reason for writing a plebeian quest romance is given in his first "Apology," that while writing in a polemical tract of the metaphoric "pilgrims and travelers" of the biblical letter to the Hebrews he "fell suddenly into an allegory/ About their journey." But soon after that fall into narrative he also realized that he was writing, as he later admits, "Romance" (151), a very dubious kind of story for Dissenters, on moralistic grounds and subliminally on grounds of class identity, since quest romance typically celebrates an emerging ruling-class hegemony. Spenser in Book I *of The Faerie Queene* had also spun out a representative Christian's quest for holiness, from the same dual scriptural metaphors of the wayfaring and warfaring Christian (Hebrews and Ephesians). Redcrosse Knight wears the Ephesian armor often, most notably in his concluding dragon fight; Bunyan's Christian most notably in his fight with the analogous dragon figure Apollyon. But Redcrosse's courted and espoused lady Una, a figure of the true Protestant church, is allegorically active in his quest throughout, so that there is no occasion for a sequel about her as there is with Christian's realistic wife, left behind as his story begins.

Readers have often sensed that Bunyan, despite his vaunted scant and plebeian reading, was in Part I somehow drawing upon Spenser (Golder), though some scholars have claimed that the similarities are merely the result of their both having started with the same two biblical tropes (Frye, 194). One fact is clear: enchanted castles, allegorical houses of instruction, and wicked waylaying giants do not occur in Protestant canonical scripture.[10] Lynn Veach Sadler, summarizing scholarship on Bunyan's reading, notes that he must have read "romances," unspecified (31). I believe he was responding closely to, even "misreading" or contestively rewriting Spenser (see notes 7 and 8). Both *Faerie Queene* I and *Pilgrim's Progress* Part I have an encounter with Despair as the last dramatically emphasized challenge of the road or Way, followed in each case by a place of refreshment and instruction — respectively the House of Holiness (I, x) and the Delectable Mountains leading to Beulah Land—where each hero is whipped for his sins and granted a mountain-top vision of the holy city. Indeed, the two plots display markedly close parallelism:

Event	Redcrosse Knight	Christian
First challenge	Error monster	Slough of Despond
Hypocrisy temptation	Hermit Archimago	Mr. Worldly Wiseman
Temporary loss of an essential help	Loss of Una/church	Loss of Scroll (Bible)
Central temptation	Two houses of pride	Two valleys of abasement

Event (continued)	Redcrosse Knight	Christian
Expose of the institutional enemy	Duessa/Catholicism stripped, scorned	Marketry of all values (Vanity Fair) exposed
Despair temptation	Peasant Despair	Castle-owner Giant Despair
Refreshment after trial	House of Holiness with Fidelia, Speranza Charissa, Mercie	Delectable Mountains, Beulah Land
Victory	Dragon conquest with baptism, eucharist	Crossing of Jordan into the Heavenly City

One might argue that the close similarity and identical ordering of these features could be coincidental, but in the climactic episode of Christian's and Hopeful's imprisonment in Giant Despair's Castle, we find parallels to Spenser, even in physical details and a name, that can scarcely be coincidental. Redcrosse, because of a moral failing, has been captured by a giant and has languished in his dark dungeon near starvation. So too Christian and Hopeful. Redcrosse's rescue involves a ring of keys that will unlock doors of the castle. So too for Christian and Hopeful (a single key there). In Spenser's rescue scene we find one Ignaro, who carries the castle keys and should be able to save Redcrosse but cannot. Likewise Christian and Hopeful, having just escaped from the dungeon, meet one Ignorance, who claims to have the secret of salvation but does not. Ignaro and Ignorance both represent the "old man" or unregenerate natural sinful person of Pauline theology.

Along with these similarities there are distinct differences, but they evince a pattern of sharp oppositions likewise showing that Bunyan was redoing and revising Spenser. First, Spenser's old man Ignaro, an intriguing dim-witted figure of unregenerate humanity, does not outlast the castle episode; but Bunyan's "brisk" lad Ignorance from there on dogs and periodically catches up to the pilgrims, figuring the unregenerate nature that does not leave a Christian entirely in this life. The fact that he is, by inversion, young rather than old (the oldness of Spenser's "old man" Ignaro was a pun on the Pauline phrase) reflects his perpetual resurgence in believers' lives—as if Bunyan thought Spenser had not given the unregenerate nature its due. Second, the key ring in Spenser is wielded by Prince Arthur, allegorical agent of divine grace, who finds, however, that the dungeon door does not open to those keys but only to his own sheer force battering it down. Bunyan, disliking a princely mediator in the agency of divine grace, puts the key into Christian's own hands, but then also gives him temporarily the dim-wittedness of Spenser's useless key-bearer Ignaro (notable for saying nothing but, four times, "I cannot tell"); this mindlessness makes Christian forget for a time the saving key (the "Promises" of God) in his pocket. Third and most significantly, Spenser's giant's castle with dungeon is an image of pride while Bunyan's is the place of despair — the fearful deep rather than the fearful height.

In fact Bunyan, in pursuing his homologous class-revisionist re-writing, has in several ways inverted Spenser's treatment of the related spiritual opposites pride and despair. Spenser's Despair is a scruffy peasant with a poor rusty dagger, a contemptible "carl" in a cave, who in weaseling fashion nearly talks Redcrosse into suicide. Bunyan's De-spair is the castle-owning giant Spenser had devised for Pride (Or-goglio), as we have just seen. Bunyan reclaims this giant for his working-class fiction partly by redefining him as a fairy-tale sort, a Jack-and-the-Beanstalk giant with a domineering wife to whom he talks in homey fashion ("And sayst thou so, my dear?") and who adroitly manages the big lummox to suit herself. This intriguing turn reminds us that figures such as giants, enchanters, and hags had in the first place been appropriated from folklore by aristocratic romance storytellers — Bunyan is reclaiming a creature of folk fantasy.

The revisionist appropriation of femaleness that would shape Part II had already begun on a small scale even early in Part I, as part of Bunyan's dealings with *The Faerie Queene*: for example, Bunyan there adopted but also notably revised Spenser's allegory of the Pauline triad of faith, hope, and charity (1 Cor. 13, and see chart, pp. 151-152), creating instead of Spenser's three sisters at the House of Holiness a pattern assigning two of the three virtues to maleness. Spenser's female Charity (in line with Bunyan's idea of compassion as a feminine trait) is kept as preeminent among the allegorical ladies at the House Beautiful (Char-ity, Prudence, Piety, and Discretion). But "faith" and "hope" are re-defined as Christian's male boon companions of the Way, Faithful, and Hopeful.[11]

Besides these matters of particular allusion, Bunyan's more general revisionist way of inverting Spenser's treatment of pride and despair (again, see the chart above) is central to his plot structure and reflects an emotional fact of working-class life: the crucial moral enemy on these pilgrims' road is not pride, as it might well be for a moneyed person, but the ego-pounding threat of humiliation. Thus at the center of Redcrosse's quest is a double instancing of the temptation to pride, the high Palace of Lucifera with its glorious parade of the seven deadly sins and, following immediately, the Castle of Orgoglio, who conquers Redcrosse because the knight is "poured out in looseness on the ground" with the treacherous Duessa, instancing the power-arousal linkage; the despair episode follows next, despair being seen as an effect of succumbing to pride and power-lust. Inversely, at the center of Christian's quest is a double instancing of the danger of abasement: the Valleys of Humiliation and of the Shadow of Death. Despair follows later, being posed as natural successor not to humiliation but to the experience of the consuming marketplace where Faithful is martyred, Vanity Fair. (Christian has only slight occasions for pride or "vain-glory," as when, crowing over having caught up with Faithful, he takes a little comical fall.)

The revision of characters is as follows (again see chart). Instead of Spenser's typical villains from chivalric romance, who are figures of appropriated folklore (giants, enchanters, witches) and once even a literal peasant Despair (the very word "villain," villager, records the class contempt whereby bad guys are considered low-born), Bunyan substitutes figures with aristocratic or moneyed-class associations: gentlemen or upstart gentlemen (Mr. Legality), land-owners seen as monsters (Apollyon) or giants (Despair), or lords such as those who authorize the martyrdom of Faithful at Vanity Fair, namely "the Lord Carnal Delight, The Lord Luxurious, the Lord Desire-of-Vain-Glory, my old Lord Lechery, Sir Having Greedy, with all the rest of our nobility" (84).

Bunyan was perhaps not aware of doing a class-specific revision; he simply says in his "Apology" that he is writing of "the way and race of Saints" in his own "gospel time" as compared to their situation in earlier times. The great institutional enemy of Protestant Christians in Spenser's time had been, Bunyan would gather, the Catholic church and related popish tendencies in the English church (Duessa as the Catholic church in *Faerie Queene* I is allied with most of the evils threatening Redcrosse). Bunyan records this perception in the odd emblematic scene of "Pope and Pagan," briefly encountered by Christian and described as remnant bug-a-boos from earlier times, who momentarily alarm but cannot hurt him.

Did Bunyan really substitute for the Catholic church a compara- bly threatening institutional evil on the "way and race" of plebeian Saints of his own milieu? The Vanity Fair episode has often been remembered as the most vivid challenge of Christian's pilgrimage, naturally so since only there is a true pilgrim's blood shed, when Faithful is martyred. As to the institutional phenomenon that the Fair is portraying, our best clue is the account of its merchandise, at first sight a hodgepodge of the most oddly discrepant items:

> [Here] should be sold all sorts of vanity. . .all such merchandise, as houses, lands, trades, places, honours, preferments, titles, coun- tries, kingdoms, lusts, pleasures, and delights of all sorts, as whores, bawds, wives, husbands, children, masters, servants, lives, blood, bodies, souls, silver, gold, pearls, precious stones, and what not (79).

What could motivate the good preacher Bunyan to throw together in one list such wicked items as "whores and bawds" and such respect- able ones as "wives and husbands"? It is the treating of diversely val- ued and meaningful items all as saleable commodities that defines Vanity Fair (theologically, the rejection of its value definition equals the emp- tying of all values but that of discipleship). To regard values primarily in terms of market categories (a wife or husband as a priced item), to devote one's primary energies to acquisition of objects according to market value, is to become a habitue of the Fair. This formulation is cast in terms of apolitical morality (as if one chooses freely whether or not to deal in the Fair). But the Marxist critique of capitalism as imposing large-scale commodification of values is not far to seek (See- hase, 210). The Way of Bunyan's pilgrims runs inevitably through Vanity Fair. There is no bypass. Christian and Faithful try to pass through and buy nothing, but when they are heard commenting on the evil of the Fair, trouble starts.

As I noted above, the encounter with Despair (by Christian and his new companion Hopeful, met at the Fair and thenceforth a substi- tute for the martyred Faithful) follows immediately upon the Vanity Fair episode, tagging it as the most entrenched and institutionalized evil of the Way; having got through it with great loss, one is at risk of despair. Just so Spenser's despair episode, following upon the ad- venture of Giant Pride, had tagged it as the most debilitating challenge on Redcrosse's road; Duessa, the Catholic church figure, had led Red- crosse into both houses of Pride. Plot structure then confirms the emo- tional perception of generations of readers, that the Orgoglio episode (with Arthurian rescue) and Vanity Fair, respectively for the two quests, embody the evil powers being painted as most entrenched and historically concrete. Bunyan of course does not speak of free-market economies or commodification of values but denounces evils associated with the "love of money": "thefts, murders, adulteries, false swearing," etc., things his later bourgeois readers could easily agree to denounce while picturing the Fair at someone else's town.

In sum, Bunyan's plebeian rewriting of Spenser's holiness quest created for himself and his first readers a deeply satisfying, class-specific, and male-centered experience of power and validation. When the pilgrim has turned up his nose at the offer of wages and rented house in the entrepreneur's town to go dragon-fighting and winning his way to the golden City instead, Bunyan and his readers have successfully overcome that obstacle he cites several times in the abstract (as well as in, among others, the "valley" allegorizations already noted), namely "the Shame that attends [working-class] religion" since members of rival social groups "are proud and haughty, and religion in their eye is low and contemptible" (135).

This Shame has earlier taken another allegorical form as a dangerous "fellow," in an account that shows why Christian's sword-swinging quest could overcome it. Faithful recounts of Shame:

> Why, he objected against religion itself; he said it was a pitiful, low, sneaking business for a man to mind religion; he said that a tender conscience was an unmanly thing; and that for a man to watch over his words and ways, so as to tie up himself from that hectoring liberty that the brave spirits of the times accustom themselves unto, would make him the ridicule of the times. He objected also that but few of the mighty, rich, or wise, were ever of my opinion. . . .
> He said also that religion made a man grow strange to the great because of a few vices, which he called by finer names, and made him own and respect the base, because of the same religious fraternity. And is not this, said he, a *shame*? (65).

Appropriation of an aggressive religious manliness from aristocratic quest romance has been the achievement of Part I. It has enabled Bunyan and his original audience to "own and respect the base, because [they are] of the same religious fraternity."

Absorbing Femaleness into the Pilgrimage

Earlier I used the terms "shoring up" or "qualifying rewriting" for the relationship of Part II to Part I in Bunyan's overall treatment of the central theological/ideological issue of *The Pilgrim's Progress*, that of chosenness or religious validation. More precisely, the relationship is one of "homology" between layers of meaning in the eventual whole text (see notes 8 and 9): in Part I, predestination determined that strong males defer initiative for contestive action to God or Evil Ones, themselves resisting or denouncing only when attacked, and this victorious deferral is the narrative equivalent of manly faith; but in Part II, in a version of this formula more agreeable to a male-dominant readership, females (and analogously weak pilgrims) gladly defer initiative for contestive action to vicariously divine male "champions" or to Evil Ones, and their deferral equals faith. In the sense of generative homology, the two layers of meaning (which are not entirely separated into Parts I and II, but rather show some overlap) are related not simply as in a static parallelism; instead "the second is seen as being generated in order to compensate for and rectify a structural lack at some lower or earlier level of production," here namely that of the male deferral paradigm of Part I (Jameson, 44; also see note 8). That structural lack and its rectification can now be illustrated concretely.

We return to the Little-Faith episode and the emergence of Part II from the quandary about the meaning of weakness and dependency. Throughout Part I, whenever frightened, Christian exhorted himself to "play the man" and stand up to the enemy. On a few occasions this meant actual fighting. But the courage was more often a matter of passive resistance through principled toleration of injury; as long as it meant asserting oneself, it could reinforce a self-esteem based on "manly" strength. Faithful "played the man" supremely, we are told, in giving himself up to martyrdom. In other words, non-violent or passive resistance was incorporated into the paradigm of plebeian manliness in Part I, reflecting the strategy of self-validation in Jesus's gospel recommendations that the Roman-occupied Jews control their rulers by the moral superiority of assertive passive resistance ("if someone requires you to go one mile with him, go two").

In Giant Despair's dungeon Christian has been challenged one last time, by Hopeful, to "play the man" in this sense by resisting the giant's pressure toward suicide: "remember how thou playedst the man at Vanity Fair. . . . Wherefore let us (at least to avoid the shame that becomes not a Christian to be found in) bear up with patience" (104). The next day Christian finally remembers his key of Promise, which effects their escape.

But from this point on, a series of perspective-shattering moments destroys their ability to rely on courageous manliness in its plebeian redefinition. Upon returning to the Way, they enter the Delectable Mountains and, having asked directions, get an astonishing answer:

> CHRISTIAN. How far is it to the Celestial City?
> SHEPHERD. Too far for any but those that shall get thither indeed.
> CHRISTIAN. Is the way safe or dangerous?
> SHEPHERD. Safe for those for whom it is to be safe; "but transgressors shall fall therein" (106).

The two then go walking on the mountains to see instructive visions, including one of some blind men stumbling perpetually among tombs. These are victims of Giant Despair, for "He that wandereth out of the way of understanding shall remain in the congregation of the dead" (108). The pilgrims suddenly realize that they, exactly as did those pitiful wanderers, strayed from the Way into the Giant's bypath Meadow and thus fully deserve to be among them: "Then Christian and Hopeful looked upon one another with tears gushing out, but yet said nothing to the Shepherds" (108). No amount of playing the man—only the key of Promise which it was somehow granted to Christian barely in time to remember—prevented them from joining the figures below. Why did they too not reach into their pockets for the key? Were their pockets empty? It is a moment of tears that reduces the two to the level of terrified children, uncomprehending of whether or why the adult in control will continue to approve of them or will determine upon denunciation, punishment, and misery. They are not yet beyond the last dangers.

As they leave the shepherds, having viewed the City through a telescope with shaky hands, Ignorance joins them, a moneyed young citizen confident in his own basic goodness and in the merits of Christ to compensate should his actions come up a little short of good. Bunyan allows him to speak his case so well that Christian has to debate him at length. Ignorance will be damned because he has not had the ecstatic experience of emptying oneself of all claim to worthiness, of radical casting of oneself on the Other, of casting down one's Crown in adoration, of "believing and coming. . .that is, running out in his heart and affections after salvation by Christ," the experience that makes Christ "a justifier of thy person," not of thy actions. Little-Faith has had this experience and clings savingly, poor fellow, to the perspective it gave him. Bunyan has framed the inquiry about Little-Faith's case with this lucid, part narrative, part expository review of his most basic doctrines: predestination and the ecstatic experience of divine love saving one's very "person" or body. It is as if, confronted with the case of Little-Faith, he reviews the basic tenets that somehow should resolve it. But they do not.

What remains to be confronted in Part II is that playing the man is only half – and that not the more fundamental half – of pilgrimage. Playing the woman is more basic. (Little-Faith managed very little more and it was enough.) For whenever Bunyan, in Part I or Part II, thinks of "running out in one's heart and affections after Christ," he thinks of the devotee as female. Christian is imaged in devotional ecstasy either as the beloved of Canticles, sick with desire for her divine lover (137), or as Ruth creeping under the skirt of Boaz's robe, by that submissive sexual self-offering requesting the boon of marriage and acceptance into the Lord's people, the people of her mother-in-law, Boaz's kinswoman. As Christian tells Ignorance, citing the Ruth paradigm, "True justifying faith . . . flies for refuge unto Christ's righteousness . . . under the skirt of which the soul being shrouded, is presented as spotless before God, is accepted, and acquit from condemnation" (130-31).

In terms of class consciousness, this valorizing of lowly submission as female ecstatic sexuality permits an affirmation of plebeian status whereby one can, by willingly bowing low, rise to spiritual heights that a "gentleman" can never know. By valorizing lowliness one also leaves behind the dizzying view down to hell (that little doorway in the hill) that is Christian's last terror before he reaches the River: lost in the wonder, love, and praise that is one's own chosenness, one no longer feels anyone's misery.

The Gentleness of Part II

Of course in portraying the soul in ecstasy as female beloved to the divine Lover, Bunyan, far from being revisionary, is perpetuating an ancient trope of Christian mystic and devotional writing that the convenient feminine grammatical gender of *anima* (soul) had always reinforced.

But Bunyan could never leave such a crusty trope safely on the shelf as a near-dead metaphor. He had to touch it with his magic fairy god-father wand, and—pop!—the next thing you knew, that *anima beata* would be up walking the Way, confessing her sinfulness with sweet little boys in tow, giving them syrup for the trots, sewing for the poor, smiling on people who "revile" her (152), and ordering the high-road cleared of bogeymen now that she had "risen a mother in Israel." For all this concrete portrayal of the female ways of his milieu, Bunyan is not presenting Christiana and her young admirer Mercy as models only for female believers;[12] rather they depict what he saw as the female side of any good pilgrim's character—the side that could be "ravished" by the Lord, the side showing compassion, gentleness, humility, and a happy willingness to be helped as well as to help and achieve, thus to be part of supportive company and community.

The Little-Faith episode had clarified for Bunyan the need to show this "other half" of pilgrimage, for there Christian had concluded, after hard traveling and many "slips," that he should have asked, that all pilgrims should ask, for a convoy rather than trying to walk the Way alone, "playing the man." Yet manliness could also not be eschewed: Bunyan could give each half of his power-weakness antinomy its due only by writing a two-layered story.

The potential guide is introduced in the Little-Faith episode, one Great-grace (precursor of the ladies' guide Mr. Great-heart), who was nearby on the road when Little-Faith was robbed, though alas not at the right spot to help him (115). The robbers—Faint-heart, Mistrust, and Guilt—are still further versions of that central "abasement" or ego-loss danger that was allegorized as the two Valleys (see chart above). To Hopeful's query why Little-Faith did not "pluck up a greater heart" and withstand them, Christian answers that few can do so in time of trial, and sometimes even great champions of faith cannot. The apostle Peter for example was once the robbers' victim, "so that they made him at last afraid of a sorry girl" [i.e. behaving badly] (116; why a girl shaming a man must have been in this colloquial sense "sorry" is not explained). Sounding like an authorial voice, as Van Dyke observes (181), Christian concludes the discussion as follows:

> When therefore we hear that such robberies are done on the King's highway, two things become us to do: 1. To go out harnessed, and to be sure to take a shield with us; for. . . "Above all take the shield of faith, wherewith ye shall be able to quench all the fiery darts

of the wicked." 2. 'Tis good, also, that we desire of the King a convoy, yea, that he will go with us himself.... I for my part have
been in the fray before now, and though, through the goodness of
him that is best, I am, as you see, alive; yet I cannot boast of my
manhood. Glad shall I be if I meet with no more such brunts (116-17).

In this "1" and this "2" are represented two homologous structural
levels of *The Pilgrim's Progress*: that each believer, male or female,
must go out armed and play the man, yet also and more fundamentally
must play the woman and go out submissively, asking ravishment and
guidance. Thickstun is correct in noting that Bunyan, in his second story,
is often unwilling to let the women play the man or show independence and assertiveness; this is the mirror image of his strength-
weakness dilemma of Part I, where men can very seldom be allowed
to act out their necessary female side. Even so, the hermaphroditic
paradigm is the over-arching one to which his visions led him.

The hermaphrodite ideal of pilgrimage emerging from the total text
has been figured, besides in the Little-Faith episode, in a more explicit image early on. In the Interpreter's House, Christian has seen
a portrait of a wonderful preacher, a figure for the witnessing believer
as a parent bringing new believers to salvation (one's spiritual "children"). The figure

> had eyes lifted up to heaven, the best of books in his hand, the law
> of truth was written upon his lips, the world was behind his back.
> It stood as if it pleaded with men, and a crown of gold did hang
> over his head....
>
> INTERPRETER. This man...is one of a thousand; he can beget
> children, travail in birth with children, and nurse them himself when
> they are born. And whereas thou seest him with his eyes lift up
> to heaven, the best of books in his hand, and the law of truth writ
> on his lips, it is to show thee...that slighting and despising the things
> that are present, for the love that he hath to his Master's service,
> he is sure in the world that comes next to have glory for his re-
> ward.... This is the only man whom the Lord of the place whither
> thou art going hath authorized to be thy guide (26-27).

But Christian, his "playing" of individualistic "manhood" still to do, leaves
the House of visions without this recommended guide — forerunner of
Little-faith's Great-grace — seemingly forgetting the lesson until much
later, when the case of Little-Faith makes him see that he could have
been helped by a guide all the way, just as Christiana later will be.

Great-grace, the escort champion in the Little-Faith episode, like Ignorance, takes his name from *The Faerie Queene*, where *Contemplation*, an inhabitant of the outlying mountain properties of the House of Holiness, shows Redcrosse the vision of Jerusalem. He keeps his piercing inner vision fixed always on "God and goodness":

> Great grace that old man to him giuen had;
> For God he often saw from heauens hight,
> ...wondrous quick and persant was his spright,
> As Eagles eye, that can behold the Sunne (I.x.47).

What evidence does Part II itself offer that Bunyan is thinking of it as the female side of pilgrimage *per se*, not just as a female pilgrimage? He says so more than once in its "Apology" (see p. 147 above), which introduces Christiana's story in a bright mood of companionship and mutual help. Gone are the lonely terrors of Christian's Way. There is a sense of traveling together, of each believer's gifts benefiting the group, weak though each alone would be. Poor Little-Faith has now been rearticulated, by reiterative homology, into a whole array of appealing weaklings, women, and children tripping down the Way. The "Apology" offers a selective preview: Master Feeble-Mind will offer his arm to Master Ready-to-Halt hobbling on crutches, and in turn will have his feeble spirits lifted by a song from the said Ready, who also offers to lend one of his crutches whenever a troublesome dog needs to be beat off. Old gray-haired Honest will chip in useful counsel, and Masters Fearing and Despondency, with the latter's daughter Much-Afraid, will swell the entourage, making it less likely to be attacked. Young Mercy, who everywhere brings the group a good name by her sewing for the poor, will faithfully support her admired mother in Faith, Christiana. The described but unseen Great-grace of Part I has become the stout champion-escort Mr. Great-heart, who retains something of the aura of his hermaphroditic precursor, the emblematic Guide of Interpreter's picture. Lent by the Interpreter at Christiana's request (after a rape attempt on her),[13] he takes the company clear to the River's edge. Christiana by the later stages of the journey has, as noted, acquired the status of respected matriarch, gently governing most of the others and democratically consulting with Mr. Great-heart about decisions.

A natural question about such fine practices of companionability, gentleness, and power-sharing is why men should make them all over to femaleness and not claim some as their own. But Bunyan had to start with the gender constructs known to his audience. He could not suddenly invent new ones.[14] For his own time, Bunyan's effort was to subsume the feminine — not into maleness — but into pilgrimage, thereby creating a hermaphroditic image of pilgrim spirituality. Yet he wanted to do it in such a way as to preserve the power and conventional identity of manliness. For example, Christiana's boys of Part II, whenever they do well, are praised for manliness, and late in Part II the group sends its able-bodied male pilgrims on a foray to demolish Giant Despair's castle, for which valor each man is awarded a medal. In fact, manliness was not to be entirely forgotten anywhere in the story, piping up periodically to claim its authority.

Concerning Part II as a second instance of, this time gender-specific, revisionism, two points remain to be made, about the centrality of the Ruth paradigm and about the male-dominated ending of Part II. The relationship between Mercy and Christiana is from the start modeled on the devotional paradigm already noted as applied by Christian to ecstatic faith, namely Ruth's devotion to her mother-in-law Naomi, and thereby to the Lord. In the Interpreter's house, Mercy is told: "Thy setting out is good, . . .Thou art a Ruth, who did, for the love she bore to Naomi and to the Lord her God, leave father and mother, and the land of her nativity" (184). Like Ruth, Mercy is humble and unassuming, claiming nothing by right but simply asking for acceptance on the pilgrim Way. It is quite to be expected that she will eventually be married to one of Christiana's sons,[15] cementing the warm adoptive mother-daughter relationship that she has had with Christiana from the start. When Bunyan calls her "Mercy the wife of Matthew" he is reiterating this constellation: he considers that he has completed the development of their friendship when Christiana "takes [Mercy] into a nearer relation" to herself by uniting her with Matthew, literally enacting the Naomi-Ruth pattern by making them mother-in-law/daughter-in-law. The matriarchal power is evident, incidentally, in Matthew's lack of any "say" in this marriage arrangement — he is shown as unproblematically content with his mother's domination.

Thickstun is right, I think, that we as modern readers would expect Mercy, rather than the newly introduced male pilgrim Mr. Standfast (who indeed seems to be a male stand-in for Mercy at the end), to receive Christiana's ring in her death-bed scene. By a later novelistic logic of relationships (not to mention a submerged potential lesbian dimension to the affection that current readers may discern), it should have been Mercy receiving the beloved mother-figure's ring and then herself, the Ruth figure, crossing into bliss. (Mr. Stand-fast's River death is recounted in distinctly sexual terms as a coming to the Lord – 280.)

Clearly at that point Bunyan wanted to reinstate male salvation as conclusive and controlling by ending with Stand-fast's passing rather than with Christiana's movingly presented death. (Of course he also wanted to keep Mercy alive a while, among the younger generation who remain in Beulah-land "for the increase of the Church.") Stand-fast's last request shows that he is a stand-in or reiteration not only for Mercy as the "Ruth" model of everyone's devotional spirituality but also for Christian, the original pilgrim, and thus again reiterates the hermaphrodite ideal: he asks Mr. Great-heart to send a message to his wife and children, who did not come on pilgrimage, urging them to follow him. Thereby the male's dominance and leadership in spirituality is ultimately reasserted, after so much importance has been assigned to femaleness. Christian and Stand-fast comprise, as it were, a before-and-after framing of Christiana's faith journey, with the ending positing a kind of indefinite cyclic repetition: for all the fundamental importance of supposed femaleness to the nature of pilgrimage, men always lead and women always follow.

Bunyan has not so much "subsumed" (that would suggest a swallowing up of something then no longer identifiable) as he has appropriated the feminine – and a strong version he got – for a plebeian male-dominant spirituality and ideology. In terms of the whole *Pilgrim's Progress* this was a second revisionary appropriation: by homology he substituted the grid of gender for that of class in the basic structures of the first appropriation, that of redefined aristocratic aggressiveness turned to the purpose of working-class self-validation. Bunyan near the end of Part I, having appropriated chivalric manliness by "playing" it, sensed that he had left too far behind his audience's actual low social status, which in the "antinomy" of irresolvable contradiction (that which is "low" claiming "height") had to be restored in the narrative. The rectifying homologous female journey was his second revisionary adjustment. And in working out a libidinal appeal of the total fiction for both women and men, it effects at least four compensations across the grids of class and gender: it recompenses the male audience for the "shame" of plebeian religion and status with a redefined sense of manly assertiveness and with a glowingly valorized influence over women through appropriation and containment of things traditionally feminine within a male-framed narrative; and it recompenses the female audience for their subjugation to adult males with a matriarchal authority over boys and household groupings and with an upgrading of their anciently maligned sexuality through revitalizing its spiritually metaphoric dimension.

Notes

1. In terms of applied theory, this essay explores the part played by systems of domination such as gender, class, or race in the revisionism fundamental to intertextuality (or transpositioning) as understood by Julia Kristeva, or hypertextuality as defined by Gerard Genette.

2. My argument opposes views such as Gordon Campbell's that Bunyan in his fiction disregarded his own theology, for example on predestination, and simply let his narrative impulses rule: "in *The Pilgrim's Progress* he eliminates the truths that are set in the mind of God, such as the doctrine of election, and presents a theology accommodated to the experience and limited perspective of man" (261).

3. My argument generally accords with Thickstun's view (86-104) that Part II is "subsuming the feminine" into a male ideal, but I am working from a different analytical perspective from hers. Her often-insightful account unfortunately includes some inaccuracies. Arguing, for instance, that late in Part II Bunyan chauvinistically suppresses Mercy and her long friendship with Christiana, Thickstun alleges as evidence that she is referred to as " 'Mercy the wife of Matthew, . . . a young and breeding woman,' . . . as if the reader would not remember who she was" (103). This takes phrases from two different contexts and combines them to create the alleged import. Grammatically, the second phrase is not a tag identifying Mercy but an explanation of why she craved something to eat at a certain time (she was pregnant): "But Mercy, being a young and breeding woman, longed for something she saw there" (258). See also notes 10 and 14.

4. A usefully detailed essay by N. H. Keeble supports portions of my argument, also citing earlier work on Bunyan that sees Parts I and II as closely linked.

5. In all three homologous fictions, incidentally, grace is actorialized (in the Greimassien sense) as a key or key ring: that wielded by Arthur at Orgoglio's castle, Christian's key in Giant Despair's dungeon (see pp. 151-152 above), and Christiana's here.

6. Georg Seehase in "Realistische Allegorie in John Bunyan's *The Pilgrim's Progress*," *ZAA* 27 (1979): 211, says it was after the aristocratic-bourgeois compromise of 1689 that puritanism served, for the ruling class, to give religious respectability to its capitalist ideology. Bunyan's background derives from earlier decades. (". . . nach dem aristokratisch-bourgeoisen Klassenkompromiss von 1688-89 diente der Puritanismus den herrschenden Klassen zur religiosen Tarnung ihrer kapitalistischen Ideologie.")

7. Jeff Hearn (35-57) argues, after summarizing recent meanings of "patriarchy," that the goal now for studies bringing together Marxism and feminism should be to develop an analytical model of social structures that eliminates "dualisms" such as those of "production and reproduction, . . . mode of production and ideology," or class and gender. He praises, for example, Mary O'Brien's study, which makes the point that capitalism

permits diverse structural functions of gender, as long as the operative ones continue to result in "a cheap labour pool of women and children which can be utilised to threaten uppish unionized male workers" (Hearn 50). But for purposes of semiotic analysis, such "dualisms" are essential concepts since they have often been central to the processes of text generation.

8. My list here is close to the one Jameson includes in his dialectic definition of homology (see also p. 161 above). But while he recommends studying homology across the levels of social mimesis, style, and narrative structure within one text, I study it across the grids of different kinds of domination, both within one text and intertextually. The "elementary logical relation" necessary for a homology in Greimassien terms is in this case the contrary "submission" (will to be obliged to do) vs. "rebellion" (will not to be obliged to do); see Greimas, 144, "homologation" entry. The three layers of the triple homology here are:

A (Redcrosse)	submits to	B (Prince Arthur as grace)
	rebels against	B (Duessa)
A' (Christian)	submits to	B' (God's grace)
	rebels against	B' ("gentlemen")
A" (Christiana)	submits to	B" (quasi-divine Mr. Great-heart/Great-grace)
	rebels against	B" (evil women neighbors)

Note how Christiana's rebellion of a woman against (evil) women turns over good femaleness to the controlling male submitted to. "Domination" in Greimassien terms would not be a sememic category like "submission" but involves the sending of a "narrative program" to a subject-Receiver (see Greimas, "factitivity" entry). Jameson's statement is as follows: "[one could posit some static homology or parallelism between the three levels of social reification, stylistic invention, and narrative or diegetic categories; but it seems more interesting to grasp the mutual relationships between these three dimensions of the text and its social subtext in the more active terms of production, projection, compensation, repression, displacement, and the like. In the case of Conrad, . . . the stylistic mannerisms have the function of symbolically resolving the contradiction in the subtext, while at the same time actively generating or projecting their narrative pretext . . . in the form of a specific category of event to be narrated" (44).

9. Oppositions such as youth-age, male-female are classemes in Greimas's terms. As another important theoretical point, in adapting Jameson's dialectic sense of homology to relate not only Bunyan's Part II to his Part I but also his Part I to Spenser's *Faerie Queene* I, I am proposing a kind of contestive intertextual homology as a substitute for the "misreading"

concept of Harold Bloom's Freudian intertextuality. My proposed intertextual homology should perhaps be termed a quasi-homology, "as if" the
new text is a revisionist continuation of the first. Bloom's "misreading"
model of intertextuality, whereby writers Oedipally attack and displace
their "father"-precursors from their texts, can be thus demythologized
(compare to Julia Kristeva's gender-neutral model of intertextuality or,
as she calls it, transposition). The Greimas/Courts definition of homology (see entries "homologation" and "conversion") is already a matter of
the dynamic rather than the static dimension of text production and already contains the potential for Jameson's dialectic sense of the term,
since "homologation" in Greimas requires recognition of contraries and
contradictories.

10. Exactly such materials were excluded by the reformers when they
    declared the deutero-canonical (i.e. apocryphal) works of the Bible to
    be of no authority—such tales as Bel and the dragon or Tobias and the
    demon lover.

11. Keeble also notes this pattern, though not as deriving from Spenser and
    not noting its implied gender structuring: "If Part I had handled faith and
    hope, Part II turns to charity. But it is the same text: Christian's faith
    resulted in charity; Mercy's charity is the result of her faith. . . . in Part
    II, there is neither contradiction, rejection, nor retraction; there is com-
    pletion of the portrait of the saint" (14).

12. Thickstun says that Christiana and Mercy are meant as models only for
    women. I also disagree with her claim that the designation "mother in
    Israel" represents an "effacement" of Christiana; in context, it clearly for-
    malizes the matriarchal authority she has attained after some years of
    pilgrimage. In the paragraph just before this "mother" phrase, she has
    courageously defied Bloody-man Grim and directed Mr. Great-Heart to
    clear him off the road.

13. For extensive treatment of the rape episode see Thickstun.

14. Perhaps he has explored possible new ones: while this is obviously not
    an absolute contrast, Part I's male pilgrims more often face down some
    quasi-physical attacker, but the women of Part II more often have
    epistemological "fights" to win understanding of some vision, so that Chris-
    tiana becomes noted for discernment in emotional dimensions of
    spirituality.

15. Thickstun finds it demeaning that Mercy should be married to Matthew,
    claiming that she had catechized him as a boy. In fact it was not Mercy
    but Prudence, an allegorical figure at the House Beautiful, who catechized
    Matthew (*Pilgrim's Progress*, II, 201-02). As the oldest of four boys, all
    able to hike and to recite the catechism pertly, Matthew must be im-
    agined as near if not into teenage years at the story's beginning. Since
    Mercy is then a young woman, possibly a teenager, their ages are close
    enough for marriage later.

References

Bloom, Harold. *A Map of Misreading*. New York: Oxford University Press, 1975.

Bunyan, John. *The Pilgrim's Progress from this World to that Which Is to Come*. Garden City, N. Y.: Collector's Library, n.d.

Campbell, Gordon. "The Theology of *The Pilgrim's Progress*," in *The Pilgrim's Progress: Critical and Historical Views*. Ed. Vincent Newey. Liverpool: Liverpool University Press, 1980, pp. 251-62.

Cantarow, Ellen. "A Wilderness of Opinions Confounded: Allegory and Ideology." *College English* 34 (1972): 215-55.

Engels, Friedrich. *Marx Engels Werke*, 39 + 2 vols. Berlin: Dietz, 1956-68.

Frye, Northrop. *Anatomy of Criticism: Four Essays*. Princeton: Princeton University Press, 1957.

Genette, Gerard. *Palimpsestes*. Paris: Seuil, 1982.

Golder, Harold. "Bunyan and Spenser." *PMLA* 45 (1930): 216-37.

Greimas, A.-J. & Joseph Courts. *Semiotics and Language: An Analytical Dictionary*. Trans. Larry Crist, et al. Bloomington: Indiana University Press, 1979.

Hearn, Jeff. *The Gender of Oppression: Men, Masculinity and the Critique of Marxism*. Brighton, Sussex: Harvester, 1987.

Jameson, Fredric. *The Political Unconscious: Narrative as a Socially Symbolic Act*. Ithaca: Cornell University Press, 1981.

Keeble, N. H. "Christiana's Key: The Unity of *The Pilgrim's Progress*," in *The Pilgrim's Progress: Critical and Historical Views*. Ed. Vincent Newey. Liverpool: Liverpool University Press, 1980, pp. 1-20.

Kristeva, Julia. *Desire in Language: A Semiotic Approach to Literature and Art*. Trans. Leon S. Roudiez, et al. New York: Columbia University Press, 1980.

O'Brien, Mary. *The Politics of Reproduction*. London: Routledge, 1981.

Sadler, Lynn Veach. *John Bunyan*. Boston: G. K. Hall, 1984.

Seehase, Georg. "Realistische Allegorie in John Bunyan's *The Pilgrim's Progress*." *ZAA* 27 (1979): 207-17.

Thickstun, Margaret Olofson. *Fictions of the Feminine: Puritan Doctrine and the Representation of Women*. Ithaca: Cornell University Press, 1988.

Van Dyke, Carolynn. *The Fiction of Truth: Structures of Meaning in Narrative and Dramatic Allegory*. Ithaca: Cornell University Press, 1985.

Walch, Günter. "John Bunyan – Dichter der Plebejischen Fraktion Revolutionärer Puritanismus und Allegorie." *ZAA* 27 (1979): 197-207.

To "Undiscovered Land": D. H. Lawrence's Horsewomen and Other Questers

Virginia Hyde

SO CENTRAL IS the quest to much of D. H. Lawrence's fiction that it has been examined in the light of Joseph Campbell's famous initiation paradigm.[1] But some of his works, on traveling women, fit at least as well into Annis Pratt's model for the quest in literature by women. I find this true even though Pratt herself has contrasted Lawrence with some women writers, for I agree with Carol Siegel that he often presents a "feminized cosmos," as projected through active female characters.[2] One of Pratt's criteria for the female quest is a "green-world lover" (or guide), not especially a "lover" at all but often an animal representing "one's Pan," serving to lead the woman quester into the realm outside her everyday life—a realm in which she encounters her own unconscious and has a chance of emotional rebirth.[3] I suggest that the rustics and horses with which Lawrence's fictive women are often associated fill this role, eventually taking them into wild terrains where they seek newness of being.

His female riders evidently originate in an orthodox enough image of a Victorian "Mary" (Anna in *The Rainbow* (1915), riding meekly into Egypt under Joseph's protection, but they progress to include powerful pioneers. With such figures, he boldly revalues a long-standing Platonic and Neo-Platonic trope, which he knew well, depicting the horseman as a representative of reason over "animal" passion. In *The First Lady Chatterley*, Plato's Phaedrus is discussed by the Chatterleys, who recall the dark and light horses that chariot the soul as embodiments of these psychic antinomies; the charioteer must control the "bad" wild horse in favor of the "good" (respectively, to them, the emotional or sensual and the mental). Significantly, in this revision of the trope, the woman "sides with" the wild horse just as Lou Carrington and Rachel Witt, in *St. Mawr*, champion the explosive horse *St. Mawr* when Lou's husband tries to destroy or geld it. It is Connie Chatterley who declares that the wild dark horse has "as much right" to its desires as does the other horse or even the charioteer,[4] somewhat as Ursula defends Gerald's mistreated horse against the man's cruel control in *Women in Love* (1920). A Neo-Platonic tradition sometimes conflates the two horses and emphasizes the Platonic charioteer as the rational faculty: a recurrent emblem celebrates man as the driver or rider of horses in triumph over animal passions.[5]

This description of the "rational" horseman does not fit all of Lawrence's male riders, for some are quite passionate individuals — Ciccio in *The Lost Girl* (1920), Jack Grant in *The Boy in the Bush* (co-authored in 1924 with the Australian writer Mollie Skinner), and Cipriano in *The Plumed Serpent* (1926). The horse, Lawrence maintains, suggests power: "Even Jesus rode an ass, a mount of humble power. But the horse for true heroes."[6] Nonetheless, Gerald in *Women in Love* (1920), Rico in *St. Mawr* (1924), and even Clifford in *Lady Chatterley's Lover* (1928) — who "rides" his wheelchair in a grotesque parody of the horseman — are clearly representations of the sterile mind as it restrains potency and dynamic impulse. In contrast, the horsewoman Lou Carrington, in *St. Mawr*, is the guardian of that potency and vitality.

Lawrence inherits from the 19th century the idea that women are more emotional, closer to nature, and less "reasonable" than men.[7] Although he sometimes casts a woman as the agent of culture in contrast to a male representative of nature (as in the case of Gertrude and Walter Morel in *Sons and Lovers* [1913]), he otherwise produces some powerful heroines who embody the life force and who even, as Sandra Gilbert shows, display characteristics of nature divinities.[8] Often, too, he depicts the transformation of the cultural woman back into the natural one — or, more accurately, shows her striking a lost balance between the two. While the widespread Romantic association of women with nature and emotion constitutes a stereotype that has often frightened men (including Lawrence at times) and dismayed women, it could not fail at the deepest level to appeal to Lawrence, who blamed reason and loss of instinctive faculties for the modern world's lifelessness. In making all of his major New World questers women — several on

horseback – he reveals, in spite of some of his own anti-feminist state-
ments, his hope that instinct (embodied in such women) might save
his world from its excessive rationality.

Lawrence raises pressing issues in literary theory – the extent to
which a writer's intentions may differ from his actual achievement and
the extent to which a man can represent female experience in literature.
But it should be no surprise that it is Lawrence who raises these questions in this book about women's journeys. Probably no man wrote more
about women's journeys than he. Moreover, many women have found
his characterizations true to their own experience, although Lawrence
has also stimulated much controversy among women critics, having
been the target of some well-known feminist criticism.[9] His appeal to
many women is understandable, however, for, more than most male
writers, he worked with female collaborators and often asked the women
close to him how they would feel about various fictive situations;[10] this
practice was so constant as to be a major aspect of his creative process.
In addition, according to Siegel, Lawrence appropriated the women's
literary tradition (of George Eliot, the Brontes, and others), thereby
becoming an important influence on later women writers.[11] Just as he
turned to a number of women writers as literary predecessors, he
adapted mythology from Jane Harrison, a classicist of his time. Famous
as a writer of travel books,[12] he often traveled with women – not only
his wife Frieda but also friends, acquaintances, and followers, including
Katherine Mansfield, the writer; Dorothy Brett, a painter; and Mabel
Dodge Luhan, a writer and patron of writers and artists.[13]

For a number of years during and after World War I, Lawrence
urged his own coterie, men and women, to flee England – which he
considered stultified, mechanistic, and doomed – and to form a new
society in the New World. This scheme to establish "Rananim"– as
Lawrence called the projected utopia – never materialized, and he eventually saw no hope of such a communal venture. To his correspondent
Lady Cynthia Asquith (the daughter-in-law of the prime minister), he
wrote his belief that, since men would not improve the potential for
life even in their own English setting, women must act for themselves.[14]
In keeping with such advice, his post-war women characters often flee.
He presents in their journeys the edge of danger, of risk, of extremity,
that accompanies the necessity of completely severing old ties and forg-
ing new beginnings. Unlike the casual traveler, these women are seldom planning to go home, nor are they simply following Campbell's

quest scheme of departure from home, initiation, and return; one Lawrence title, "The Woman Who Rode Away," expresses the radical nature of their departure. This particular character's fate – her death – underscores how perilous it can be to undertake such sweeping change. Campbell's paradigm depends on an intimate commitment to the original society, but Lawrence's characters, like some of the women protagonists studied by Pratt,[15] do not find it worth the return.

Lawrence's development of the female traveler and bold, horse-riding female quester is the more remarkable because, in non-fiction, he makes a blatant pronouncement that man should be "the pioneer of life, adventuring onward into the unknown" while woman awaits him "by the campfire"[16] (a passage written in 1921). But his fiction shows how little the artist in him meant the statement. Most of his male travelers – like the bumbling Aaron Sisson in *Aaron's Rod* (1922) and the "henpecked" Lovett Somers in *Kangaroo* (1923) – are inept. L. D. Clark, studying these "pilgrimage novels," comments, "The relative position of men and women in Lawrence's ideal scheme. . .is not, in the world of the novels, the hierarchy he propounds in theory in the essays."[17] In literary criticism Lawrence advises, "Never trust the artist, trust the tale" because the writer himself is "usually a dribbling liar."[18] In this study, I therefore take his actual fiction practice to supersede his non-fiction statement.

The earliest work in this discussion will be *The Rainbow* (1915), in which Anna and Ursula Brangwen make the journey of life, often in terms of biblical iconography that limits them to patriarchal models yet sometimes lends mythic dimensions to their efforts at expanded self-discovery. I will then turn to the more active adventure of Lou Carrington, whose flight from England to America with the horse St. Mawr brings her into a rugged, even threatening Western landscape, one which she recognizes as the goal of her quest and which brings her to a kind of rebirth. In such works as *St. Mawr*, "The Princess," and "The Woman Who Rode Away," the American frontier is cast as the last-chance arena in which the characters may discard the old civilization's deathly grip upon them – or not. In these tales, then, Lawrence is the spokesman of the woman so desperate to encounter vital purpose that she will face the utmost existential crisis. Despite centering on *The Rainbow* and *St. Mawr*, this study also ranges somewhat more widely into Lawrence's tales of journeying women so as to reveal the larger contexts for these examples.[19]

I

In *The Rainbow,* marriage is seen as a journey in human advancement, and this progress requires both sexes, though the man is at least nominally the leader.[20] Lawrence's patriarchalism is often compensatory, existing side by side with demonstrations of female power (and fear as well as adoration of the Magna Mater). A specifically biblical form of the patriarchal ideal guides the relationships in many of his works, presenting man and woman in terms of biblical typology[21] – as Adam and Eve with the world before them, or as children of Israel passing through the wilderness toward the Promised Land. Lawrence's own paintings, as well as his fiction and non-fiction, depict the first parents journeying away from or back toward paradise. In one painting, "Throwing Back the Apple" (1927-28), they pause, when leaving the Garden of Eden, to toss the apple of knowledge back at God; in another, "Flight Back into Paradise" (1927), a large, rudimentary Adam helps Eve to free herself from the entanglement of modern gadgetry that blocks the way back into Eden.

In *The Rainbow* one character, Tom Brangwen, looking at a stained glass window in church, sees a vision of his life and his wife's: "He felt himself tiny, a little, upright figure on a plain circled round with the immense, roaring sky: he and his wife, two little, upright figures walking across this plain, whilst the heavens shimmered and roared about them."[22] This scene can stand as a paradigm of marriage in many Lawrence works. The two figures, "like two children camping in the plains," seem at least vaguely biblical. In this example they seem equal, and they are, of course, together: the journey of love is the journey of life. It can succeed as long as the characters retain their awareness of the cosmic setting–"the heavens" that "shimmered and roared"– and their sense of the deep mystery and glamour of life. Always they must "journey" onward, for human advancement is an exigent if not literally divine imperative; at the same time, they must not lose contact with the elemental world.

In a later generation in this novel, Anna Brangwen's life (apparently in the late Victorian era) is cast in terms of the journey of Moses to the Promised Land and, in an early version, of Mary on the flight into Egypt. The journey means progressing as a human being, not stagnating. Because her husband (rather ironically named Will) is a weak man who progresses little, Anna finds her own development stymied.

She longs to follow the sun, "a magnificent traveller surging forward," and the moon that "signalled her to follow" (*Rainbow*, 182), but she finds she can not. An early manuscript copy of the novel contained the following passage: "The sun knew, and the moon knew, that she could not go alone, save the man took her, as Joseph took Mary to Egypt" (*Rainbow*, 293).[23] Although Lawrence eventually eliminated this line from the novel,[24] the meaning of this section remains very much the same in the published version. Although Mary is the rider on the donkey in the flight into Egypt, she is the mild wife and mother guided by the man, quite unlike Lawrence's later horsewomen. By references to sun and moon (masculine and feminine), the text suggests an eternal order of things: sun and moon are both journeyers but, as the sun's is the greater orbit and as the moon gains its light from the sun, so the man's purpose, Anna thinks, should provide direction for the woman; since this idea is in Anna's consciousness, the author shows that she is herself resigned to "journeying" in subordination to her husband. But purpose is lacking in him. At this stalemate, redeemed only by her sense of satisfaction in her pregnancies, Anna's "journey" ends: "Sun and moon travelled on, and left her, passed her by. . . . She should go also. But she could not go, when they called, because she must stay at home now. . . . She was bearing her children" (*Rainbow*, 182).

Because of the children she can still feel some connection with the future, the Promised Land, so that her home seems to her like Pisgah, the mountain where Moses could see the goal of his wilderness trek although he was not allowed to enter Canaan itself. Somewhat like Noah, too, she envisions, "a long way off," a rainbow of promise: "If she were not the wayfarer to the unknown, if she were arrived now, settled in her builded house. . ., still her doors opened under the arch of the rainbow, her threshold reflected the passing of the sun and the moon, the great travellers, her house was full of the echo of journeying" (*Rainbow*, 182). An essay of 1914 shows how far Lawrence was from accepting this *hausfrau* stereotype. "That she bear children is not a woman's significance," he wrote. "But that she bear herself, that is her supreme and risky fate. That she drive on to the edge of the unknown, and beyond."[25] The very fact that critics generally find Anna a sympathetic character, empathizing with her even in her frustrations and compromises, shows how complex is Lawrence's use of the patriarchal pattern that binds her; for her case points movingly to shortcomings in that pattern.

Her daughter, Ursula, is one of the greatest female "travelers" in Lawrence's works, and he presents her this way blatantly in the original book-jacket description of *The Rainbow* (a paragraph which he apparently wrote himself)[26]: she is "the leading-shoot" of her family, "waiting at the advance-post of our time to blaze a path into the future." If she is not quite a frontier horsewoman in this passage, she is certainly an active pioneer. Whereas Anna has been house-bound, Ursula hates houses and the very idea of "the little grey home in the west."[27] Her early travel is geographically limited but significant as she moves outward from her home into the "widening circle" of school and work (*Rainbow*, 259, 413), "the man's world" (*Rainbow*, 352), and into expanded relationships that are all inadequate – but all initiatory in her passage to an unencumbered future. At last she can look "into the undiscovered land before her –"the unknown, the unexplored, the undiscovered upon whose shore she had landed, alone" (*Rainbow*, 493). At the novel's conclusion, she is the only character to have a positive vision of the future: seeing a rainbow, she envisions the transformation of an ugly mining town, representing a sordid civilization, into a beautiful new city, something like the New Jerusalem.

It should perhaps not be surprising that Lawrence casts a woman in a commanding role in this 1915 novel, for, in that year, he wrote to his acquaintance, Lady Cynthia Asquith, of his disillusionment with men during World War I. Hoping for a new beginning –"another epoch of civilisation"– he stated, "It is a question for the *women* of the land now to decide: the men will never see it. I don't know one single man who would give the faintest response to this. *But I still have some hope of the women* [my emphasis]." He even urged Lady Cynthia to consider a move to the new society with her children: "Perhaps now the true living is defeated in [your husband]. But it is not yet defeated in you."[28] It is obvious that he means a woman should act on her own without waiting for a man's guidance.

Despite Lawrence's real-life appeal for women to act alone if necessary, Ursula Brangwen is not long alone. In *Women in Love*, a kind of sequel to *The Rainbow*, she gains a husband, Rupert Birkin, and the two travel away from England together, seeking "Rupert's Blessed Isles," as one character puts it ironically (*Women in Love*, 438) – attempting to move toward this novel's equivalent of Lawrence's Rananim. During their sea passage by night to the continent, Ursula's visionary optimism renews itself: "In the midst of the profound darkness, there seemed to glow on her heart the effulgence of a paradise unknown and unrealised" (*Women in Love*, 388). The woman again travels with the man somewhat as in the biblical models suggested earlier and recalled by the reference to paradise. A certain restoration of the patriarchal pattern, perhaps of "paradise regained" for Adam and Eve, seems to have occurred for the couple. But the possible utopia, not to be found in wartime Europe even with their closest friends, utterly eludes them at the novel's end.

II

If Ursula herself is not ultimately independent of a male partner, like some characters studied by Pratt, she is the forerunner of a protagonist who is. Ursula's bold development at the "advance-post" in *The Rainbow* suggests the later Lawrence horsewoman Lou, who explicitly detaches herself from men, going to the American West in quest of fullness of life and self-identity. Ursula even has her own remarkable encounter with horses, and their meaning has been the subject of protracted debate.[29] Near the end of *The Rainbow*, Ursula is menaced by a herd of horses while attempting to make her way across a field. In her fear she has a strange awareness of the animals, "pressing, pressing, pressing to burst the grip upon their breasts, pressing for ever till they went mad, running against the walls of time, and never bursting free" (*Rainbow*, 487). These horses, running wild against all restraints, suggest the degree to which Ursula, at this point, lacks control of her own life, not the rider of her destiny but one "ridden down" by it.

But the famous Rainbow horses also function in some measure as "green world lovers" or tokens of the call to her unconscious depths. Such figures, says Pratt, are not the goal or reward of the woman's search but further her toward a recognition of stereotypes she must discard and toward reconciliation with her matrilineal heritage and self-realization.[30] Ursula is expecting a child which will, she thinks, bind her to an unsuitable man and place her in the unacceptable domestic conditions she hated in her mother's life. Contrary to the critical views that the horses represent masculine forces,[31] Cornelia Nixon demonstrates that they suggest female activity, actually signifying the pangs of labor by which Ursula suffers a miscarriage but, at the same time, gives birth to herself, a new self in "new ground" (*Rainbow*, 402).[32] At last Ursula knows that the child "would have made little difference," that she would have raised it alone without submitting to a mistaken marriage (*Rainbow*, 493). Her growth as an individual amounts to re-birth. She comes to terms not with the "man's world" or its stereo-types but, as in Pratt's account, with her female identity. It is not, of course, her mother's domestic traditionalism but a new female posi-tion that she reaches.

In *Women in Love* the actual rider is the cruel mine owner, Ger-ald, whose treatment of his horse accurately predicts his insensitivity to his lover (and his literary descendant is Lou's hollow and distasteful husband in *St. Mawr*). Gerald, the novel's representative of misguided reason and mechanization, forces his horse to stand beside a railway train that frightens it, thus attempting to bend the animal's nature to conformity with an inorganic milieu. Another horseback figure has gone virtually unnoticed in the same novel: a statue of *Lady Godiva* is the focal point of a revealing scene. The depicted horsewoman is not at all the powerful figure of *St. Mawr*—nor is she at all the defiant real-life Godiva who, in medieval English history, dared to ride naked, fulfill-ing a bargain in order to relieve the oppression of suffering people.[33] On the contrary, she is the opposite of such heroines—being a man's fantasy object—and Lawrence directs scathing satire at her creator, a degraded modernist sculptor who is the villain of the novel's late chap-ters. The rider is modeled after a small, child-like girl student whom the corrupt sculptor has brutalized before casting her, ironically, as Lady Godiva. In the sculpture she sits helpless, head in hands "as if in shame and grief" (*Women in Love*, 429), on a disproportionately large horse—one which Ursula identifies with the sculptor himself: "The horse is a picture of your own stock stupid brutality, and the girl was a girl you loved and tortured and then ignored" (*Women in Love*, 431). Even Gerald feels "some pain" looking at a picture of this sculpture, for the sculptor Loerke is far more advanced in perversity than Gerald, glorying in the subjugation of warm spontaneous life, upholding the superiority of cold, calculated artifice.

Later Lawrence horsewomen are far more powerful figures than this negative example, repudiating both the meek mother riding into Egypt and the prurient male tradition of Godiva as a sex object. Such women seem to assimilate something from the heroic version of Godiva favored by women writers of the day.[34] Four years after the publica-tion of *Women in Love*, in 1924, the horsewomen appear in a "cluster" in the Lawrence canon. What, then, does the woman on horseback gain as a character? She is in a position of some command, one that requires both trust of another creature and skillful handling of it. She is mobile, clearly ready to travel, able to change her setting. For Lawrence, it is important, too, that the rider is in literal touch with a powerful live creature, a life source. (When he taught Dorothy Brett to ride, he emphasized to her " 'the flow' between the horse and herself.")[35] In a letter of 1924 he stated, "It would be a terrible thing if the horse in us died for ever," referring to the horse as a representative of horse sense, "horse laughter," the passions, and the capacity to kick down constrictive walls.[36] Clearly he has in mind the wild horse, like that in the Platonic myth discussed in *The First Lady Chatterley*. In this work, even Clifford Chatterley feels tragedy at the thought that this horse might be "dead in him." His very rage is seen as a perverted remainder of the creature, but it is Connie who still represents its wholesomeness and vitality (*First Lady Chatterley*, 30-32).

Lawrence's interest in horses was stimulated when, in 1922, the Lawrences moved, via Australia and other points, to New Mexico. Because of his collaboration in 1924 with Mollie Skinner on *The Boy in the Bush*, he was aware of the Australian frontier on which rugged riding was common for both sexes, as it was on the American frontier. In this novel, however, men are still the dominant riders until the last chapter (one of Lawrence's additions to Skinner's work).[37] Jack, the stereotypically *macho* hero, is often seen on horseback. Suddenly, though, a female character, Hilda Blessington, rides up to him on a particularly dynamic grey horse so well-matched with his own red one that the two mate. The two animals are, in fact, described by the cosmic metaphors of sun and moon. By implication, the hero has at last, perhaps, met his match among women, one who can "keep up with him" in his wandering and unorthodox lifestyle. It is probable that this chapter embodies some of Lawrence's riding experience in America, where he wrote it.

After leaving Australia the Lawrences had accepted an invitation to New Mexico from Mabel Dodge Stern, who, during the writer's second stay in 1924, traded Frieda a remote, wild ranch for the manuscript of *Sons and Lovers*. This was their Lobo Ranch (later Kiowa), and here Lawrence, Frieda, and Dorothy—the last Rananim pilgrim—all rode regularly, as did Mabel. In a letter of 1923, Lawrence thanked Mabel and Tony Luhan (later her husband) for teaching him and Frieda to ride horses.[38] Despite a troubled relationship between the dominating patron and the irascible author, Mabel's effect on Lawrence's creative work is noteworthy. A powerfully self-motivated woman, she had moved from New York to Taos, where she took up the cause of Native Americans. At one time she and Lawrence began a collaborative work based on her life, but the project got no further than opening pages.[39] Mabel is sometimes seen, however, as one model for both Mrs. Witt and her daughter Lou in *St. Mawr,* for the heroine of Lawrence's Mexican novel *The Plumed Serpent* (1926), and for "the woman who rode away."[40] In fact, the embittered Mabel finally referred to the last tale as one in which Lawrence "thought he finished [her] up" by killing off his heroine.[41] Another source for Lou may be a character imagined by Lawrence's friend, the English writer Catherine Carswell, who, in 1924, suggested to him the outline of a tale about a woman set apart from the rest of society. The plot did not originally include the American journey, but it led to at least one Lawrence story that does—"The Princess"—and possibly also to "The Woman Who Rode Away" as well as *St. Mawr.*[42] L. D. Clark, noting that Lawrence's American questers are all women, connects them with "the Christian and pagan tradition of regarding the seeking soul as female."[43] This allegorical dimension takes nothing from the individual urgency of their dissatisfaction and search but broadens the significance of both. In the largest sense, they represent the deep, instinctive human life force that, frustrated with existing conditions, seeks out other viable directions.

In *St. Mawr,* both Lou and her mother endure a trivial round of tea parties and artificial relationships in post-war England, but they insist on riding each morning. While this is not an unusual activity among people of their class, who can afford horses, their riding clearly takes on special meaning, identifying them as active, seeking figures— especially when they befriend the horse St. Mawr, in whom they can see vivid life and even the spirit of Pan. All about them, despite the forced gaiety of life, "the dead hand of the war lay like a corpse decomposing" (*St. Mawr,* 70),[44] and people "secretly, viciously, potently undermine the natural creation. . .destroy it from the inside" (*St. Mawr,* 80). On the personal level, Lou feels "the complete futility of her living" and finds her empty, rather frivolous husband Rico "the symbol of the futility" (*St. Mawr,* 51). A young baronet, he is, like the more familiar Clifford Chatterley in *Lady Chatterley's Lover,* one of Lawrence's caricaturistic embodiments of sterile society. But St. Mawr seems to call to Lou from "another world" (*St. Mawr,* 19, 27).

Rico fails a revealing test when he mismanages St. Mawr on a ride so that the horse shies at a dead snake and injures Rico by falling backward on him. Riding behind her husband, Lou witnesses "his fear, his impotence as a master, as a rider, his presumption" (*St. Mawr*, 79). She senses that the horse waits "in vain for someone noble to serve" (*St. Mawr*, 84), and she has already realized that men are woefully lacking (as Rico's "impotence" suggests), that "the animal [in them] has gone queer and wrong" and that none can "think quick . . . as a woman" (*St. Mawr*, 61). The word "quick," to Lawrence, always refers to genuine, spontaneous vitality: thus, according to Lou's statement, men, unlike some women, lack a living, creative faculty after the monstrous destructiveness of the war. Seeing the life force still present in St. Mawr, Mrs. Witt and Lou defend the horse against Rico. To save it from being shot or gelded by "the eunuch cruelty of Rico" and his friends and countrymen (*St. Mawr*, 96), Mrs. Witt kidnaps the stallion, riding crosscountry with a groom to meet Lou; and the two women take St. Mawr by ship to Texas, where we last see him free and mated in a setting deemed worthy of him.

Commenting on St. Mawr's sudden disappearance from the story, Keith Sagar likens the horse's role to that of John Bunyan's Evangelist, who in *Pilgrim's Progress* sets the pilgrim on the path to salvation: he "awakens Christian to the realization that he inhabits the city of destruction, strengthens his resolve to sever all the ties which bind him to it, and shows him the way towards the new life."[45] Margot Norris points out, St. Mawr is an "allegory of the salvation of [the] dark, wild, true, animal self [in Lou],"[46] while another critic sees St. Mawr as one of the "tutelary presences" giving Lou guidance and having a "surviving influence" on her even after he leaves the story.[47] The "green-world lover" discussed by Pratt is similarly a transitory aid to the woman's recognition of her deep inner reserves.

Lou's journey to the new life continues. Having left her husband, country, and lifestyle, she is in search not of another mate but of cosmic forces that can give meaning to her existence. It has occurred to her that mankind is like a horse with an "evil rider," one "riding mankind past the dead snake, to the last break" (*St. Mawr*, 80). This snake is not merely a phallic image but represents the life force in both genders, the force Lou seeks to save both in the male (St. Mawr) and in the female (herself). At the same time, she acts in accord with the author's statement that "the individual can but depart from the mass and try to cleanse himself" (*St. Mawr,* 80). Thus the tangible object of her quest proves to be an isolated ranch in the Rocky Mountains of New Mexico, where she sees herself as a priestess "serving the eternal fire" of life:

> Because, after all, it seemed to her that the hidden fire was alive and burning in this sky, over the desert, in the mountains. She felt a certain latent holiness in the very atmosphere, such as she had never felt in Europe, or in the East. . ."For me [she said], this place is sacred. It is blessed" (*St. Mawr,* 139-40).

If this is not the communal utopia of Rananim, it is one of the few locations in Lawrence's fiction actually offering satisfaction to the refugee from a doomed civilization. While Lou acts at the level of lone personal necessity—even of survival—her journey has some expanding reverberations for others, at least for St. Mawr and perhaps for her mother and servants. The only nucleus of a new lifestyle, Lawrence knew, must at first be a new individual.[48] In any case, Lou's arrival at the ranch seems to at least one critic "a *Heimkehr,*" a homecoming, offering Lou a sense of "belonging" in constrast to her feeling of rootlessness in England.[49]

Yet Lou's ranch is no idyllic spot despite its "holiness," for it has already defeated a determined New England woman who tried to live there: "It had broken something in her. . . . It had maimed her for ever in her hope, her belief in paradise on earth" (*St. Mawr,* 153). Describing the "spirit" of the land, Lou acknowledges and accepts the hardships she will face:

> "It's something wild, that will hurt me sometimes and will wear me down sometimes. . . . But it's something big, bigger than men, bigger than people, bigger than religion. It's something to do with wild America. And it's something to do with me. It's a mission, if you like" (*St. Mawr,* 158).

Lawrence interrupts his account of struggle on the ranch to comment that "man is only himself when he is fighting on and on" in such an effort, "to win from the crude wild nature the victory and the power to make another start, and to cleanse behind him the century-deep deposits of layer upon layer of refuse" (*St. Mawr,* 153-4). Despite the masculine noun and pronouns, Lawrence undoubtedly includes Lou in his reference, for he casts her as virtually the only pioneer of her age. Interestingly, Lawrence has adapted the history of his own Lobo

Mountain ranch to fit a story of female endeavor, thus creating something of a matrilineal heritage for Lou. While the earlier settlers in real life had been men,[50] Lou's predecessor is a woman.

To Lawrence, the human journey always occurs between opposites of primitivism and over-civilization; having escaped one extreme, Lou will evidently grapple with the other, but she can do so with a new vitality—and with more realism than many other Lawrence seekers.[51] As for the possibility of her finding a male helpmate, it is all but ruled out. She is still in touch with one of St. Mawr's grooms, but, after all, the "green world lover," says Pratt, is "antimarital."[52] Lou declares, "Either my taking a man shall have a meaning and a mystery that penetrates my very soul, or I will keep to myself.—And what I know is that the time has come for me to keep to myself. No more messing about" (*St. Mawr*, 158). Her feeling for the land is itself erotic and satisfying.

III

Another story written in 1924 features a horsewoman whose fate is far harsher. The unnamed protagonist in "The Woman Who Rode Away" enacts a dark fairy tale, even an inverted version of the Lady Godiva syndrome. Her American location does not give her the new life experienced by Lou. Rather, it simply presents the old society in a state of entropy: in Mexico, with a mine-owner husband who is doubtless another representative, like Rico, of the decadent *status quo*, she has an overwhelming sense of nullity. Her "journey" of life had ceased when she arrived in her husband's house: "Her conscious development had stopped mysteriously with her marriage, completely arrested" (*Complete Short Stories*, 2: 547).[53] Her deadened feeling is the less surprising since her husband has "downed her, kept her in an invincible slavery," "admired his wife to extinction, kept her guarded," and refused to let her leave home alone (*Complete Short Stories*, 2: 547, 550).

The story begins with a splendid defiance as she suddenly "rides away" from all this to seek a savage Indian tribe that may, she thinks, have more to offer. Unfortunately, she escapes into the extreme of primitivism; and, as the story turns into a narrative of captivity, she becomes a human sacrifice at the winter solstice, dying in keeping with the Indians' belief that this death will usher in a new era. Although she is stripped of her clothing (and reclothed, as in initiation), the tribesmen have absolutely no interest in her sexuality, only in her utility in their rituals.

The story has been seriously examined in terms of Campbell's quest pattern (and the woman even likened to Christ in the roles of initiate and savior),[54] but its end is actually a parody of such patterns – and a parody, as well, of the patriarchal and the primitive. Although my reading is far from the common interpretation of the tale (one critic even thinks Lawrence hints at "a recovered Eden" in the village where she is sacrificed),[55] the text bears me out.[56] Before her journey, the woman had sustained "a foolish romanticism," feeling "it was her destiny to wander into the secret haunts of these timeless, mysterious, marvellous Indians of the mountains" (*Complete Short Stories*, 2: 549); this dream is completely reversed as Lawrence, who never endorsed unmediated primitivism, portrays savagery as savagery.

Revealing this quality in a typical Lawrentian fashion (as in Gerald's actions in *Women in Love*), the Indians start by abusing the woman's horse with many "resounding" blows (*Complete Short Stories*, 2: 555-56). Her own ultimate voluntarism in her sacrifice must be seriously questioned. As she begins to fall in with the tribe's plans, the woman says "what they wanted her to say" (*Complete Short Stories*, 2: 260), and the author terms her "foolhardy" for doing so (*Complete Short Stories*, 2: 260). Only when drugged intermittently on an emetic drink does she feel acquiescent. Knowing "she was a victim" (*Complete Short Stories*, 2: 577), sick at soul, she still states, "I am dead already. What difference does it make, the transition from the dead I am to the dead I shall be, very soon!" (*Complete Short Stories*, 2: 579).

Naturally, the distastefulness of this tale has not gone unnoticed, Kate Millett labelling it "sadistic pornography"[57] and Julian Moynahan finding in it "one of the most depressing images in all Lawrence."[58] Nevertheless, the story has been highly praised. Graham Hough calls it Lawrence's "profoundest comment on the world of his time,"[59] and L. D. Clark justifies it in terms of real modern crises: "any observant human today," says Clark, can see "that the life-urge of the present technological age. . . is well on its way to exhaustion" and that "the frustrated instincts of mankind incarnated in the woman [the one who "rode away"] must seek some way out of its dilemma."[60] This brings us closer to the tale's importance as a testament of crisis, set at the existential edge, the "sickness unto death." The title and the opening pages of the story present memorably the definitive image of one who journeys irrevocably, one with no desire to return home, one who flees from the unbearable. We do not need to know the specific circumstances to feel her despair. Lawrence is at his best in rendering that state of mind in which the woman knows only that "she must get out" (*Complete Short Stories*, 2: 548) – a feeling echoed, moreover, in her desire "to go out" from her later imprisonment by the Indians (*Complete Short Stories*, 2: 568). She appears consistently as someone so disspirited by the tyranny she has already known as to be unable to resist the more savage paternalism of the tribe.

Another horsewoman's story, also written in 1924, similarly inverts its promising beginning. Partly based on the story idea Catherine Carswell had imparted to Lawrence, "The Princess" presents Dolly Urquhart (nicknamed "the Princess") with a chance to be more than "an empty vessel" (*The Princess*, 31),[61] the last of a line of Scottish introverts. With "her face...turned west" (*The Princess*, 32) in repudiation of Europe, she arrives in New Mexico looking for a husband – looking, really, for any human contact that may be possible to her. Developing an interest in the wild landscape and in a guide, Romero, she makes a journey with him to the very center of the Rocky Mountains: "She wanted to look over the mountains into their secret heart.... She wanted to see the wild animals move about in their wild unconsiousness" (*The Princess*, 41). No doubt the animals suggest the deep sensuous being, the natural self as opposed to the limited superficial self, that might come to life in her. Lawrence's account of the journey is especially dynamic in this story, in which he follows the rider's perspective, as in this example:

> Sometimes, crossing a stream [she] would glance upwards, and then always her heart caught in her breast. For high up, away in heaven, the mountain heights shone yellow dappled with dark spruce firs, clear almost as speckled daffodils against the pale turquoise blue lying high and serene above the dark-blue shadow where [she] was. And she would snatch at the blood-red leaves of the oak as her horse crossed a more open slope, not knowing what she felt (*The Princess*, 44).

These vivid colors suggest the life (and death) possibilities in the wild setting. But she, having no capacity to grow or to change from this experience, becomes afraid of the journey she has desired. Similarly, when she and Romero become lovers, we are told, "She had *willed* that it should happen to her" but, paradoxically, "she never wanted it" (*The Princess*, 62). The story ends tragically as Romero is shot by a forest ranger, and Dolly goes somewhat mad, later recollecting the incident as "my accident in the mountains, when a man went mad and shot my horse from under me" (*The Princess*, 72). Her journey's failure to cause change is emphasized in that she seemingly "recovered herself entirely" as "a virgin intact" before marrying an elderly man (*The Princess*, 72).

A short story of the following year, however, shows an opposite responsiveness in a woman traveler. In "Sun," a narrative about a "health cure," the heroine, Juliet, gains in Sicily the vitality that a poor marriage has sapped from her. We have already seen in *The Rainbow* and at the beginning of "The Woman Who Rode Away" Lawrence's ability to show the sense of arrested life in a bad marriage. This is a matter given well-known prominence in the opening pages of *Women in Love*, when one woman supposes marriage would at least be some kind of "an experience" but another (Ursula) answers, "More likely to be the end of experience" (*Women in Love*, 7). The repercussions of this arrest on a woman's health are never lost on the author. The woman who "rode away" had once had to be taken to El Paso for three months when her "nerves began to go wrong" (*Complete Short Stories*, 2: 548), and "Sun" begins with the doctor's decree, "Take her away, into the sun" (*The Princess*, 116).

Sailing from New York to Sicily, Juliet not only sunbathes, as ordered to do, but develops a healing, sensuous relationship with the sun: "By some mysterious will inside her, deeper than her known consciousness and her known will, she was put into connection with the sun," and it begins "an activity which would bring another self awake in her" (*The Princess*, 125, 127). In fact, says the author, "She was like another person. She *was* another person" (*The Princess*, 123; my emphasis). In New York, she had been pale and silent, a "ghost woman," her emotions "reversed even against herself" in helpless anxiety and hostility (*The Princess*, 138). The husband, with his "little etiolated body. . .city-branded," represents the general alienation from nature that she has escaped, and the very sight of him, when he turns up unexpectedly in Sicily, throws "a cold shadow" over her very womb (*The Princess*, 134). Even he can see, however, that she is reborn, agreeing with her that she cannot return to her old life but must remain in the sun. Unfortunately, the down side of his acquiescence is that Juliet, after having mated so splendidly with the sun, will evidently have to bear the unwanted husband another child (as Lawrence comments wryly).[62]

Lawrence presents great variety in his works on women's journeys. Sometimes he disturbs deeply and sometimes he delights. Whether he depicts Anna Brangwen on her Pisgah Mountain at the end of her "journey" or Lou Carrington in her triumphant move westward—whether the housewife or the horsewoman (even the one who "rode away")—Lawrence demands attention in a study of women's journeys. His female characterizations often seem surprisingly "lived through." Anne Robinson Taylor, in *Male Novelists and Their Female Voices*, believes, with many other critics, that men, including Lawrence, cannot present real women but only men impersonating women; such male authors, she holds, must have a strong "androgynous" quality,[63] and no doubt Lawrence as an artist possesses it. But Carol Dix argues that "Lawrence's women are not men in women's clothing."[64] And his practice of collaboration with women writers, friends, and acquaintances helps to explain his characters' sense of authenticity, as does his appropriation of women's literary tradition.

Lawrence demands our attention for another reason. Throughout his works he has a profound awareness of the ancient matriarchal mythologies that he, following Jane Harrison, believed to predate more familiar patriarchal patterns: mythologies frequently dealing with traveling goddesses such as the Greek Demeter, questing for her lost daughter, and the Egyptian Isis, seeking all over the world for the slain Osiris. The tale of Persephone and Demeter is a well-known staple in Lawrence's works, including one of his last poems, "Bavarian Gentians."[65] Isis in Search appears in two late Lawrence works: a poem, "For a Moment," and the novella, *The Man Who Died* (1928). In the latter work a Christ figure, still alive after crucifixion, is healed of his wounds by a priestess of Isis, representing the Egyptian goddess. Looking at a statue of the goddess, the "man who died" sees her as a dauntless traveler, forever furthering the human race by seeking the man who must be restored from death:

> . . . he saw the goddess striding like a ship, eager in the swirl of her gown, and he made his obeisance.
> "Great is Isis!" he said. "In her search she is greater than death. Wonderful is such walking in a woman, wonderful the goal."[66]

The very term "striding like a ship" stamps her not only as a voyager but as a vessel of life's ongoing voyage. She is seen as the source of life in a double sense, both as a potential mate and mother and as an agent of resurrection from the dead. This mythic pattern perhaps suggests why Lawrence's major quest figures are women. His very belief in the power of the female myths accounts in part for his own frequent advocacy of compensatory patriarchal patterns. His continuing urgency to regain the wellsprings of life brought such strong female archetypes inevitably to the fore—in company with his horsewomen, questers themselves who act from the deep, instinctive life force, tending the Phaedran horses of the soul. "The ancient worship of goddesses suggests truths vital for the survival of the human race today," writes Pratt.[67] No English writer believed this more deeply, or with more complexity, than D. H. Lawrence.

Notes

1. See James C. Cowan, *D. H. Lawrence's American Journey: A Study in Literature and Myth* (Cleveland and London: Case Western Reserve University Press, 1970), 64-80, applying Campbell's quest "monomyth" to several tales. See also Joseph Campbell, *The Hero with a Thousand Faces*, 2nd ed., Bollingen Series 17 (Princeton, N.J.: Princeton University Press, 1968), 384-85, outlining the initiation paradigm of the quester's separation from society, initiation, and return to society.
2. Annis Pratt, "Women and Nature in Modern Fiction," *Contemporary Literature* 13 (1974): 476-90; Carol Siegel, *Lawrence Among the Women: Wavering Boundaries in Women's Literary Traditions* (Charlottesville: University Press of Virginia, 1991), 10.
3. Pratt, with Barbara White, Andrea Loewenstein, and Mary Wyer, *Archetypal Patterns in Women's Fiction* (Bloomington: Indiana University Press, 1981), 140. Northrop Frye, too, in his *Anatomy of Criticism: Four Essays* (Princeton, N. J.: Princeton University Press, 1957) also finds that "helping animals" are "conspicuous in romance," especially the horses transporting questers.
4. Lawrence, *The First Lady Chatterley* (New York: Dial Press, 1944), 30-32. For the source of the *Phaedrus* myth see *The Collected Dialogues of Plato, Including the Letters*, ed. Edith Hamilton and Huntington Cairns, Bollingen Series 71 (New York: Pantheon, 1961), 499-502. On some of Lawrence's references to Plato, see also Dennis Jackson, "Literary Allusions in *Lady Chatterley's Lover*," in *D. H. Lawrence's 'Lady': A New Look at 'Lady Chatterley's Lover*,' ed. Michael Squires and Dennis Jackson (Athens: University of Georgia Press, 1985), 173-87, and Barry J. Scherr, "Lawrence's 'Dark Flood': A Platonic Interpretation of 'Excurse,' " *Paunch* 62-63 (1990): 209.
5. See also *Marsilio Ficino and the Phaedran Charioteer*, trans. Michael J. B. Allen (Berkeley, Los Angeles, and London: University of California Press, 1981), 184-88. Related to this model is the well-known Renaissance image of a charioteer, representing reason, reigning in the untamed passions, as in George Whitney's *A Choice of Emblemes* (London, 1586), 6. Carl G. Jung, in *The Practice of Psychotherapy: Essays on the Psychology of Transference and Other Subjects*, 2nd ed. rev., Bollingen Series 20 (New York: Pantheon Books, Inc., 1966), 159, says horses represent "animal impulses" of the "lower" body.
6. D. H. Lawrence, *Apocalypse and the Writings on Revelation*, ed. Mara Kalnins (Cambridge: Cambridge University Press, 1989), 101-102.
7. See, for example (besides Pratt's previously cited works), Pratt, "Spinning Among Fields: Jung, Frye, Levi-Strauss," in *Feminist Archetypal Theory: Interdisciplinary Re-Visions of Jungian Thought*, ed. Estella Lauter and Carol Schreier Rupprecht (Knoxville: University of Tennessee Press, 1985), 106-18; Sherry B. Ortner, "Is Female to Male as Nature Is to Culture?" in *Woman, Culture and Society*, ed. Michelle Zimbalist Rosaldo and

Louise Lamphere (Stanford, Cal.: Stanford University Press, 1974), 67-87; Susan Griffin, *Woman and Nature: The Roaring Inside Her* (New York: Harper and Row, 1978); and Nan Bowman Albinski, *Women's Utopias in British and American Fiction* (London and New York: Routledge, 1988), 4-5. See also Aidan Burns, *Nature and Culture in D. H. Lawrence* (Totowa, N. J.: Barnes and Noble, 1980). When Lawrence presents women as the guardians of culture or "the spoken world" (as he does early in *The Rainbow*), he is often describing the Victorian woman's reaction against her supposed affinity with nature to the exclusion of culture.

8. Sandra Gilbert, "Potent Griselda: 'The Ladybird' and the Great Mother," in *D. H. Lawrence: A Centenary Consideration*, ed. Peter Balbert and Phillip L. Marcus (Ithaca and London: Cornell University Press, 1985), 130-61.

9. See, for example, sympathetic writers Carol Dix, *D. H. Lawrence and Women* (Totowa, N. J.: Roman and Littlefield, 1980), 12 ("Lawrence understood women, and the novels are written from that feminine point of view"), and Anais Nin, *D. H. Lawrence: An Unprofessional Study* (Paris: Edward Titus, 1932), 70 ("It is the first time [in Lawrence's works] that a man has so wholly and completely expressed woman accurately"). On the other hand, see, for example, hostile critics Kate Millett, *Sexual Politics* (New York: Ballantine, 1969), and Simone de Beauvoir, *The Second Sex*, trans. and ed. H. M. Parshley (New York: Vintage, 1974). "The Woman Who Rode Away," one of the tales with which I deal, is a particular target of Millett, 409-410. See also Cornelia Nixon, *Lawrence's Leadership Politics and the Turn Against Women* (Berkeley, Los Angeles, and London: University of California Press, 1986), dealing with the earlier period of *The Rainbow* and *Women in Love*; Hilary Simpson, *D. H. Lawrence and Feminism* (DeKalb: Northern Illinois University Press, 1982), placing Lawrence historically in the feminist movement of his time; and Judith Ruderman, *D. H. Lawrence and the Devouring Mother: The Search for a Patriarchal Ideal of Leadership* (Durham, N. C.: Duke University Press, 1984).

10. For details of his biography and its relation to his writing, see, for instance, Keith Sagar, *D. H. Lawrence: Life into Art* (New York: Viking, 1985) and *The Life of D. H. Lawrence* (New York: Pantheon, 1980); Jessie Chambers [E. T.], *D. H. Lawrence: A Personal Record* (London: Jonathan Cape, 1935); Frieda Lawrence, *Not I, But the Wind . . .* (New York: Viking, 1934); Dorothy Brett, *Lawrence and Brett: A Friendship* (Philadelphia: Lippincott, 1933; rpt. with additional material, Santa Fe, N. Mex.: Sunstone, 1974); Helen Corke, *D. H. Lawrence: The Croyden Years* (Austin: University of Texas Press, 1965); Catherine Carswell, *The Savage Pilgrimage: A Narrative of D. H. Lawrence* (London: Chatto and Windus, 1932); and Mabel Dodge Luhan, *Lorenzo in Taos* (New York: Knopf, 1932).

11. Siegel, *Lawrence Among the Women*.

12. On Lawrence as a travel writer, see Billy T. Tracy, Jr., *D. H. Lawrence and the Literature of Travel* (Ann Arbor, Mich.: UMI Research Press,

1983); Maya Hostettler, *D. H. Lawrence: Travel Books and Fiction* (Bonn, Frankfurt, and New York: Peter Lang, 1985); and Jeffrey Meyers, "Lawrence and Travel Writers," in *The Legacy of D. H. Lawrence*, ed. Jeffrey Meyers (New York: St. Martin's Press, 1987), 81-108.

13. I gratefully acknowledge the assistance of Enid (Hopkin) Hilton, a life-long friend of Lawrence, who graciously wrote to me from her California home about Lawrence's travels with women as well as about some of his interests in art.

14. See note 28 below. For the origins of the term *Rananim* (apparently from Hebrew), see George J. Zytaruk's introduction to *The Quest for Rananim: D. H. Lawrence's Letters to S. S. Koteliansky, 1914 to 1930*, ed. George J. Zytaruk (Montreal: McGill-Queens University Press, 1970), xxxiii-xxxiv. See also Zytaruk's essay, "Rananim: D. H. Lawrence's Failed Utopia," in *The Spirit of D. H. Lawrence: Centenary Studies*, ed. Gamini Salgado and G. K. Das, with a Foreword by Raymond Williams (Totowa, N. J.: Barnes and Noble Books, 1988), 266-94.

15. Pratt, *Archetypal Patterns in Women's Literature*, 141-42.

16. Lawrence, *Fantasia of the Unconscious*, in *Psychoanalysis and the Unconscious and Fantasia of the Unconscious*, introd. Philip Rieff (New York: Viking, 1960), 143-44.

17. L. D. Clark, "Making the Classic Contemporary: Lawrence's Pilgrimage Novels and American Romance," in *D. H. Lawrence and the Modern World*, ed. Peter Preston and Peter Hoare (Cambridge: Cambridge University Press, 1989), 202. See also Clark's *The Minoan Distance: The Symbolism of Travel in D. H. Lawrence* (Tucson: University of Arizona Press, 1980).

18. Lawrence, *Studies in Classic American Literature* (New York: Viking, 1961), 2, and "The Novel," in *Study of Thomas Hardy and Other Essays*, ed. Bruce Steele (Cambridge: Cambridge University Press, 1985), 190.

19. Among Lawrence's works are instances of several types of narratives discussed elsewhere in this volume—accounts of the "health cure" ('Sun'), the captivity tale ("The Woman Who Rode Away"), the allegory of pilgrimage (*The Rainbow*), the quest romance (*St. Mawr*), and even versions, perhaps not always conscious, of the Lady Godiva story (explicit in *Women in Love*, implicit in *St. Mawr* and "The Woman Who Rode Away").

20. Yet the ancestral Brangwen women had always taken the lead in conscious development, as shown in the opening pages of the novel. The question of when Lawrence begins his "patriarchal" ideal is a vexed one, but I see it already implicit in his use of biblical typology even in quite early works. Tracy, in *D. H. Lawrence and the Literature of Travel*, 15, discusses the author's preference, during at least one period of his life, for matriarchy (such as he studied in Pueblo cultures). But a number of Lawrence's works clearly show the patriarchal pattern, as suggested by Judith Ruderman's very subtitle, *The Search for a Patriarchal Ideal of Leadership*. And Barbara A. Miliaras, *Pillar of Flame: The Mythological Foundations of D. H. Lawrence's Sexual Philosophy* (New York: Peter

Lang, 1987), 188, sees the focus early in *The Rainbow* on "the father as protector, patriarch, and nurturer of the family."

21. See my book, *The Risen Adam: D. H. Lawrence's Revisionist Typology* (University Park: Pennsylvania State University Press, 1992) and my article, "Aaron's Rod: D. H. Lawrence's Revisionist Typology," *Mosaic* 20 (1987): 111-26. On Lawrence's frequent use of Adam and Eve imagery, see also Judith Ruderman, "The New Adam and Eve in Lawrence's The Fox and Other Works," *Southern Humanities Review* 17 (1983): 225-36. See also Anne Smith, "A New Adam and a New Eve – Lawrence and Women: A Biographical Overview," in *Lawrence and Women*, ed. Smith (New York: Harper and Row, 1978), 9-48.

22. Lawrence, *The Rainbow*, ed. Mark Kinkead-Weekes (Cambridge: Cambridge University Press, 1989), 131.

23. See notes in Kinkead-Weekes's edition, giving passages from the holograph manuscript (located at the Harry Ransom Humanities Research Center, the University of Texas at Austin).

24. See Charles L. Ross, "The Revisions of the Second Generation in The Rainbow," *Review of English Studies* 27 (1976): 280, and Kinkead-Weekes's introduction to the novel in the Cambridge Edition.

25. Lawrence, *Study of Thomas Hardy*, 52.

26. Sagar, *The Life of D. H. Lawrence* (New York: Pantheon, 1980), 96 (facing plate), shows the book jacket.

27. Lawrence, *Women in Love*, ed. David Farmer, Lindeth Vasey, and John Worthen (Cambridge: Cambridge University Press, 1987), 374. Ursula quotes satirically from a popular song of 1911, "Little Grey Home in the West" (by D. Eardley-Wilmot and Hermann Lohr), glorifying domestic life.

28. *The Letters of D. H. Lawrence*, vol. 2, ed. George J. Zytaruk and James T. Boulton (Cambridge: Cambridge University Press, 1981), 425, 438.

29. Nixon, *Lawrence's Leadership Politics*, 91-93, comments that the meaning of Lawrence's horses is different in different works. Cowan, in *D. H. Lawrence's American Journey*, 88, shows the importance of horses in several stories besides those I discuss: "Strike Pay," "The Blind Man," "The Horse-Dealer's Daughter," and "The Rocking Horse Winner." In the first three examples the horses represent the instinctive "animal" faculties valued by Lawrence. In the fourth example, a negative one, the horse has been replaced by a false surrogate. For some further studies of Lawrence's horse symbolism, see also Mary Freeman, *D. H. Lawrence: A Basic Study of His Ideas* (Gainesville: University Press of Florida, 1955), 46-47; Jennifer Michaels, "The Horse as a Life Symbol in the Prose Works of D. H. Lawrence," *The International Fiction Review* 5 (1978): 116-23; Ann L. McLaughlin, "The Clenched and Knotted Horses in The Rainbow," *The D. H. Lawrence Review* 13 (1980): 179-86; and Cornelia Nixon, "To Procreate Oneself: Ursula's Horses in The Rainbow," *English Literary History* 49 (Spring 1982): 123-42.

30. Pratt, *Archetypal Patterns in Women's Literature*, 241-42.

31. See, for example, H. L. Daleski, *The Forked Flame: A Study of D. H. Lawrence* (Evanston, Ill.: Northwestern University Press, 1965), 123-4.

32. Nixon, *Lawrence's Leadership Politics*, 93-100. See also Nixon, "To Procreate Oneself," 123-42.

33. Lady Godiva was an eleventh-century woman in Coventry, where the people were suffering because of the taxation levied by her tryannical husband. She told him she would do anything to relieve them, and he suggested what he supposed (wrongly) she would not do—ride naked through the town. She is associated, therefore, with both defiance and humanitarianism. Lawrence's source might be any of numerous accounts, including, for example, Alfred Tennyson's poem "Godiva."

34. See Diane Gillespie's essay in this volume.

35. Luhan, *Lorenzo in Taos*, 169.

36. *The Letters of D. H. Lawrence*, vol. 4, ed. James T. Boulton, Elizabeth Mansfield, and Warren Roberts (Cambridge: Cambridge University Press, 1987), 769.

37. Because Skinner's original manuscript (which Lawrence revised) is lost, it is impossible to be certain at all times which sections of *The Boy in the Bush* are Lawrence's; but, according to Skinner as well as literary scholars, the conclusion is entirely his. See Paul Eggert's introduction to the Cambridge Edition of the novel (1990) and Charles Rossman, "The Boy in the Bush in the Lawrence Canon," in *D. H. Lawrence: The Man Who Lived*, ed. Robert B. Partlow, Jr., and Harry T. Moore (Carbondale and Edwardsville: Southern Illinois University Press, 1980), 187-88. See also M. L. [Mollie] Skinner, *The Fifth Sparrow: An Autobiography* (Sydney: Sydney University Press, 1972).

38. *The Letters of D. H. Lawrence*, vol. 4, 515.

39. This beginning, dealing with a train trip west, has been published under the title "The Wilful Woman" in Keith Sagar's edition, *The Princess and Other Stories* (Harmondsworth: Penguin, 1971), 15-21.

40. Lois P. Rudnick, "D. H. Lawrence's New World Heroine: Mabel Dodge Luhan," *The D. H. Lawrence Review* 14 (1981): 85-111. See also Rudnick's *Mabel Dodge Luhan: New Woman, New Worlds* (Albuquerque: University of New Mexico Press, 1984).

41. Luhan, *Lorenzo in Taos*, 238.

42. Catherine Carswell, *The Savage Pilgrimage*, 201-4, gives the outline of this story. For the possibility that it is a forerunner to all three of Lawrence's stories of horsewomen in America, see Keith Sagar's introduction to T*he Complete Short Novels of D. H. Lawrence*, ed. Keith Sagar and Melissa Partridge (Harmondsworth: Penguin, 1982), 14.

43. L. D. Clark, *Dark Night of the Body: D. H. Lawrence's 'The Plumed Serpent'* (Austin: University of Texas Press, 1964), 14. Clark, pointing out that "Lawrence chose a woman for his central surrogate in the American works" (13) identifies these characters with "Lawrence's soul, speaking religiously as well as artistically" (14). He adds that the American heroines "stand near an ancestral crowd of yearning female spirits in search. Cybele,

Isis, Venus, and Freya went in quest of their male consorts. Centuries of Christian mysticism have made the soul incarnate in the form of a woman" (14). See also Rosemary Radford Ruether, *New Woman, New Earth: Sexist Ideologies and Human Liberation* (New York: Seabury Press, 1975), 45-46: "The soul or mind is normally imagined as masculine in relation to the body" but not in relation to God; influenced by the Song of Songs, "Every Christian mystic. . .took on, then, a feminine persona in relation to the divine lover. This is as true for John of the Cross as for Teresa of Avila."

44. Lawrence, *St. Mawr and Other Stories*, ed. Brian Finney (Cambridge: Cambridge University Press, 1983), 70, 80.

45. Sagar, introduction to *Complete Short Novels*, 28.

46. Margot Norris, "The Ontology of D. H. Lawrence's St. Mawr," in *D. H. Lawrence*, ed. Harold Bloom for Modern Critical Views (New York: Chelsea, 1986), 297.

47. Frederick P. W. McDowell, " 'Pioneering into the wildnerness of unopened life': Lou Witt in America," in *The Spirit of D. H. Lawrence: Centenary Studies*, ed. Gamini Salgado and G. K. Das (Totowa, N. J.: Barnes and Noble, 1988), 92-105.

48. In a letter to Lady Cynthia Asquith in 1917, Lawrence had written of his plan "to go far west" to prepare for a more communal life: "I hope in the end other people will come, and we can be a little community." *The Letters of D. H. Lawrence*, vol. 3, ed. James T. Boulton and Andrew Robertson (Cambridge: Cambridge University Press, 1984), 70.

49. Norris, "The Ontology of D. H. Lawrence's St. Mawr," 308.

50. Lawrence, *The Letters of D. H. Lawrence*, vol. 5, ed. James T. Boulton and Lindeth Vasey (Cambridge: Cambridge University Press, 1989), 110-11, refers to the ranch's earlier settlers as a man who squatted there while seeking gold and then "a man called McClure."

51. Lawrence had learned a great deal about rugged pioneering since he wrote to Catherine Carswell in 1917, "The only way is the way of my far-off wilderness place which shall become. . .an Eden and a Hesperides, a seed of a new heaven, and a new earth." *The Letters of D. H. Lawrence* (Cambridge), vol. 3, 71-2.

52. Pratt, "Spinning Among Fields," 103.

53. Lawrence, *The Complete Short Stories*, vol. 2 (New York: Viking, 1972), 547, 550.

54. See, for example, Cowan, *D. H. Lawrence's American Journey*, 170-78.

55. R. P. Draper, "The Defeat of Feminism: D. H. Lawrence's 'The Fox' and 'The Woman Who Rode Away,' " in *Critical Essays on D. H. Lawrence*, ed. Dennis Jackson and Fleda Brown Jackson (Boston: G. K. Hall, 1988), 167. Draper says the tale shows "enmity towards the independence of women."

56. See also Kinkead-Weekes, "The Gringo Senora Who Rode Away," *D. H. Lawrence Review* 22 (Fall 1990): 251-65; Sheila McLeod, *D. H. Lawrence's Men and Women* (London: Heinemann, 1985); Peter Balbert, "Snake's

Eye and Obsidian Knife: Art, Ideology, and 'The Woman Who Rode Away,' " *D. H. Lawrence Review* 18 (1985-86): 271, and Balbert, *D. H. Lawrence and the Phallic Imagination: Essays on Sexual Identity and Sexual Misreading* (New York: St. Martin's, 1989), 130-31.

57. Millett, *Sexual Politics*, 410.

58. Moynahan, *The Deed of Life: The Novels and Tales of D. H. Lawrence* (Princeton, N. J.: Princeton University Press, 1963), 178.

59. Hough, *The Dark Sun: A Study of D. H. Lawrence* (New York: Macmillan, 1957), 146.

60. Clark, *The Minoan Distance*, 310-311.

61. Lawrence, *The Princess and Other Stories*, ed. Keith Sagar (Harmondsworth: Penguin, 1971), 31.

62. One of the two versions of "Sun" contains an Italian peasant who attracts Juliet although, since her husband returns, she never gets to know him as she might have. Being glimpsed from afar, this character seems to serve some of the function of a "lover" from the "green world."

63. Anne Robinson Taylor, *Male Novelists and Their Female Voices: Literary Masquerades* (Troy, N. Y.: Whitston Publishing Co., 1981). See also Declan Kiberd, *Men and Feminism in Modern Literature* (London: Macmillan, 1985), 136-67.

64. Dix, *D. H. Lawrence and Women*, 24.

65. On the particularly female dimension of the Persephone-Demeter tale, see, for example, Pratt, "Spinning Among Fields," 112-115. For Lawrence's use of the Persephone-Demeter myth, see my essay, " 'Lost' Girls: D. H. Lawrence's Versions of Persephone," in *Images of Persephone*, ed. Elizabeth T. Hayes (Gainesville: University Press of Florida, 1993); George Ford, *Double Measure: A Study of the Novels and Stories of D. H. Lawrence* (New York: Norton, 1965), 26-60; Gilbert, "Potent Griselda," 130-61; and "D. H. Lawrence's Uncommon Prayers," in *D. H. Lawrence: The Man Who Lived*, 73-93.

66. Lawrence, *The Man Who Died* (New York: Knopf, 1928), 70.

67. Pratt, "Spinning Among Fields," 134. See also Carol Christ, *Diving Deep and Surfacing: Women Writers on Spiritual Quest* (Boston: Beacon Press, 1980), 128: "to speak the word 'Goddess' again after many centuries of silence is to reverse age-old patterns of thinking in which male power and female subordination are viewed as the norm."

Unwriting the Quest:
Margaret Atwood's Fiction and
The Handmaid's Tale

Susanna Finnell

> *I want to break*
> *these bones...*
> . . . .
> *erase all maps,*
> *crack the protecting*
> *eggshell of your turning*
> *singing children:*
>
> *I want the circle*
> *broken.*
> Margaret Atwood, *The Circle Game*

> *If they were conscious that the narrative dynamics and the erotics of*
> *reading they were expounding were specifically tied to an ideology of*
> *representation derivable only from the dynamics of male sexuality,*
> *would they not at least feel uncomfortable making general statements*
> *about "narrative," "pleasure," and "us"?*
> Susan Winnett, "Coming Unstrung: Women, Men, Narrative,
> and Principles of Pleasure"

CRITICS OFTEN RECOGNIZE in Margaret Atwood someone who writes novels of female self discovery, quest novels of sorts. The quest, of course, resembles the journey, with its dynamics of beginning, middle, and end. Like a journey, a quest embraces a linear narrative trajectory that suggests a reading pleasure based on an oedipal model that presumes as the desired outcome a reaching of the end. Presenting alternative models of narrative structures and, subsequently, alternative models of reading, are problematic since writers and readers may not yet possess the critical tools necessary to become "unstrung" as Susan Winnett points out in her telling article "Coming Unstrung: Women, Men, Narrative, and Principles of Pleasure."[1] Winnett begins to offer insight into possible ways of becoming extricated from patterns of reading and writing that do not question the positionality of the text's subject in relation to a dominant and male-inflected ideology of reading and writing. Neither would it question the reader's positionality in relation to the desire and pleasure of meaning-making. Margaret Atwood's fiction, especially her novel *The Handmaid's Tale*,[2] becomes in this essay the vehicle for exploring those issues. What happens when a writer tries an old form (the quest based on a journey motif) on a new model (the female)? What happens to the sense-making operation of the subsequent reader, who tries to come out of reading "in drag" to understand her "other" as a subject in a community of discourse?

Self-discovery in the form of the "quest or journey" is, according to Northrop Frye in the *Anatomy of Criticism*, one of the common structures akin to a symbol, or archetype. According to him such archetypes have "communicable power which is potentially unlimited."[3] He goes on to argue that these symbols are universal, although there might be "groups of people" who might have known them and then forgotten, or those who "do know and won't tell, or are not members of the human race."[4] Although she would never "tell" directly, Margaret Atwood takes issue with this supposedly most universal of archetypes, most directly in some of her poetry, but also in her novels, and perhaps especially, as I will argue, in *The Handmaid's Tale*.

Frye sees the symbolic structure of the quest at work in a three-staged movement: "the successful quest. . . has three main stages: the stage of the perilous journey. . . ; the crucial struggle. . . ; and the exaltation of the hero. . . [or] the recognition of the hero, who has clearly proved himself to be a hero even if he does not survive the conflict."[5] A beginning, a middle, and an end, generated on a narrative trajectory that implies a getting to the end. A quester may struggle inside, outside, or on the margins of a larger structure. However, at the end of the struggle, at the end of the journey, he can be, in Frye's words "exalted," or recognized, that is, brought back within the fold. This integration may occur at the level of mimesis, thematically, in the society mirrored in the story. It could also occur as a matter of form, as a narrative confirmation. A traditional quest then is a narrative wherein the ideals and hopes of the protagonists are finally mirrored positively in a prevailing, larger structure that in a sense has the means to control and confirm the production of the subject's making.

The quest pattern, therefore, fits the orgastic pattern of fiction as articulated by Robert Scholes when he writes:

> The archetype of all fiction is the sexual act. In saying this I do not mean merely to remind the reader of the connection between all art and the erotic in human nature. . . . For what connects fiction— and music—with sex is the fundamental orgastist rhythm of tumescence and detumescence, of tension and resolution, of intensification to the point of climax and consummation.[6]

But what if, as Winnett proposes, female pleasure differs? Can we presume that we all read as "men"? Could it be that Atwood refuses to comply with this pattern, offers different narrative poses, sequenced to trouble the arbitrarily "universal" understanding of correct form?[7]

While critics refer to Atwood's novels, especially *Surfacing* and *The Edible Woman*, as personal quest novels, they do not examine them in light of the narrative structure that such a quest would entail.[8] The critics ignore the fact that in all of Atwood's novels, the quest pattern does not measure up if examined against a traditional form. In each case Atwood's protagonist, although having lived through some perilous journey or crisis point, never comes back to be integrated in, or successfully adapted to, the world that she had fought. On thematic grounds alone Atwood's female selves cannot successfully be re-inscribed in its traditional notion of the place from where they break away.

Another critic, Robert Lecker, thinks that Atwood uses traditional patterns in order to expose them as sham.[9] If she uses the romance patterns, he argues, but does not provide the usual happy ending, it is for the reason that in the quest "the mythical pattern of separation, initiation and return must itself be seen as a sham in a culture where rituals have lost their potency."[10] While Lecker rightly exposes the sham of the ritual, Atwood challenges more than that. Frank Davey recognizes what so many Atwood critics seem to ignore, namely "that the comic or romance patterns are themselves patriarchal second-order constructions from which, to be 'free' in any meaningful way, Atwood characters will have to escape."[11] She not only points out the meaninglessness of certain rituals, but also the impossibility of structures that, as Davey remarks, remain patriarchal and prison-like, structures within which it is perhaps not possible to validate the female experience.

Margaret Atwood herself has undertaken an overt critique of the traditional quest pattern as a narrative structure in her sequence of poems entitled "Circe/Mud Poems" from *You're Happy*, tackling the most classic of quests, the Odyssey. Critic Estella Lauter demonstrates how Atwood rethinks Circe, the enchantress, and her presumed complicity in the quest plot.[12] Atwood envisions the old structure of the myth as a story that has become a prison, where the hero and the minor characters are helpless and doomed to reenact the same roles. The quest is exposed here as a sequenced narrative structure that repeats itself over and over, each time becoming faster and jerkier, within which the roles assigned can never be changed. Things in this kind of a space run their course predictably; it is a language game that is repetitive, and improvement of the game is not possible. The only way to change it is to undo the basic form, to break the circle. Lauter concludes that "[t]he poem is not so much a rebirth journey (there is no journey) as it is an exploration of what might happen if we *stopped* questing and made the most of the capabilities for relationship that we have 'Right now I mean. See for yourself.'"[13] Atwood implies that the quest is obsolete and no longer a powerful discursive mechanism.

With *The Handmaid's Tale*, Atwood further rethinks the quest, this time involving the question of gender. The exploration still makes use of the elements of a quest, but shakes up the form, putting it all under question: the actual journey is unseen and presented as a lacuna, the struggle is veiled, and the official validation with its parodic twist becomes a discursive control mechanism that fails. Seen this way, the narrative thematic assumes a negative presence, and the form, standing like an ironic shadow from the past, destroys its own function. The linear journey through the text troubles assumptions of sense-making, and forces the reader to look for other readings and understanding.

The Quest/Struggle

Every quest begins with the desire to be somewhere else, to be someone else. That desire is present in Offred, the protagonist of *The Handmaid's Tale*. The struggle of the quester in its most basic form plays out between two main characters: a hero, and the obstacle to the hero's success, the antagonist. Offred is caught up in a veiled struggle with the antagonist, who, mythical in proportion, does not have a face, but is the repressive Gileadean society itself. As in any quest structure, the relationship between the two is dialectical, but the reader is forced to focus on the conflict of the heroine as she struggles to come to terms with the antagonist. Our reading values are bound up with her as we move along in the text.

Offred's autobiographical rendering describes her efforts to survive and make meaning out of existence in Gilead, a repressive theocratic society in the early 1990s created following a right-wing military takeover. A female *1984*, the novel speculates on practices established by a puritanical vision for society that must assure its progeny at a time when procreation has become difficult and problematic. The most precious natural resource is a viable womb; women in the reproductive years. Assigned as handmaids to the men in charge (the commanders), they assure the future of the race. Under the guise of protection for women, the regime gains complete control over women's bodies and minds.

Free speech and free movement are not allowed. Offred, in the early stages of the dictatorship, had planned a carefully orchestrated journey to flee to Canada with her husband and daughter. This was a struggle designed to win, with every step accounted for: the daughter drugged to make it easier to get through check points, the cat drowned and disposed of so as not to tip off neighbors. The escape misfired, leading to her capture and separation from her husband and daughter and her subjugation as a handmaid to a commander whose name she is given, Fred. Offred tells of another attempt to flee. Her friend Moira outwitted the overseers at the handmaid's training center. As Offred learns much later, her friend's attempt was as unsuccessful as her own. Moira, too, gets caught and reintegrated into the new social order. Since Moira is not retrainable, and therefore presents a risk, she is placed at Jezebel's, a clandestine but tolerated brothel located at the fringes of Gilead. Both these journeys, planned and willed, failed.

All movement in Gilead is carefully controlled and prescribed. There are daily rituals, journeys that take Offred along prescribed routes to accomplish her assigned shopping tasks. These are circular, within the walls of the city, always returning her to the commander's home. She is not allowed to wander, not even with her eyes, as her bonnet-like headdress protrudes like blinders on a horse. Trips are orchestrated around participatory community events that highlight Gilead's values. Handmaids and wives gather to celebrate newborn babies at communal birthings. At "salvagings" (public hangings), the handmaids symbolically participate by touching the cord. Their direct participation is required and monitored during "particicutions," executions which involve the violent tearing apart of a man's body. Gatherings of a religious nature ("prayvaganzas") allow the groups to affirm the common belief. Attendance is required at these events; they present a structured release for such emotions as joy, fear, and anger. Offred even participates in an "illegal" outing, when her commander takes her out for a night of illicit fun at Jezebel's. But all these minor displacements are for the handmaid orderly, precise steps not planned by her, none of them fulfill any of her desires to accomplish her own quest.

She does in the end succeed, if escaping her condition is the aim of her quest. There is a successful journey that starts precisely at the moment when she gives up thinking that she can outwit her enemy. She relinquishes her struggle after having weighed several modes of action to escape (including suicide). She decides not to choose, all options being equal, none preferable. She does not save herself, but gets saved by unknown agents. This occurs the moment when she lets go of her own motto *Nolite te bastardes carborundorum* (schoolboy Latin for "Don't let the bastards grind you down"). It is the rallying cry that had been scratched into the wood by the commander's previous handmaid, who did exit by committing suicide. When fatigue has overcome Offred's will, her faith in the meaning of the motto is lost: "[f]atigue...is what gets you in the end. Faith is only a word, embroidered."[14] We only see the beginning of this successful journey as she is escorted from her room. At this moment she, and the reader, do not know whether she is being led to a better or worse fate, her last words being "And so I step up, into the darkness within; or else the light."[15]

Unlike the quest, this becomes an anti-quest, being saved rather than an exercise of the fighting will. While we see the beginning of this journey, the rest happens some place where we as readers are not allowed to participate. It remains an enigma, even if the subsequent "Historical Notes" on *The Handmaid's Tale* at the end of Offred's autobiographical narrative attest to some proof of its having occurred. The journey that has taken place becomes a lost trace, a lacuna, a negative space. It literally took place in the blank pages that separate the autobiographical rendering of her desire to be somewhere else, to be someone else, from the historical and academic recapturing and validating of her traces 200 years later.

The Historical Confirmation

Reintegration of the hero into the fold is necessary to a successful quest. Ostensibly this is what the "Historical Notes on *The Handmaid's Tale*" set out to accomplish. In an apparent authoritative gesture the Notes play on the discursive practice of verifying and authenticating the first story. But the ritual of recognizing the hero fails.

The historians depicted in the epilogue to the tale feel it to be their task to provide proof of the narrator's identity in order to establish her status as a subject. Since Offred told her story on tape, not in writing, they must rely on them as clues. Going back to the tapes' origin as far as they can, they find the U. S. Army issue metal footlocker in a house near the Canadian border that used to be a connecting link of the Underground Femaleroad (or as they joke, The Underground Frailroad). The play on the Underground Railroad no doubt parallels the treatment of the handmaid's oral account with that of slave narratives.[16] Undertakings such as these highly prosecuted journeys to freedom require its participants to cover their tracks so as not to compromise themselves or others. Or else, if traces are found, as is the case with Offred's tapes, the process of historicizing effectively questions the little evidence left. Worse yet, it may have the effect of discrediting it completely.

Having found satisfactory proof that the 30 tapes from the period of the 1980s were spoken by the same female voice, the professors are still not convinced that the tale is a "true" autobiographical rendering. Pompous Professor Pieixoto, in his talk at the Twelfth Symposium on Gileadean Studies held as part of the International Historical Association Convention (from whence the "Historical Notes" are derived), questions the nature of the autobiography because what they have now is not "the item in its original form."[17] What he refers to is his transcribed, textual version of an oral account. His discomfort about the nature of the autobiographical rendering is betrayed by his uncertainty and uneasiness on how to refer to it. "Document," "item," and "material" are safe and cautious words that allow him to keep his distance and his skepticism. The question of the tale's authenticity and its origin remains. The document, after all, is unauthored, so to say, as the "I" of the narrative never names herself, referring to herself only by her assigned patronymic name, Offred. Even worse, she never put the proverbial pen to paper to sign and authenticate.

Since there are no further diaries, and since no other evidence could be found to tie her to any relationship or family, the only remaining alternative is to inquire and link her to the commander to whom she had been assigned. The professors narrow down their choices to two, favoring one, in the process of which they are able to amplify the historical importance of both men, at Offred's expense. Neither historian can, however, add any evidence to her account; in fact, what the researchers are after is more substantiation of the Gileadean regime: "She could have told us much about the workings of the Gileadean empire, had she had the instincts of a reporter or a spy."[18] What they really want is a print-out from one of the commander's computers, the equivalent of some locus of power. They do not hear, or care about, the female voice and its struggle for meaning outside the ascribed and prescribed formula of her role by the regime.

Even though the female voice has produced a moving personal account of considerable breadth and depth about her past, present, and desire for a different life, the scholars insist that not much is known about her.[19] What counts as knowledge, according to them, is what she does not supply. The "Historical Notes" section of Atwood's work must be read with all of the ironies intended, especially the fact that the two male professors in this once and future world continue the academic practice of not reading, or misreading, or marginalizing accounts of women's experience. Accounts of such desire do not seem to fit and cannot be recognized, rewarded, and redeemed. It is fitting that this reported symposium (staged with applause, laughter, and groans) that supposedly seeks to affirm the protagonist's identity and account is in fact denying it, as the name of the place of where it is held—at the University of Denay at Nunavit—seems to indicate.

Since she cannot be named because she cannot be linked with any certainty to any male, and because the conditions under which she will "give" her name are not noticed by those at the symposium, Offred becomes a factor of uncertainty to the historian, who wishes to lift his object of research into a rationalized, historical space—lifting it, as in moving into, and as in stealing, to make possible his own narration, his own graft. The threat of the female remains though, and underlies Professor Pieixoto's misogynistic tone in delivering the paper, comprising almost the whole of the "Historical Notes." It is especially evident in the title that he assigns to the "document," *The Handmaid's Tale*, of which the professor assures us that all puns were intended, "particularly that having to do with the archaic vulgar signification of the word TAIL; that being, to some extent, the bone, as it were, of contention, . . ."[20] Precisely. This tale/tail's particular bone of contention is about this quest's other absence, the pen, linked however sardonically with penis, as shall become evident, as a locus of power and origin.

The second text in Atwood's book (the "Historical Notes"), then, in an apparent authoritative gesture, tries to establish the identity and name of the author of the first text, but fails and falters, because her voice is not recuperable in male terms as a subject. There was no meaningful position for her in Gilead, other than the one ascribed to her by the political system. Neither can she accede to a position of purpose within the ideology of history, or of the academy. It is clear that the parodic presentation of this second account plays on the discursive practice of "fixing" the first reading: it acts as a controlling fiction that seeks to appropriate the first text into an ideologically determined space. Yet the attempt to fix the meaning-making production fails because of its self-conscious presentation and the overdetermined knowledge the reader had gained traversing the linear space of both fictions. In other words, the reader knows better, and cannot settle with this ending; satisfaction must be elsewhere. The failure to produce the closure (detumescence) draws attention to itself, forces the question, and that is why the reader must begin again.

Coming Home

Reading becomes in this particular instance an adventure of an undoing. Having first moved through the retrospective autobiographical account of a female protagonist trapped in an authoritarian, theocratic society, the reader then arrives at the second account, a commentary on the first text entitled "Historical Notes on *The Handmaid's Tale*." This later body of supposed academic scholarship seeks to locate the voice of the first text within a historical framework. The two texts are at odds, each undermining the other; personal, female experience as "authority" is set against male authority of historical and academic research. While both accounts are fictional, the second text may be considered a "reading" of the first. Yet its overall tone arouses the suspicion and attention of the reader. The historical attempt of restoration and closure fails to deliver the "truth" the reader had hoped for. All that seems closest to the purpose of the struggle of the protagonist is absent.

Reaching the end of the book, the non-fulfilled anticipation forces a reflective third reading, one that refocuses once more on missing items: the voice that wasn't heard. In this segue, validation and confirmation are possible.

Despite the discursive failure to account for the subject, the first account still is about an economy of desire, a wishing to be somewhere else, inscribed in a movement of time and space that does not (or cannot) assert itself in any traditional combative sort of way. There is no winning; she does not emerge victoriously, expecting her due rewards. But most assuredly this voice looks for confirmation. Validation is sought, directly contracted by the "I" of the autobiographical account, who pleads with a "you," the listener/reader as the agent who holds the power to recognize and validate. This implied "you" is asked to confirm, mediate, and locate "the value" of this quest.

The main character in the *The Handmaid's Tale* pursues a quest in circumstances that situates her in an extreme position of powerlessness. Offred is not just barred from selective participation in her given society, but from all meaningful, self-directed participation. Since the act of writing and the ideology of individual agency and power are tightly bound together, it will be useful to examine what form individual agency and power may take in such circumstances. What sense does Offred have of her own power? With what tools, weapons, support can she hope to accomplish her quest, to find her home?

In Gilead, human drives, urges, and emotions are regulated through public manifestations. Joy, fear, and anger are supposed to replace self-generated feelings in a structured way, through publicly organized events such as birthings, hangings, salvagings, and particicution. In this way, emotions are supposed to have been purged. No one ought to want, to desire more, or to wish for a quest. Yet desire, or the pulse of the intimate body, is the fomenting fact that cannot be totally accounted for. It is the wild card that threatens to undo this society at every level. Fundamentally it is also what drives any quest.

Power for Offred is a secret thing, having to do with her own body. She is conscious of the fact that she can use her body to tease, and enjoys it like the "power of a dog bone."[21] She is also aware of her body as a commodity, and of its concomitant possibility of exchange or bargaining. She knows she would earn tolerance (if not respect) from the commander's wife, Serena Joy, if she could produce a baby for the household. She therefore agrees to an arranged clandestine mating with

Nick, the commander's chauffeur, in exchange for a cigarette and a recent photograph of her daughter (now adopted into another commander's family). When the commander requests to see her outside of their functional relationship, she knows she is in a position to extort: "It's a bargaining session, things are about to be exchanged.... I'm not giving anything away: selling only."[22] The power that her body holds gives her some sense of self.

While her body is the equivalent of currency or exchange, it is the control over her self-spun words that seems to reassure her. The narrative voice resorts to wordplay, often to just pass the time, to fill up space, but perhaps also to constitute herself. Since women in Gilead are not allowed to read or write, Offred repeats, explores, and exploits words in her mind as if they were things to try on. This wordplay is also an activity that transforms an unbearable assigned empty space into a space of a self, a fiction of a self being projected into space, or inscribed on the "blank." Words make substance, they become the flesh of her imagined and rationalized existence: "These are the kind of litanies I use, to compose myself." Or as she articulates it in another instance of waiting in her room for time to pass: "I wait. I compose myself. My self is a thing I must now compose, as one composes a speech. What I must present is a made thing, not something born."[23]

These words become limits, walls, a way to fence in the self, and a way to create something to fill the unbearable empty space of herself. There is an empowering sense in the fiction of this self-composed fact. It's her way to escape: "Where should I go?" she asks, as she faces another lonely night in her room.[24] It is her way to travel back to her past, to her lost daughter, mother, and husband, as well as into the future and possible better times. But it is a fiction, and the narrating self knows it.

The power words hold is translated in the forbidden scrabble game. The commander requests to see her secretly, but not to have uninhibited or non-prescribed sex. What he asks for instead is a game of scrabble. The squares that hold the letters of the scrabble game are magical to Offred, full of promise: "The feeling is voluptuous. This is freedom, . . . luxury."[25] She compares the feeling to the taste of edible things: candies, peppermint, humbugs, tartness of lime. She would like to taste the words, put them in her mouth. As she continues to play scrabble on consecutive evenings, the words associate with things of the past, bodily pleasures associated with eating: "My tongue felt thick with the effort of spelling. It was like using a language I'd once known but had nearly forgotten, a language having to do with customs that had long before passed out of the world: café au lait at an outdoor table, with a brioche, absinthe in a tall glass, or shrimp in a cornucopia of newspaper; things I'd read about once but had never seen."[26]

The sensuousness or fleshliness of words, their power, is even greater when she is given the first opportunity to write with a pen in the commander's library:

> The pen between my fingers is sensuous, alive almost, I can feel its power, the power of the words it contains. Pen Is Envy, Aunt Lydia would say, quoting another Center motto, warning us away from such objects. And they were right, it is envy. Just holding it is envy. I envy the Commander his pen.[27]

The unnamed female voice, with this tongue-in-cheek reference to penis envy (and implicitly to oedipal models), knows about the use and promise of words and the stories they can make up. She knows exactly what she can do with it, and how far she can go with it. She knows she can provide the illusion, and that she can destroy the illusion, which she does as the narrator of the multiple, unreliable versions of her night with Nick, who becomes her secret lover.

When and how exactly her story gets recorded, not with a pen on paper but with a microphone and tape, we do not know. But we do know that the story is made like a pleading, offered to someone called "you." It is intended to reach an invented "you"– her husband Luke (who is probably dead), or someone like a lover, but intended also for any reader, the historians, for example, or just "you," the reader:

> But if it's a story, even in my head, I must be telling it to someone. You don't tell a story only to yourself. There's always someone else.
>> Even when there is no one.
>> A story is like a letter. DEAR YOU, I'll say. Just YOU, without a name. Attaching a name attaches YOU to the world of fact, which is riskier, more hazardous: who knows what the chances are out there, of survival, yours? I will say YOU, YOU, like an old love song. YOU can mean more than one.
>> YOU can mean thousands.[28]

In this relationship of her self and her presumed listener/reader she places her hope for understanding and confirmation. "You" is refused a name, just as is the narrating "I." Perhaps her addressing the interlocutor as the "you" of a popular love song seeks a more direct communication. It counts on a relation of trust, one within which it will be possible to release the name, just as she told Nick, whom she so desperately trusted and loved, "I tell him my real name, and feel that therefore I am known."[29] It is not the "you" of the "world of fact," because then "you" would be like a word, like a structure that is enclosed. She wants a receptive "you" that, like the extending "I," exists in some other kind of understanding. A "you" that can hear, under the right circumstances. A "you" of the underworld, just like the "I."

> I keep on going with this sad and hungry and sordid, this limping and mutilated story, because after all I want you to hear it, as I will hear yours too if I ever get the chance, if I meet you or if you escape, in the future or in heaven or in prison or underground, some other place. What they have in common is that they're not here. By telling you anything at all I'm at least believing in you, I believe you're there, I believe you into being. Because I'm telling you this story I will your existence. I tell, therefore you are.[30]

The "chance of survival" depends somehow on the presence of this "you," who may be able to hear this underground communication that insinuates itself into and through the language, one that is more erotic than the world of fact.[31]

The loyalty articulated by the speaking subject must remain open to an active process. This moment ceases when her desire is consummated in her sexual relation with Nick. Desire consummated asks for more, and she goes back to Nick over and over, not just for the mating arranged by Serena Joy to produce a child, but for her own pleasure, illicitly and illegally. She did it for herself, she says, and each time the meeting is taken as if it is the last ever, each became "always a surprise, extra, a gift."[32] But she feels a need to apologize: "I would like to be without shame. I would like to be shameless."[33] She sees that moment as reader betrayal: "And I thought afterwards: this is a betrayal. Not the thing in itself but my own response."[34] While she clearly thinks this in relation to Luke, as a sort of explanation and apology to her husband, should he still be alive, this explanation also includes the reader. It's adultery, and it is co-extensive with the illusion of having control over one's textual and sexual representation.

She asks the interlocutor, her "you," for forgiveness: "[y]ou'll have to forgive me. I'm a refugee from the past, and like other refugees I go over the customs and habits of being I've left or been forced to leave behind me, and it all seems just as quaint, from here, and I am just as obsessive about it."[35] Clearly she invests the reader with the power to forgive: "remember that forgiveness too is a power. To beg for it is a power, and to withhold or bestow it is a power, perhaps the greatest."[36] This apology insists that even while she makes herself into a subject—a composed fact—she wishes to refuse the illusion of a stable identity, because whatever that would be would be false. It would be an instance of dominant static space, over the active, subversive relationship, and it would be betrayal, of Luke, of the reader. Nevertheless, is this not the very act that begs for understanding, integration, and confirmation? The one act that redeems the quest?

This is where the story ends. Like so many of Atwood's endings it is awkward, forced and faked, but that is again conscious strategy: "[d]on't be deluded by any other endings, they're all fake, either deliberately fake, with malicious intent to deceive, or just motivated by excessive optimism if not by downright sentimentality."[37] In some sense Offred's voice is guilty of representation, of truth, and that is what she apologizes for. In the interest of the plot she had to serve up her own body, to which we as reader respond and follow in an itinerary of our own pleasure. We as reader participate in the staging of her body, in this foregrounding of her mental torment. We consume her body of desire and its hoped-for fulfillment, and our pleasure in this activity is not innocent. To witness the spectacle of her body, of her secret mind, to follow her desire that cannot close, we possess as readers a certain power. The reader is in the position to understand the means—the linear space of the narration—to which she must resort to make her story, a tricky space that could be seen as static. But the reader also has the option of understanding this unfolding as an experience in space and time, as a process that subverts the logic of the static space.

The Handmaid's Tale, with its strategy of narrative techniques, sets out to break the circle of discursive closure in the traditional quest structure. Atwood's strategy challenges the notion of the quest based on the conquest of identity achievable through mastery of speech, language, and subject. Just as she consciously excludes the journey toward a new identity, she also disallows confirmation of the identity of the subject within an ideologically situated framework. Confirmation of the subject would result in the freezing of the subject as its own system, as well as in its appropriation into a larger structure or system. Margaret Atwood moves beyond this structuring appropriation.

Rather than letting the text exercise the contract of confirming the subject, she places this responsibility into the hands of the reader. Unlike the historians, we can validate, confirm, and bring home (that is, understand) this journey for what it is: a ritual of different narrative erotics, of reading otherwise.

Notes

1. Susan Winnett, "Coming Unstrung: Women, Men, Narrative and Principles of Pleasure," *PMLA* (May 1990): 505-518.
2. Margaret Atwood, *The Handmaid's Tale* (Boston: Houghton Mifflin Company, 1986).
3. Northrop Frye, *Anatomy of Criticism: Four Essays* (Princeton: Princeton University Press, 1973), 118.
4. *Ibid.*
5. *Ibid.*, 187.
6. As quoted in Winnett, "Coming Unstrung," 506.
7. Is it coincidence that Atwood in *The Handmaid's Tale* uses the words "traveling" and "journey" most consciously within a male sexual context? Referring to the male organ as an "eye" that is "traveling forward. . .avid for vision"? (p. 88) Sex becomes a means by which to gain vision and is a "journey into a darkness that is composed of women, a woman, who can see in darkness while he himself strains blindly forward" (p. 88). Twice the narrator describes the commander as "intent on his inner journey, that place he is hurrying towards, which recedes as in a dream at the same speed with which he approaches it" (p. 95) and later seeing him on "his single-minded journey" (p. 162).
8. Annette Kolodny enlists Atwood in *The Edible Woman* as a writer who depicts her female protagonist as "discovering herself," or as becoming woman. See "Some Notes on Defining a 'Feminist Literary Criticism,' " in *Feminist Criticism: Essays on Theory, Poetry and Prose*, edited by Cheryl L. Brown and Karen Olson (Metuchen, N.J. & London: The Scarecrow Press, Inc., 1978) 42, 26. R. L. Widmann discusses the search of the main protagonist in *Surfacing* as a search "away from civilization in search of her father and her self" in "The Poetry of Cynthia Macdonald" in *Ibid.*, 191. In addition, *Surfacing* is read as a quest novel by Catherine McLay; as a "woman's rebirth fiction" by Annis Pratt; while Barbara Rigney declares that in this novel the protagonist woman "can descend and return, sane, whole, victorious." Cited in Frank Davey, *Margaret Atwood: A Feminist Poetics* (Vancouver: Talonbooks, 1984). Elizabeth A. Meese in *Crossing the Double-Cross* (Chapel Hill and London: The University of North Carolina Press, 1986), p. 124 finds that the central character in *Surfacing* "attempts a female self-definition."
9. Robert Lecker, "Janus Through the Looking Glass: Atwood's First Three Novels," in *The Art of Margaret Atwood: Essays in Criticism*, ed. Arnold Davidson and Cathy N. Davidson (Toronto: Anasi, 1981).
10. *Ibid.*, p. 194.
11. Davey, *Margaret Atwood: A Feminist Poetics*, 62.

12. Estella Lauter, "Margaret Atwood: Remythologizing Circe," in *Women as Mythmakers: Poetry and Visual Art by Twentieth-Century Women* (Bloomington: Indiana University Press, 1984), p. 62-78. See also the discussion of this poem using a "revisionary strategy . . . to gain release from a colonial tale" by Rachel Blau Du Plessis in *Writing Beyond the Ending: Narrative Strategies of Twentieth-Century Women Writers* (Bloomington: Indiana University Press, 1985), 110-112.

13. Estella Lauter, "Margaret Atwood: Remythologizing Circe," in *Women as Mythmakers: Poetry and Visual Art by Twentieth-Century Women* (Bloomington: Indiana University Press, 1984) p. 76.

14. Atwood, *Handmaid's Tale*, 292.

15. *Ibid.*, 295.

16. See, for example, Thomas F. Soapes's discussion on the value of oral histories of slavery in "The Federal Writers' Project Slave Interviews: Useful Data or Misleading Source" in *The Oral History Review*, 1977.

17. Atwood, *Handmaid's Tale*, 300.

18. *Ibid.*, 310.

19. *Ibid.*, 305.

20. *Ibid.*, 301.

21. *Ibid.*, 22.

22. *Ibid.*, 138.

23. *Ibid.*, 66.

24. *Ibid.*, 37.

25. *Ibid.*, 139.

26. *Ibid.*, 156.

27. *Ibid.*, 186.

28. *Ibid.*, 40.

29. *Ibid.*, 270.

30. *Ibid.*, 268.

31. Davey elaborates on Atwood and her concept of "underground" as being one of her most important signs in her poetry, one that asserts "the dominance of temporally active space over static space, of the female over the male." Time and process become subversive, and subsist beyond traditional space.

32. Atwood, *Handmaid's Tale*, 268.

33. *Ibid.*, 263.

34. *Ibid.*

35. *Ibid.*, 227.

36. *Ibid.*, 135.

37. Margaret Atwood, *Murder in the Dark* (Toronto: Coach House Press, 1983), 40.

Housekeeping in the Western Tradition: Remodeling Tales of Western Travelers

Sheila Ruzycki O'Brien

IN HIS 1893 SPEECH, "The Significance of the Frontier in American History," Frederick Jackson Turner said about the American character that "movement has been its dominant fact" (Turner 228). A sense of movement has indeed dominated fictional and historical narratives of the American West, and various narrative patterns are recognizable as part of the genre of the Western. Yet just as canonized American literature provides a limited sense of what is distinctly American, traditional Westerns provide a limited sense of Western life and stories.[1] In her novel *Housekeeping*, set chiefly in Idaho, Marilynne Robinson incorporates and refigures patterns evident in canonical and non-canonical literature, and her reshaping of travel narratives of the American West is particularly striking. Robinson earned a doctorate in literature before writing the novel, and she was raised in the Northwest, so her reshaping of canonical and non-canonical Western stories — from *Adventures of Huckleberry Finn* to *Shane* — is not surprising. Critical attention, however, has focused largely on *Housekeeping's* feminist qualities at the expense of its relationship to a wide range of texts, including classic male adventure tales. Martha Ravits does note Robinson's debt to both "aunts and uncles," but Ravits chiefly relates *Housekeeping* to the Transcendental tradition and not to the Western (Ravits).[2] *Housekeeping* clearly claims kin with Western travel stories, yet Robinson's approach is distinct;[3] she makes her central travelers anti-hierarchical female "drifters" and emphasizes the sustained bond between them which mitigates their sense of isolation.

One Western pattern that permeates *Housekeeping* is that of the lone traveler/adventurer. The adventurer appears in fictional narratives as well as in history turned legend, and is almost always a male figure. Jane Tompkins notes "the importance of manhood is an ideal" in Westerns. "It is not one ideal among many," she claims, "it is *the* ideal" (Tompkins, 17-18). Martin Green concurs that Westerns are a mainstay of the gender-defining adventure-tale genre, which

> has been the main literary means by which males have been taught to take initiatives, to run risks, to give orders, to fight, defeat, and dominate; while females have been taught, both by being ignored by the genre and by being reduced to passive roles within it, *not* to do those things (Green, 1-2).

Lone adventurers are legion within the genre of the Western: Daniel Boone, the trailblazer who escapes from Indians and always yearns for more "elbow room;"[4] Jim Beckwourth, the son of a slave who became a famous mountain man, scout, and member of the Crow tribe (marrying a series of Crow women before heading out to California);[5] Shane, the good-hearted gunslinger of both novel and screen, riding off into the sunset away from civilization before he gets too emotionally involved there; and Ethan Edwards (played by John Wayne) in *The Searchers*, who quietly learns something about love and acceptance before lumbering through the homestead door and off into the sunset alone. These men and many others reject the possibility of sustained relationships in favor of adventure and freedom from social constriction.

Robinson uses some aspects of the classic Western loner, both in creating the family background of Ruth, the narrator, and in detailing how Ruth and her transient aunt, Sylvie, revise this pattern. Loners who avoid the constrictions of town society comprise Ruth's known ancestry; all her forebears, both male and female, with the exception of her grandmother and great aunts, were travelers. They were also all lonely or disconnected from affection, and by the time Ruth reaches her teens all are dead or gone. The first loner/ancestor Ruth discusses in detail is her grandfather. While Elizabeth Meese, Thomas Foster, and Phyllis Lassner all claim that men are only marginal or merely a point of departure left behind in *Housekeeping*, the centrality of Ruth's grandfather Edmund as a solitary ancestral quester, evidenced by Ruth's recurrent visions (and her revisions) of him, clearly counters this. Edmund looms as a mythic Westerner in the novel, a man known to Ruth only through others' tales of him. Ruth focuses much of the opening of her book on her grandfather, on his yearning for mountain heights during his childhood in a subterranean house on the plains, on his journey west in search of mountains, and on his life as a railroad man based in the northern Idaho community of Fingerbone.[6]

Robinson also links Edmund's loner status to a rejection of society's strict gender code, and so this railroad man prefigures the remodeling of the classic loner figure that Robinson will accomplish in both Ruth and Sylvie. Edmund possesses an artistic soul as well as an adventurous spirit, and, to a limited extent, defies the societal norms of masculinity. Contrary to Turner's definition of the frontier man as "lacking in the artistic" (Turner, 228), not only does Edmund paint, he even embellishes one of the bibles of cultural order—the dictionary—in a poetic way, by filling it with wildflowers. (He does attempt to put the flowers in alphabetical order.) He also walks long distances from town to see beautiful wildflowers, and tries—unsuccessfully—to replant them at home.

Ruth's meditative narrative often focuses on Edmund's intense individualism. Ruth imagines that after his death (in a train that slips into Fingerbone Lake), her grandmother, Sylvia, accepted his disappearance as part of his life's pattern: his death "seemed to her a kind of defection, not altogether unanticipated. How many times had she waked in the morning to find him gone?" (Robinson, 10). Ruth also envisions Edmund and Sylvia on walks together, Sylvia imagining her husband as a wild man, "a soul all unaccompanied" (17), more alarming than death as he calmly puts fragments of once-living things into his pockets and forgets about all civilization—including herself.

No sharp distinctions exist between male and female travelers in Robinson's novel, and women as well as men are isolates, characters disconnected from emotional bonds. While Sylvia does not travel beyond the woods near Fingerbone, she does think of her life "as a road down which one traveled, an easy enough road through a broad country, and that one's destination was there from the beginning." (9). Although she is not adventurous, Sylvia shares the family's loner qualities, both spiritually and then physically, through abandonment. She likes her husband Edmund best on their sojourns in the woods because his solitary soul reminds her of her own; she does not "resent" his "wordless and impersonal courtesy. . . because she had never wished to feel married to anyone" (17). Sylvia enjoys her daughters' presence, but does not teach them "to be kind to her"; instead, she fosters their independence, their "unconsciousness" of her own desires or of others' (19, 18). After her three daughters leave her, Molly for a missionary's life in China, Sylvie to become a transient, and Helen first for marriage and then finally by committing suicide, Sylvia does not become a social person, but instead clings to ordinary household chores to give her a sense of stability and of autonomy in her socially unstable world.

Sylvia's daughter Helen (Ruth's mother) is indeed her parents' child, another loner who reaches out to no one. She marries a man who "traveled" (52), and who, in one classic loner tradition, abandons his family. Like her mother, Helen takes a material approach to her children's security, tying anchored clothesline through their belts to keep them from tumbling from a high porch. Yet emotional ties are tenuous. In fact, during her short life she is apparently disconnected from any strong bonds. After getting stuck in the mud, she calmly eats strawberries until she solicits a push and drives into the lake, and so, like her father, takes a lonely trip to the bottom.

Sylvia's loner perspective continues beyond her relationship with her daughters and is especially prominent in her relationship with her granddaughters, Ruth and Lucille. Sylvia does not attempt to form emotional bonds with the children, but she does have nightmares in which the symbols of good housekeeping prove ineffectual during disaster, particularly travel-related disasters: she tries to catch a baby in her apron after it fell from an airplane, and she attempts to save a baby who had fallen down a well by employing a tea strainer. While her dreams tell her of the dangers of unaccompanied travel for children, she reads them only on a material level. She watches her grandchildren, Ruth and Lucille, and cares for their needs. She feels helpless, however, knowing that her "scrupulous care" is not enough, but not knowing what else to do (25). By living a life in which the female role of supposedly secure housekeeper uneasily coexists with her spiritual lonesomeness, Sylvia, too, portends Ruth and Sylvie's remodeling of the Western loner pattern.

Edmund's sisters, Lily and Nona, are women who are adamantly neither travelers nor adventurers; they form the antithesis of the loner tradition, to the point of finishing each other's sentences. In Stephen Greenblatt's view of culture as shaped by the dynamic interplay between "constraint" and "mobility"—cultural forces between which individuals must negotiate—Lily and Nona have both internalized the concept of constraint. For them the world is a place fraught with dangers, and so they are extreme versions of the staid, overly strict representatives of the church and the law who inhabit *Housekeeping* as well as most classic Westerns. When Sylvia dies they care for her grandchildren briefly, but while they would like to instill their sense of correct female behavior in Ruth and Lucille, they find the movements and imagined movements of both the children and their rickety old house in Fingerbone too disconcerting. They scuttle back to the more controlled society of their child-free apartment building and regain their basement apartment—the subterranean life their brother had fled— when substitute child care arrives in the form of Sylvia's daughter, the supposedly reformed transient, Sylvie. While Lily's and Nona's joined lives and their lack of a social network foretell Sylvie's and her niece Ruth's future bond, their terror of taking risks and of moving in the world indicate the life that Ruth eventually escapes. Their behavior echoes the fear-ridden early stage of Ruth's development, before Sylvie helps her to accept her fears so that she can travel more freely. As embodiments of "constraint," they form the opposition to Sylvie's solitary "mobility" before she returns to Fingerbone and to her nieces.

The bond that Robinson develops between Ruth and Sylvie incorporates and refigures the pattern of the Western loner evident in Ruth's family. They reject extreme isolation, isolation that resulted in suicide and abandonment, and they also reject intensive care for material things. While the women maintain their loner status, this solitude is linked to sharing, and to an emotional bond that allows for one's inherent lonesomeness.

This bond develops slowly. At first Ruth's and Lucille's wandering aunt exhibits the family tendency to remain isolated. Recipient of her mother's training for independence and endowed with her father's wandering feet, for a while after her arrival she seems chiefly concerned with her own world rather than with that of her dependent nieces. The girls, trying to cajole her into a parental role, skip school for weeks, but to no avail. Yet, Ruth recalls, Sylvie does seem pleased by her familial status even on the first night of her return, after Lily and Nona had contacted her about her mother's death and her nieces' presence in Fingerbone:

> I remember that, as she sat there in a wooden chair in the white kitchen, smoothing her borrowed-looking dress and working her feet out of her loafers, sustaining all our stares with the placid modesty of a virgin who has conceived, her happiness was palpable (49).

This passage practically shouts out problems with Sylvie's initial relation to her recovered family, as she expresses contentment without involvement.

Sylvie's sense of contentment within a semi-traditional family structure as well as within the walls of a house and the walls of a restrictive society is fleeting. At root she is a loner. Even her continuing bond with Ruth is, Ruth claims, based on her desire to keep Ruth's image from multiplying via loss and further invading her privacy. Ruth reflects on Sylvie's state of mind after Lucille leaves home:

> Sylvie did not want to lose me. She did not want me to grow gigantic and multiple, so that I seemed to fill the whole house, and she did not wish me to turn subtle and miscible, so that I could pass through the membranes that separate dream from dream. She did not wish to remember me. She preferred my simple, ordinary presence. . . . She could forget I was in the room. . . . But if she lost me, I would become extraordinary by my vanishing (195).

While Sylvie prefers not to be haunted by Ruth, she does acknowledge the anguish both she and Ruth feel at Lucille's abandonment and the implied haunting that goes along with such absence.

This desire for solitude coupled with her sympathy for Ruth helps Sylvie learn to be a guide and a companion. Before Lucille moved out, Sylvie had occasionally cared for her nieces, but her care, like her housekeeping, was off-handed. Only after Lucille leaves home for the supposed normality of life with the home economics teacher does Sylvie take action, not only for Ruth's sake, but also for her own. Wanting to create a tighter bond, Sylvie takes Ruth on a journey away from civilization. Ruth plays hookie on a day that Sylvie knows is a test day, the first morning after Lucille's abandonment is certain. Sylvie awakens her niece before dawn and cajoles her to go forth into the cold, night world, leaving behind the comfort of her bed and home.

Sylvie teaches Ruth through sharing her experience, an empathetic, traditionally female approach to knowledge Mary Field Belenky calls "connected knowing" (Belenky, 112-130). Sylvie shares her experience of solitude and of the ensuing acceptance and fearlessness by telling Ruth narratives of her wandering life and by letting her niece experience it first-hand.

The two travel in a stolen boat (reminiscent of Huck Finn's stolen boats and rafts, and emphasizing the travelers' extra-legal status) to a deserted homestead where Sylvie leaves Ruth, encouraging her to look for "lost children." The beauty of the valley as the frost becomes fluid begins to warm Ruth, who imagines that lost children could find love here. Soon, however, she is overcome by a sense of lonesomeness. Once before, when she spent a night in the woods with Lucille, Ruth felt the boundaries between herself and nature fade. As she notes, however, "[h]aving a sister or a friend is like sitting at night in a lighted house" (154), and here she was alone, uselessly seeking shelter in the ruins of an abandoned homestead. While Ruth feels the presence of lost, solitary children, the only lost child she confronts is herself, separated from the dead children and her dead mother by her living body. As Ruth tells Sylvie of her failure to find the other lost children, her aunt rocks her, responding to their shared lonesomeness by repeatedly crooning "I know, I know" (160). Sylvie guides her to accept her losses and to accept that houses cannot shelter the soul. She puts her oversized traveler's coat over Ruth to protect her from the cold—but it is more than a mere garment. Ruth wears the coat "like beatitude" and feels that Sylvie's arms about her "were as heartening as mercy" (161). The coat also signals that Ruth has moved beyond Lucille's world, the realm of pre-cut patterns for stylish matching outfits; she has become a fellow lone traveler and an acknowledged outsider. The town dogs recognize Ruth's new status immediately (and harass the girl), just as the boy Joey in the book and movie *Shane* knows (probably seeing by his outfit) that Shane is not a farmer but an itinerant gunslinger.

While their boat floats by the railroad bridge at the spot where Edmund's train derailed and sank, and after the two have hummed "Goodnight, Irene," Sylvie gives Ruth another lesson in accepting fear, death, and lonesomeness. It is this acceptance that provides the basis for friendship. Sylvie scoops up water that had seeped into the boat and says, "There is nothing to be afraid of. . . . Nothing to worry about. Nothing at all. . . . The lake must be full of people" (168). Instead of having nightmares about those drowned, Ruth's next sleep brings a dream of accepting a new way of life, envisioning

> that Sylvie was teaching me to walk under water. To move so slowly needed patience and grace, but she pulled me after her in the slowest waltz, and our clothes flew like the robes of painted angels (175).

This first overnight journey firmly knits together Ruth and Sylvie— and they stand together against the forces of the traditional community. This community tries to separate Ruth from her unconforming aunt, presuming, as one churchwoman says, that for girls, an "orderly life"

(185) is essential, and, in particular, they should not travel in unacceptable ways or at unusual times. The concerned churchwomen, humanized versions of the women's moral society in the 1939 film *Stagecoach*, are upset by Ruth and Sylvie's having caught a ride on a freight car; they are even more disconcerted by their discovery that the two had spent the entire night in a boat. While an overnight trip by a boy and an older male relative would likely not have caused such worry, females, traditional representatives of stability, become frightening when mobile. Sylvie and Ruth threaten the town's tidy sense of itself – much like the moving flood waters that invade rigorously tidy households and yards and disrupt the town's desire for security and certainty. The text, however, counters the town's desire; as Anne-Marie Mallon notes, "*Housekeeping* says that transience, not fixity, is our natural human condition" (Mallon 97).

As Ruth grows to maturity, her acceptance of her quirky female "otherness"– an otherness related to that of the Western loner – leads her to break her family pattern of emotional isolation and welcome the companionship of her sister outsider, her aunt Sylvie. Emotionally bonded with Sylvie, Ruth refuses to join the Fingerbonians; she knows "[i]t is a terrible thing to break up a family" (190), and she flatly refuses to let the sheriff lure her away from Sylvie to his house with the promise of his wife's home-made apple pie. Because Sylvie and Ruth either cannot or have no wish to maintain a highly constrained, ordered, hierarchical lifestyle, they flee. However, they do maintain their union by living outside established society and its norms and requirements.

In fact, in Robinson's revised myth of Western travelers, the community of two women overturns a sense of hierarchy. In her analysis of feminist revisionist mythmaking, Alicia Ostriker has noted that emotional bonding can be "derived from acknowledged likeness, not from the patriarchal relationships of dominance and submission" (Ostriker, 327). In traditional Western narratives, cross-racial bonds between travelers are common but unbalanced and cross-gender bonds less common but also unbalanced. These tales elevate the handsome, powerful, mobile white male hero. The reader will undoubtedly think of numerous examples of this, including the Lone Ranger and Tonto and Wild Bill Hickok and Calamity Jane. Sometimes the hierarchy has more than two levels. In *Red River*, for example, the macho white hero, Tom Dunson, has a white sidekick associated with the female gender through his name (Nadine Groot) as well as through his role as cook; he, in turn, has a Native American sidekick, Kuo.

In cross-racial male bonds, as Leslie Fiedler has noted, the white male learns lessons about nature and emotion from his traveling mate, such as in the Western tales of Mark Twain's Huck and Jim, and James Fennimore Cooper's Natty Bumppo and Chingatchgook. This sensitivity to nature and emotion, however, is just what relegates these "dark" characters to a lower status, and the author chooses to focus on the continuing journey of the white male. One striking aspect of the hierarchy within traveling Western pairs is that, as Max Westbrook discusses, the hero often sets himself up as a man outside the constrictions of a class-based social system; he does, however, carry within himself the cultural baggage to establish a private hierarchy (Westbrook). In *Adventures of Huckleberry Finn*, for example, young Huck does move toward respect for Jim as the two move down the river, but he continues to link him to the class of people below his own "white trash" status by such comments as Jim "had an uncommon level head, for a nigger" (Clemens, 109). The power structure is particularly evident when Huck omits Jim from his narrative after a steamboat runs over the raft. Although he does call out for Jim, the runaway slave drops out of the text as Huck gets caught up in the feud between the Grangerfords and the Shepherdsons, two elite families. Huck also succumbs to middle-class Tom Sawyer's literary influence and tortures Jim instead of freeing him.[7] Twain's having Huck "light out for the Territory ahead of the rest" (336) emphasizes that this is one male's story and that Jim's position in the relationship, not only as an African American but also as a devoted family man, is subordinate.

In contrast to these lopsided unions, the relationship between Ruth and Sylvie is one of "acknowledged likeness," although the two must break old patterns to develop their equal bond. At first Ruth, along with her sister Lucille, wants to be punished for flaunting established norms, and in particular, for playing hookie. Soon, however, Ruth recognizes that her own wayward spirit is in accord with Sylvie's. The assumed rightness of the societal structure that kept them apart—the dominant/submissive, vengeful mother/sinful daughter relationship— disintegrates. Sylvie and Ruth become mother and daughter, sister and aunt to each other. Thus Sylvie is not the sole guide; Ruth is a guide as well. Significantly, Ruth instigates the night-time search for herself that draws the sheriff's attention and determines that she and her aunt must quit their housekeeping and hit the road.

Ruth's decision to accept transience with Sylvie occurs in response to Sylvie's brief zeal for normality and her adoption of the typical hierarchy between mother and daughter. Since the town is questioning her ability as a guardian, Sylvie attempts to keep Ruth and herself together and at home in Fingerbone by conforming to the town members' sense of what is proper. Sylvie temporarily abjures what Joan Kirby calls her "union with the forces of nature," a union that indicates her rejection of American patriarchal values (Kirby, 92). She clearly has a fair sense of what the town requires to achieve normality; she cleans, sweeping assorted varieties of wildness from her house: nests and leaves and cats as well as her own collections of newspapers and tin cans. She then talks of church and new clothes "in very good taste"– as she burns anything that might be considered inappropriate by the imagined "judicial gentlemen in the orchard" (201) who felt Ruth should have a "normal" life. She assumes a tone of control here, saying about a library book, "That isn't the sort of thing you should be reading. . . . I don't know how it got in the house" (200). When Ruth says, "We should go in," Sylvie's response is "Yes. . . . You go in and I'll put some dirt on the ashes" (202).

Ruth thinks about this potential new life that emphasizes containment rather than mobility, a life like the one her sister Lucille had chosen over family bonds, a life in which a woman always had to imagine critical observers who judge normality. (Like Sylvie with the judicial watchers in the orchard, Lucille has "a familiar, Rosette Browne. . .through whose eyes she continually imagined she saw" (103).) She envisions going to church with Sylvie "in pillbox hats" (201), and she slips into the darkness of the orchard, away from the brightly lit, tidy house, afraid that by entering it, she would "be transformed by the gross light into a mortal child," afraid that like Noah's wife, she might "stand in the window and realize that the world was really lost" (204). Ruth knows that her flight might draw attention, and it does. A "judicial gentleman" in the form of the sheriff appears and demands to see Ruthie. Her appearance "out in the cold with no coat on, in the middle of the night, with school tomorrow" (206) seals her fate, from the town's perspective. This brief trip also frees her aunt and herself from a future of pillbox hats, a future in which they would have to subvert themselves and lose the magic from their lives. The two shift from burning the abnormal in the house to burning that symbol of traditional female values, the house itself, and so they become equal partners in life. As Ruth states, "that night we were almost a single person" (209).

This joint decision to leave the constriction of Fingerbone modifies another common hierarchical pattern in the Western – that of the rescuer and the rescued. Here the rescue is not from Indians, but from the clutches of normality. No hero emerges here to wrest a helpless woman or child from danger with guns or money. In Westerns, usually that danger means bandits or Indians, as in *Lonesome Dove, The Searchers, True Grit*, and an early Western narrative (when the East was West), *A Narrative of the Captivity and Restauration of Mrs. Mary Rowlandson*. (For Rowlandson, God was her hero, savior, and "partner" more than the ransomers.) In contrast, Ruth and Sylvie each must face the dangers of the bridge-crossing alone in order to effect escape.

In addition to reshaping the prominent Western pattern of unequal traveling companions, another narrative pattern also common in relation to paired Western travelers is that of separation or death. Separation occurs in *Adventures of Huckleberry Finn* with the parting of Huck and Jim. In many of the Leatherstocking tales, Natty Bumppo and Chingatchgook also part at the tale's end, and in *The Pioneers* Chingatchgook dies. One or both members of a traveling pair often die, and so the pair is either truncated or decimated. Mattie lives on without Rooster Cogburn in the novel *True Grit*. (In contrast, the film doesn't kill off John Wayne (Rooster), but it does kill off Mattie's potential love interest, played by Glen Campbell.) In Rudolfo Anaya's *Bless Me, Ultima*, the traveling curandera Ultima dies, leaving behind her young male apprentice. Death of one partner occurs in Faulkner's two most Western tales: Faulkner kills off Sam Fathers (and Old Ben, the bear) in his tale of the death of wilderness, "The Bear," leaving young Ike to become a lonesome man; in *The Wild Palms*, Faulkner also kills off Charlotte after she and her lover Harry run away from civilization to Utah.[8]

While inter-racial, cross-cultural, and occasionally heterosexual friendships expand a sense of community among those Western traveling pairs, the central character's isolation at the end of the narratives provides an emphatic sense of closure, a closure that often pushes community back to the past and to abstraction. These narratives tell us friendship can be supportive – even life-saving – but the heart of the matter is that you can't depend on it; you can depend only on yourself. So patriarchal authors tend to kill these darker, frequently more feminine characters, liberating their heroes.[9]

Double deaths of paired outsiders on the road are also common, particularly in buddy films of the past few decades that glorify death over difficult survival, such as *Thelma and Louise*, a narrative that accepts the Western outsider genre with little modification despite the change in the travelers' gender. Some other dead buddy films are based on Western folk heros, such as *Bonnie and Clyde* and *Butch Cassidy and the Sundance Kid*. These films do not grapple with the central issue in *Housekeeping*: surviving as best as possible. And so although Robinson maintains the pair pattern from the Western, she rejects separation and death for her pair just as she rejects for them the pattern of the loner committing suicide.[10]

By debunking hierarchical relationships as the norm, and by concluding her novel with the women leaving home and traveling together as transients (a situation that exists as the present in this retrospective narrative), Robinson joins the forefront of those writers who are reshaping American myths. Phyllis Lassner, in "Escaping the Mirror of Sameness," rightly claims that the two women "create a new kind of interdependent relationship" (Lassner, 51).

Another Western pattern that Robinson remodels is that of the drifter. Like the wanderers in Jack Keroac's *On the Road* and Tom Wolfe's *Electric Kool-Aid Acid Test*, the women's main impetus to become transient is to escape an oppressive society. Not only do Sylvie and Ruth reject and avoid the restrictive goal of marriage in the 1950s—which for the male drifter was also considered restrictive—they also avoid establishing any goals at all except staying together. Ruth makes the distinction that she and her aunt are "drifters" rather than "travelers" (213, 216). Neither woman leads the way in choosing routes since "we had no particular reason to stay anywhere, or to leave" (216). Even Sal and his crew in *On the Road* have a goal: motion itself. Sal claims the group's goal to be "leaving confusion and nonsense behind and performing our one and noble function of the time, *move*" (Keroac, 133). Ken Kesey and his Merry Pranksters define a similar goal by naming their bus "Furthur."[11]

While Huck purposefully heads further west at the end of his story, as Susanna Finnell notes in her essay in this volume, there is no destination for women who live outside traditional society. Some real-life drifters who were the subject of literature, such as Ken Kesey and Jack London, became reintegrated into society. In fact, in some of his hobo stories, London depicts the present as the time of his success as a writer; his hobo days merely comprise a curious aspect of his past. But for women like Ruth and Sylvie who accept their outsider status, maintaining symbols of normality becomes pointless. While Lucille yearns for the right clothes and the right shoes so that she'll fit in, her aunt and sister wear what they please, no matter how quirky. Unlike Victorian women travelers who often exaggerated their normality through their outfits – so they could respectably "travel under cover" and return to their traditional way of life – Ruth and Sylvie live in both legal and self-imposed exile. "Magic cloaks" of respectability are for those with a valued home and social status at the end of the journey, not for those with wandering as their fate. Ruth and Sylvie, as Elizabeth Meese notes, live with "the absence of certainty" (Meese, 63).

What the women do have that sets them apart from other drifters is their continuing emotional bond, their sense of family. As Janis Stout notes, the "lost and wandering" pattern in American fiction usually coincides with the characters' loss of "spiritual direction" (Stout, 107), but Ruth and Sylvie's spiritual sharing breaks this pattern. While the novel does depict the tearing of one female bond – the close tie between Ruth and Lucille – the narrative focuses on the growing attachment between Ruth and Sylvie, a bond clearly distinct from a marital relationship, one that traditionally limited women's activities and frequently, as in the case of Ruth's grandparents, enforced a sense of isolation rather than of unity.

As drifters, Ruth and Sylvie delight both in each other and in the present, taking pleasure in life's curiosities. Sylvie's favorite place to work is a truck stop, where simple things delight travelers:

> I like to overhear stories strangers tell each other, and I like the fastidious pleasure solitary people take in the smallest details of their small comforts. In rain or hard weather they set their elbows on the counter and ask what kind of pie you have, just to hear the old litany again (214).

To Ruth, a "pleasant" life means "Sylvie and I see all the movies" (214).

While the portrayal of an unbroken travelers' bond sets Robinson's *Housekeeping* apart from many other tales of Western travelers, the novel is not an anomaly. Some Western narratives that emphasize community and emotional depth of commitment emerge as trailblazers if not progenitors, such as Native American tales and pioneer journals. For example in the Zuni emergence story, *Talk Concerning the First*

Beginning, the Zuni people emerge from the fourth womb as an entire nation and travel together, caring for each other, until they find their center, their home. Even before they settle, however, their mutual care provides a sense of home. Leslie Marmon Silko's *Ceremony* provides a similar sense of community. Although the central character, Tayo, often travels alone physically, or with selfish "friends," powerful spiritual beings and old stories help him heal himself and his homeland.

Housekeeping also echoes historical accounts of women travelers who create a sense of home on the road. American pioneer women are clear antecedents, particularly for a book set chiefly in north Idaho, written by a native Idahoan. As with these women, Ruth not only focuses on her family member/traveling companion, but also on her sense of loss for the family left behind when she decided to travel. The novel is mostly a reminiscence, and while it does end with Ruth's sense of delight in Sylvie's company as the two women hop trains from place to place in their oversized coats, comb their hair with their fingers, and enjoy the jumbled contents of their pockets, the ending is complicated by Ruth's longing for her sister and her assumed sense of Lucille's longing for her—and waiting "in a fury of righteousness" (217). Such sorrow is often mentioned but glossed over in tales of male travel, since a macho ability to repress sorrow forms an integral part of the ethos of the Western male. Pioneers coped with physical distance between themselves and loved ones. For example, in her diary of 1891, Martha Farnsworth (Martha Shaw at the time) repeatedly writes of her sadness in leaving Topeka for Colorado, claiming "It breaks my heart to leave my friends here" and "my heart is so full of sorrow" (Farnsworth, 82). But Martha maintains the family that is with her, including an abusive husband. Pioneers often, like Ruth, also had to confront the psychic chasm created by moving beyond the pale of middle-class acceptability. For Ruth, this chasm continually widens as time passes. As she nears the close of her narrative, Ruth still thinks of visiting Lucille "[s]omeday when I am feeling presentable," but she also acknowledges that "such days are rare now" (217). As a drifter and hobo, she has lost the acceptable "look" that accompanies socially defined normality, and she has lost much more.

While *Housekeeping* does include elements of such narratives as those that highlight the importance of emotional bonds on and off the road, what distinguishes Robinson's novel from this pattern is that Ruth and Sylvie are not searching for a home. For these women, who have adopted elements of the Western loner and drifter patterns, home is not an option.

In shaping her narrative, Robinson wends her way between various accounts of Western travelers. To Ruth and Sylvie in *Housekeeping*, as to mythic men on the move, traveling provides an escape from difficult situations and also offers a means of moving forward; the women live lives that suit them better than town life, rather than fitting a culture's blanket standards. Aunt and niece do maintain their own small community, but this bond is based on love rather than rules and a hierarchical order. Such freedom, however, comes at a cost not acknowledged by Huck Finn and Daniel Boone. In *Housekeeping*, a sense of loved ones lost and left behind lingers on.

In *Writing Beyond the Ending: Narrative Strategies of Twentieth-Century Women Writers*, Rachel Blau DuPlessis notes a pattern among 20th century women writers (and evident in *Housekeeping*) of rejecting "the ending in death and the ending in marriage, once obligatory goals for the female protagonist" (DuPlessis, 142). By reshaping various elements of Western traditions, including aspects of the surviving loner, the buddy tradition, and communities finding a sense of home in transit, Robinson provides a new twist to old narrative forms and an ending that indicates one outcome for women who don't die and won't accept what is, at the time the novel is set, a socially accepted subordinate role.

And so Ruth and Sylvie's love endures in the same way that Marilynne Robinson's novel prevails, by unifying disparate elements and thus fulfilling one of Ruth's dream images—gathering disconnected things together in a fishing net and putting "an end to all anomaly" (91). Robinson's net is prodigious, drawing together widely different elements of Western literature, mythology, and history, as well as traditionally male and traditionally female experiences and desires. The novel is not solely about resistance, or the value of an equal female bonding, or the glories of adventuring in the Western expanse. Robinson's eclectic approach provides her readers with the groundwork for a new Western mythology. While the song "Good Night, Irene" floats through the novel, offering its options of either escape or settling down, aunt and niece do both and neither. They do not "sit by the fireside bright"—nor do they "jump in the river and drown." "Sometimes [they] live in the country; sometimes [they] live in town"—and together they take the fireside with them on their Western road.

Notes

1. For cogent arguments about canon formation in American literature, see Nina Baym (1981), Annette Kolodny (1985), and Henry Louis Gates (1990). Recent works by feminist historians and critics have focused on women's roles in the West and in Westerns. See Susan Armitage (1987), Patricia Nelson Limerick (1976), Annette Kolodny (1984), and Jane Tompkins (1992).
2. In addition to Ravits's work with the canon, Dana Heller discusses the "lighting out" and the "on the road" motifs common in Western narratives, but Heller uses it as a springboard to discuss differences without analyzing similarities (Heller 1990).
3. For an analysis of how the film version of *Housekeeping* revamps the novel into a traditional Western, see my article in *Old West, New West* (O'Brien 1993).
4. Although married, Boone's folkhero status is chiefly that of a loner.
5. An account of Beckwourth's life in the form of interviews with Thomas D. Bonner (originally published in 1854) made Beckwourth a celebrity. Jack Oakie plays Beckwourth in the 1950 film *Tomahawk*—but not as an African American.
6. The town of Fingerbone is based on the Idaho community of Sandpoint. In a conversation I had with Marilynne Robinson in June of 1989, she mentioned that while she grew up in Coeur D'Alene rather than Sandpoint, she was a frequent visitor to her grandparents' home there.
7. I disagree with Myra Jehlen's view (Jehlen 1990) that Huck Finn transcends all aspects of his character except gender—including class.
8. John R. Milton also notes Faulkner's Western leanings (Milton 1980).
9. For discussions of male fear of the female and the feminine, see Judith Fetterley (1978), Susan Griffin (1981), Margaret Hallissy (1987), and Dorothy Dinnerstein (1977).
10. Jane Tompkins (1992) discusses the centrality of death in traditional Westerns.
11. Numerous feminist theorists and critics have discussed masculine and feminine narrative forms, often focusing on the goal-orientation of phallocentric writers and thinkers. Some notable analyses of narrative theories include work by Luce Irigaray (1974, 1977), Helen Cixous (1972), Mary Daly (1978), and Rachel Blau DuPlessis (1985).

References

Armitage, Susan. "Through Woman's Eyes: A New View of the West," in *The Woman's West*. Edited by Susan Armitage and Elizabeth Jameson. Norman: University of Oklahoma Press, 1987, 9-18.

Baym, Nina. "Melodramas of Beset Manhood: How Theories of American Fiction Exclude Women Authors," *American Quarterly* 33 (1981): 122-39.

Beckwourth, James Pierson. *The Life and Adventures of James P. Beckwourth as told to Thomas D. Bonner*. Lincoln: University of Nebraska Press, 1972.

Belenky, Mary Field, et al. *Women's Ways of Knowing: The Development of Self, Voice, and Mind*. New York: Basic Books, 1986.

Bunzel, Ruth. "Zuni Origin Myths," in *Forty-Seventh Annual Report of the Bureau of American Ethnology*, 1930.

Cixous, Helene. *The Exile of James Joyce*. Trans. Sally A. J. Purcell. New York: D. Lewis, 1972.

Clemens, Samuel. *Adventures of Huckleberry Finn*. Scranton, Pennsylvania: Chandler, Facsimile ed. 1962.

Daly, Mary. *Gyn/ecology: The Metaethics of Radical Feminism*. Boston: Beacon, 1978.

Dinnerstein, Dorothy. *The Mermaid and the Minotaur: Sexual Arrangements and Human Malaise*. New York: Greenwood, 1977.

DuPlessis, Rachel Blau. *Writing Beyond the Ending: Narrative Strategies of Twentieth-Century Women Writers*. Bloomington: Indiana University Press, 1985.

Farnsworth, Martha. *Plainswoman: The Diary of Martha Farnsworth 1882-1922*. Edited by Marlene Springer and Haskell Springer. Bloomington: Indiana University Press, 1988.

Faulkner, William. *The Wild Palms*. New York: Random, 1939.

_____ "The Bear," in *Go Down, Moses and Other Stories*. New York: Random, 1942.

Fetterley, Judith. *The Resisting Reader: A Feminist Approach to American Fiction*. Bloomington: Indiana University Press, 1978.

Fiedler, Leslie. *Love and Death in the American Novel*. New York: Stein and Day, Rev. ed. 1966.

Foster, Thomas. "History, Critical Theory, and Women's Social Practices: 'Women's Time' and *Housekeeping*," *Signs: Journal of Women in Culture and Society* 14 (1988): 73-99.

Gates, Henry Louis. "The Master's Pieces: On Canon Formation and the African American Tradition," *South Atlantic Quarterly* 89 (1990): 89-112.

Green, Martin. *The Great American Adventure*. Boston: Beacon, 1984.

Greenblatt, Stephen. "Culture," in *Critical Terms for Literary Study*. Edited by Frank Lentricchia and Thomas McLaughlin. Chicago: University of Chicago Press, 1990, 225-232.

Griffin, Susan. *Pornography and Silence: Culture's Revenge Against Nature*. New York: Harper & Row, 1981.

Hallissy, Margaret. *Venomous Woman: Fear of the Female in Literature*. New York: Greenwood, 1987.

Heller, Dana. "Happily at Ease in the Dark: Marilynne Robinson's *Housekeeping*," in *The Feminization of Quest-Romance: Radical Departures*. Austin: University of Texas Press, 1990, 93-104.

Irigaray, Luce. *Speculum D'autre Femme*. Paris: Editions de Minuit, 1974.

_____. *Ce Sexe Qui N'en Pas Un*. Paris: Editions de Minuit, 1977.

Jehlen, Myra. "Gender," in *Critical Terms for Literary Study*. Edited by Frank Lentricchia and Thomas McLaughlin. Chicago: University of Chicago Press, 1990, 263-273.

Keroac, Jack. *On the Road*. New York: Viking, 1959.

Kirby, Joan. "Is There Life after Art? The Metaphysics of Marilynne Robinson's *Housekeeping*," *Tulsa Studies of Women in Literature* 5 (1986): 91-109.

Kolodny, Annette. *The Land Before Her: Fantasy and Experience of the American Frontiers 1630-1860*. Chapel Hill: University of North Carolina Press, 1984.

_____. "The Integrity of Memory: Creating a Literary History of the United States," *American Literature* 57 (1985): 291-307.

Lassner, Phyllis. "Escaping the Mirror of Sameness: Marilynne Robinson's *Housekeeping*," in *Mother Puzzles: Daughters and Mothers in Contemporary American Literature*. Edited by Mickey Pearlman. New York: Greenwood, 1989, 49-58.

Limerick, Patricia Nelson. *The Legacy of Conquest: The Unbroken Past of the American West*. New York: Norton, 1976.

London, Jack. *On the Road: The Tramp Diary and Other Hobo Writings*. Edited by Richard Etulian. Logan: Utah State University Press, 1979.

Milton, John R. "The Novel in the American West," in *Critical Essays on the Western American Novel*. Edited by William Pilkington. Boston: G. K. Hall, 1980, 3-19.

Mallon, Anne-Marie. "Sojourning Women: Homelessness and Transcendence in *Housekeeping*," *Critique* 30 (1989): 95-105.

Meese, Elizabeth. *Crossing the Double-Cross: The Practice of Feminist Criticism*. Chapel Hill: University of North Carolina Press, 1986.

O'Brien, Sheila Ruzycki. "*Housekeeping*: New West Novel, Old West Film," in *Old West, New West: Centennial Essays*. Edited by Barbara Howard Meldrum. Moscow: University of Idaho Press, 1993.

Ostriker, Alicia. *Stealing the Language: The Emergence of Women's Poetry in America*. Boston: Beacon, 1986.

Ravits, Martha. "Extending the American Range: Marilynne Robinson's *Housekeeping*," *American Literature* 61 (1989): 644-666.

Red River. Dir. Howard Hawks. United Artists, 1947.

Robinson, Marilynne. *Housekeeping*. New York: Bantam, 1982.

Shane. Dir. George Stevens. Paramount, 1953.

Stout, Janis. "Lost and Wandering," in *The Journey Narrative in American Literature: Patterns and Departures*. Westport, Connecticut: Greenwood, 1983, 105-119.

Tompkins, Jane. *West of Everything: The Inner Life of Westerns*. New York: Oxford, 1992.

Tomahawk. Dir. George Sherman. Universal, 1950.

Turner, Frederick Jackson. "The Significance of the Frontier in American History," in *The Early Writings of Frederick Jackson Turner*. Madison: University of Wisconsin Press, 1938, 185-229.

Westbrook, Max. "The Themes of Western Fiction," in *Critical Essays on the Western American Novel*. Edited by William T. Pilkington. Boston: G. K. Hall, 1980, 34-40.

Wolfe, Tom. *The Electric Kool-Aid Acid Test*. New York: Farrar, Straus and Giroux, 1968.

Contributors

Susan Armitage, Professor of History and Women Studies, directs Washington State University's undergraduate and graduate program in American Studies. She is the co-editor of *The Women's West* (University of Oklahoma Press) and *So Much to Be Done* (University of Nebraska Press) and numerous articles on Western women's history. She is currently at work on an anthology of writings on multicultural Western women's history and on a community study that focuses on women's role in settlement and development.

Joan Burbick, Professor of English and American Studies at Washington State University, is author of *Thoreau's Alternative History: Changing Perspectives on Nature, Culture, and Language* (University of Pennsylvania Press), and *Healing the Republic: The Language of Health and the Culture of Nationalism in Nineteenth-Century America* (Cambridge University Press, forthcoming), as well as articles on Emily Dickinson, William Carlos Williams, and Jackson Pollock. At present, she is researching the political and economic language of women's writings in 19th-century America.

Susanna Finnell is the Associate Director of the Office of Honors Programs and Academic Scholarships at Texas A&M University. Previously, at Washington State University, she consumed the shared bread of knowledge with women from other disciplines through the Women in Literature Research Group. A specialist of French Canadian Literature, she translates Suzanne Jacob's short stories and fiction works. Among her translations are *A Beach in Maine* (Guernica Press) and *Life, After All* (Press Gang Publishers), portions of which have been reissued in *Resurgent: New Writing by Women* (University of Illinois Press) and *Ink and Strawberries: An Anthology of Quebec Women's Fiction* (AYA Press, Toronto).

Bonnie Frederick, Associate Professor of Spanish at Washington State University, has written on a variety of subjects dealing with 19th-century Argentine literature, such as the contrast between folkloric and literary narrative frames, scientific and literary discourses, and the image of the captive woman. Currently she is writing a book on 19th-century Argentine women writers; an anthology of their works is forthcoming from Feminaria Press in Buenos Aires.

Diane Gillespie, Professor of English at Washington State University, is author of *The Sisters' Arts: The Writing and Painting of Virginia Woolf and Vanessa Bell* (Syracuse University Press), co-editor of *Julia Duckworth Stephens: Stories for Children, Essays for Adults* (Syracuse University Press), editor of *The Multiple Muses of Virginia Woolf* (University of Missouri Press), and author of articles on modern British women novelists as well as modern drama. Currently she is editing Virginia Woolf's biography of Roger Fry and preparing an edition of early 20th century British women dramatists.

Jo Hockenhull is a painter and printmaker. She is a member of Artemisia Gallery in Chicago and the Northwest Print Council in Portland. Her work is in the permanent collections of the Seattle Art Museum, the Seattle Arts Commission, the Washington State Arts Commission, American Oil Company, and the Portland Center for Contemporary Prints. She has completed commissions for Columbia Records (No. 39215), Washington State Arts Commission, Northwest Print Council, and I. Reed Books. Recently, her work has been traveling throughout Colombia, South America ("Latina/Americana: Tierra Fertil") and the United States ("Computers and the Creative Process"). She is the author of "Eastern Washington: Pullman and Spokane, 1970-1990," in *Modernism and Beyond: Women Artists of the Pacific Northwest* (Midmarch Art Press) and has curated several exhibitions including "Spirits Keep Whistling Us Home: Contemporary Plateau Indian Women Artists" at Sacred Circle Gallery in Seattle, 1993. She is a Professor of Fine Arts and Director of the Women Studies Program at Washington State University.

Virginia Hyde, Professor of English at Washington State University, is the author of *The Risen Adam: D. H. Lawrence's Revisionist Typology* (Pennsylvania State University Press) and of articles in such journals as *Contemporary Literature, D. H. Lawrence Review, Victorian Poetry, Papers on Language and Literature, Mosaic, Modernist Studies,* and elsewhere. She has published on Lawrence, George Eliot, Robert Browning, W. B. Yeats, W. H. Auden, Franz Kafka, and other topics. She is presently working on a long iconographic study involving Yeats and several Victorian writers, including Elizabeth Barrett Browning.

Birgitta M. Ingemanson, Associate Professor of Russian and Director of Russian Area Studies at Washington State University, has published articles on Alexander Pushkin, the Russian poet; Ingmar Bergman, the Swedish film director; and Aleksandra Kollontai, the Bolshevik feminist. Current research interests include travel literature, the lives of Russian women, and the city of Vladivostok (a most remarkable creation in the Russian Far East). Her recent article, "The Journey as Life: /Female Travellers in Early 20th Century Russia," will be published in the Russian journal *Problems of Style and Genre* [Vladivostok]. She is presently writing a social and literary portrait of Vladivostok, to be titled *Window to the East*.

Susan H. McLeod is Professor of English and Associate Dean of the College of Liberal Arts, Washington State University. She also directs WSU's Writing Across the Curriculum faculty seminars. Her publications include *Writing Across the Curriculum: A Guide to Developing Programs; Writing About the World* (a multicultural anthology developed for freshman composition at WSU); and *Strengthening Programs for Writing Across the Curriculum*, as well as articles on emotions and the writing process, writing across the curriculum, and writing program administration.

Sheila Ruzycki O'Brien is Assistant Professor of English, American Studies, and Film at the University of Idaho. She is the author of articles in *Old West, New West: Centennial Essays, Computers and Composition* (University of Idaho Press), and *ATAC Forum*. Her research interests include narratives about women in the West, composition theory, and the teaching of literature.

Louise Schleiner is Associate Professor of English at Washington State University. Her work includes *The Living Lyre in English Verse from Elizabeth Through the Restoration* on poetry and music, two books forthcoming (*Cultural Semiotics and the Elizabethan Captive Woman* and *Tudor and Stuart Women Writers*), and articles in literary and archival scholarship, such as Kristevan studies of *Hamlet* and Greek drama (*SQ* 1990) and Milton and gendered pastoral (*LIT* 1990).

Marina Tolmacheva is Associate Professor of History at Washington State University. She is the editor and translator, from the Swahili, of *The Pate Chronicle* (Michigan State University Press) and co-editor of *Arabic Sources of the 12th & 13th Centuries on the Ethnography and History of Africa South of the Sahara* (Nauka Publishers, in Arabic and Russian). Her articles deal with the history of Arab geography and the

Islamic frontier. Her current research focuses on intercultural trans-
mission of ideas and information in medieval Islam.

Annette White-Parks, Assistant Professor of English at University
of Wisconsin-La Crosse, holds a Ph.D. in American Studies and has
authored various articles on Chinese-American literature and culture.
Her dissertation study, *Sui Sin Far: A Writer on the Chinese-Anglo
Borders of North America*, is forthcoming from the University of Illinois Press. Also forthcoming are: *Collected Writings by Sui Sin Far*,
co-edited with Amy Ling (University of Illinois Press); and *The Trick-
ster in Turn-of-the-Century Literature*, co-edited with Elizabeth Am-
mons (University of New England Press). She is currently involved
in editing selected proceedings from the National Asian American Con-
ference, University of Wisconsin-La Crosse, March 25-27, 1993, for
a collection to be published by Highsmith Press.